Language in African American Communities

Language in African American Communities is essential reading for anyone with an interest in the language, culture, and sociohistorical contexts of African American communities. It will also benefit those with a general interest in language and culture, language and language users, and language and identity. This book includes discussions of traditional and non-traditional topics regarding linguistic explorations of African American communities that include difficult conversations around race and racism. *Language in African American Communities* provides:

- an introduction to the sociolinguistic and paralinguistic aspects of language use in African American communities; sociocultural and historical contexts and development; notions about grammar and discourse; the significance of naming and the pall of race and racism in discussions and research of language variation and change;
- activities and discussion questions which invite readers to consider their own perspectives on language use in African American communities and how it manifests in their own lives and communities; and
- links to relevant videos, stories, music, and digital media that represent language use in African American communities.

Written in an approachable, conversational style that uses the author's native African American (Women's) Language, this book is aimed at college students and others with little or no prior knowledge of linguistics.

Sonja Lanehart is Professor of Linguistics; Teaching, Learning and Sociocultural Studies; and Africana Studies at the University of Arizona, USA. Her scholarship focuses on language and education in African American and Black communities; language and identity; sociolinguistics; raciolinguistics; and critical sociolinguistics from Black feminisms, critical race theory, critical discourse analysis, and intersectionality perspectives. She is particularly interested in African American Women's Language and pushing the boundaries of research in sociolinguistics, language variation, and education to be anti-racist, inclusive, diverse, and equitable in the fight for social and linguistic justice. Her publications include *Sista, Speak! Black Women Kinfolk Talk about Language and Literacy* (2002); *African American Women's Language: Discourse, Education, and Identity* (ed., 2009); and *The Oxford Handbook of African American Language* (ed., 2015).

Routledge Guides to Linguistics

Series Editor: Betty J. Birner is a Professor of Linguistics and Cognitive Science in the Department of English at Northern Illinois University.

Routledge Guides to Linguistics are a set of concise and accessible guidebooks which provide an overview of the fundamental principles of a subject area in a jargon-free and undaunting format. Designed for students of Linguistics who are approaching a particular topic for the first time, or students who are considering studying linguistics and are eager to find out more about it, these books will both introduce the essentials of a subject and provide an ideal springboard for further study.

This series is published in conjunction with the Linguistic Society of America. Founded in 1924 to advance the scientific study of language, the LSA plays a critical role in supporting and disseminating linguistic scholarship both to professional linguists and to the general public.

Titles in this series:

Bilingualism
Shahrzad Mahootian

Language in African American Communities
Sonja Lanehart

More information about this series can be found at www.routledge.com/Routledge-Guides-to-Linguistics/book-series/RGL

Linguistic Society of America

Language in African American Communities

Sonja Lanehart

LONDON AND NEW YORK

First published 2023
by Routledge
4 Park Square, Milton Park, Abingdon, Oxon OX14 4RN

and by Routledge
605 Third Avenue, New York, NY 10158

Routledge is an imprint of the Taylor & Francis Group, an informa business

© 2023 Sonja Lanehart

The right of Sonja Lanehart to be identified as author of this work has been asserted in accordance with sections 77 and 78 of the Copyright, Designs and Patents Act 1988.

All rights reserved. No part of this book may be reprinted or reproduced or utilised in any form or by any electronic, mechanical, or other means, now known or hereafter invented, including photocopying and recording, or in any information storage or retrieval system, without permission in writing from the publishers.

Trademark notice: Product or corporate names may be trademarks or registered trademarks, and are used only for identification and explanation without intent to infringe.

British Library Cataloguing-in-Publication Data
A catalogue record for this book is available from the British Library

Library of Congress Cataloging-in-Publication Data
Names: Lanehart, Sonja L., author.
Title: Language in African American communities / Sonja Lanehart.
Description: Abingdon, Oxon ; New York, NY : Routledge,
  2023. | Series: Routledge guides to linguistics | Includes
  bibliographical references and index.
Identifiers: LCCN 2022017051 (print) | LCCN 2022017052
  (ebook) | ISBN 9781138189690 (hardback) | ISBN
  9781138189706 (paperback) | ISBN 9781003204756 (ebook)
Subjects: LCSH: Black English—United States. | English
  language—Variation—United States. | English language—
  Social aspects—United States. | African Americans—
  Intellectual life. | African Americans—Communication.
Classification: LCC PE3102.B54 L36 2023 (print) | LCC PE3102.B54
  (ebook) | DDC 427/.97308996073—dc23/eng/20220803
LC record available at https://lccn.loc.gov/2022017051
LC ebook record available at https://lccn.loc.gov/2022017052

ISBN: 978-1-138-18969-0 (hbk)
ISBN: 978-1-138-18970-6 (pbk)
ISBN: 978-1-003-20475-6 (ebk)

DOI: 10.4324/9781003204756

Typeset in Times New Roman and Gill Sans
by Apex CoVantage, LLC

Contents

Acknowledgments   *x*
International Phonetic Alphabet (IPA) for English in the Continental U.S.   *xii*

1   *Talkin and Testifyin*   1

Introduction: My Subjectivities and Positionalities 1
Name a Thing a Thing: *About Definitions and Naming 9*
What to Expect 11
Questions, Discussion, and Further Inquiry 15
References 15
   Filmography 16
   Discography 17
   Digital Media 17

2   A Seat at the Table: What Are You Bringing to the Table Before We Even Get Started?   18

Introduction: Real Talk 18
Linguistic Prejudice 19
Linguistic Shame and Denial 23
Linguistic Pride and Acceptance 25
Contradictions and All 26

*What You're Not Going to Do: Definitions, Naming,
and Pet Peeves* 27
*To HEL—or HEC—and Back: The Messiness of
Having the Army and the Navy* 28
Questions, Discussion, and Further Inquiry 36
References 38
  Filmography 39
  Discography 40
  Digital Media 40

3 "*Put Some Respeck on My Name!*": Language and Uses of Identity in African American Communities   41

Introduction: How We Gon Play This? 41
Who Do People Say That I Am? 43
A Word on Ebonics 44
What Does It Feel Like to Be a Problem? 46
Say My Name! 52
Questions, Discussion, and Further Inquiry 54
References 54
  Filmography 57
  Digital Media 57

4 "*Where Your People From?*": Problematizing Origins and Development   58

*Introduction: Controversial History, Development, and
Contested Origins* 58
The Deficit Hypothesis 59
(Neo-)Anglicist and (Neo-)Creolist Origins Hypotheses 61
*Consensus Hypotheses: Substratist, Restructuralist, and
Ecological* 67
The Divergence/Convergence Hypothesis 69
My Conclusion: **Periodt!** 70
Questions, Discussion, and Further Inquiry 71
References 71

Filmography 74
Discography 74

5 *What's Good?*: A Concise Descriptivist Meta-Grammar of Language Use in African American Communities 75

Introduction: **We Bout to Ride Up on** *This Elephant 75*
Why Y'all so Interested in Language Use in African American Communities? 78
Patterns, Systems, and Structure, Oh My! 103
Lexical Level: Word Classes and Word Formation 104
Syntactic Level, Part 1: Verbal Markers 104
Syntactic Level, Part 2: From Multiple Negation to Patterns in Question Formation 109
Morphosyntactic Level: Inflections 111
Phonological Level 111
Speech Events, Discourse, Pragmatics, Nonverbal, and Paralinguistic Levels 113
Where Does This Leave Us? 115
Questions, Discussion, and Further Inquiry 117
References 117
   Digital Media 121

6 *Where Your People At?*: Regional and Geographic Variation 122

Introduction: A New Day Is Dawning 122
Gullah Geechee 126
Urban and Rural 127
CORAAL, et al. 131
From Regional to Social Variation 133
Questions, Discussion, and Further Inquiry 134
References 134
   Filmography 138
   Digital Media 138

7 Where My *Shawtys* At?: Social and Gendered Variation   139

Introduction: **It's About to Be Lit Up in Here** *139*
Black American Sign Language, or Black ASL 140
Standards in Language Use in African American Communities 141
Middle-Class Language Use in African American Communities 148
African American Women's Language, or AAWL 152
Hip Hop Nation Language, or HHNL 158
Sexuality and Gendered Identity in Language Use in African American Communities 164
Questions, Discussion, and Further Inquiry 166
References 167
   Filmography 174
   Discography 175
   Digital Media 175

8 This Is Why We Can't Have Nice Things: Pop Culture, Social Media, and Digital Media   177

Introduction: **Whatcha Know Good?** *177*
Afrofuturism and Ebonics 178
Ya Man, Steve Harvey: **Blacktainment** *Extraordinaire 181*
The Queen of Soul to Spoken Soul 184
Black Twitter and Language Use in African American Communities 186
Digital Media and the Performance of Language Use in African American Communities 187
I Refuse to **Eat the Cake** *189*
Questions, Discussion, and Further Inquiry 189
References 190
   Filmography 191
   Discography 192
   Digital Media 192

9 *It's Not the Shoes, Bruh!* You Black!: African American Language Use in AmeriKKKa's Educational ApparatU.S.   194

Introduction: **That's the Way of the World** *194*
How and When We Enter *White Educational Spaces . . . and Some Definitions 196*
We Ain't Havin It!: Let's **Get on the Good Foot** *201*
We Come From a Remarkable People *204*
The Research: Language and Linguistic Justice for Black Children 207
Language of Black America on Trial: The Ann Arbor "Black English" Trial and the Oakland Ebonics Controversy 211
As My Dad Would Say, "Stop **Pussyfootin Roun** *the Issue:" Because Racism 214*
Questions, Discussion, and Further Inquiry 216
References 217
   Filmography 221
   Discography 221
   Digital Media 222

10 *"If You Don't Know Me by Now . . ."*   223

Introduction: "**You Cain't Do Wrong and Get By**" *223*
Things I Didn't Discuss That You Might Consider 225
"**Whatcha Know Good?**": *What I Hope You Did, Learned, and Hope to Do 227*
Questions, Discussion, and Further Inquiry 227
Reference 228
   Discography 228

AAL and Black culture words and phrases   229
Index   233

Acknowledgments

Community. (Black) women writing together. Prayers and blessings; mercy and grace. I want to acknowledge that I did not do this on my own. It took more than five years after this book was due to the publisher for me to complete it. I wasn't ready before now. But I got ready in 2021 thanks to the help of my dear, dear friend Joycelyn Moody and her amazing faith and trust in me to get me to walk this journey back to daily writing. That was followed by and built up by Michelle Boyd's InkWell and her Composed Writing Retreat in May 2021 followed by Roxanne Donovan's WellAcademic and her Focus Fridays writing program—where I found my people, my community. Even though the program only meets for a few weeks at a time on Fridays during the fall and spring semesters and then again in the summer, I asked people to write with me at 7am or 8am Mountain Standard Time for two hours Monday through Friday (and oftentimes longer) because I knew that was the only way I could get this done. And they did. Thank you to my Focus Fridays Sistas: April Langley, Lisa Jennings, Jacqueline Koonce, Jessica Retis, Carol Bunch Davis, Andrea Harris, Meghen Jones, Marisol "Mari" Negron, Dana Gathers, Lizzie Ngwenya-Scoburgh, Ching-In "Chingy" Chen (they/them), Alissa Hochman, and Susan Cook. Thank you, also, to the Black Language and Linguistics Scholars (i.e., BlacTOP) who always show up and show out. Thank you, Jamie Thomas, for helping provide the spark for what this book looks like now as opposed to what it would have looked like five years ago. Thank you, Rachel Weissler and Arthur Spears, for providing feedback on the *whole* book; Candis Smith for feedback on

Chapter 2; Adam Carpenter, deandre miles-hercules, and H. Samy Alim for feedback on Chapter 7; Jamie Thomas and Dani Lalonders for feedback on Chapter 8; and John Rickford for feedback on Chapter 9. Special thanks and much love to Ayesha Malik, who critiqued the *entire* book despite having moved on from academia to being a full-fledged, passed the bar, lawyer. Thank you for your love, Ayesha, and much love to you. Thank you to my family—Paul, Isaac, and Mom—for always having my back and always being patient and gracious for the times I'm so laser focused that I may neglect to tell or show you how priceless you are and how much you contribute to my motivation and ability to do this work. And, always, thanks be to God for His mercy and grace that endure forever and ever. Amen!

International Phonetic Alphabet (IPA) for English in the Continental U.S.

Table 0.1 International Phonetic Alphabet (IPA) for English in the Continental U.S.

Consonants	Word Examples				Vowels	Word Examples		
	initial	medial	final	cluster		initial	medial	final
/p/	peace	Stickpin	recoup	kept	/i/	eat	seat	bee
/b/	boot	lobster	crib	blend	/ɪ/	it	women	coffee†
/t/	time	empty	hurt	stain	/e/	aid	vacation	slay
[ɾ] (flap)	*	water/ladder	*	*	/ɛ/ (epsilon)	essay	west	meh
[ʔ]	*	certain/uh-oh	bad†	*	/æ/ (ash)	ask	plait	baa
/d/	daily	leader	paid	words	/u/	ooze	recruit	crew
/k/	cap	napkin	book	next	/ʊ/ (upsilon)	oomph	should	*
/g/	geese	igloo	rogue	grain	/o/	open	motor	go
/m/	movie	lemon	fame	amp	/ɔ/	awl	fog	law
/n/	gnat	banana	alone	tent	/ɑ/	option	mop	pa
/ŋ/ (eng)	*	monkey	bring	think	/ə/ (schwa)	about	people	sofa
/f/	phone	after	laugh	phrase	/ʌ/	other	enough	duh
/v/	vest	oven	glove	loved	**Diphthongs**	**initial**	**medial**	**final**
/θ/ (theta)	theta	Athens	heath	thwart	/aɪ/	eye	height	imply
/ð/ (eth)	these	rather	breathe	writhed	/aʊ/	oust	snout	how
/s/	scent	taxi	voice	stream	/ɔɪ/	oil	soil	toy
/z/	zipper	busy	owes	dazed	[eɪ]	ale	lame	sway
/ʃ/ (esh)	chute	mission	dish	shrimp	[oʊ]	old	bold	slow
/ʒ/ (yogh)	genre	azure	beige	*	**R-colored**	**initial**	**medial**	**final**
/h/	hay	behind	*	*	/ɪr/	ear	pierce	near
/tʃ/	chip	peachy	witch	bench	/ɛr/	err	tears	there

International Phonetic Alphabet (IPA) for English

Consonants	Word Examples				Vowels	Word Examples		
	initial	medial	final	cluster		initial	medial	final
/dʒ/	jump	major	bridge	orange	/ær/	air	Claritin	bare
/j/	use	onion	*	music	/ər/ or /ɚ/	urbane	injured	harbor
/w/	once	always	*	language	/ʌr/ or /ɝ/	early	terse	infer
/ʍ/	whip	nowhere	*	*	/ʊr/	Urdu	lurid	tour
/ɹ/	write	zero	bear	spring	/ɔr/	orb	hormone	more
/l/	leap	island	ball	zilch	/ɑr/	are	start	car
[ɫ]			general		**Nasalized**	**initial**	**medial**	**final**
[ɾ]			toll		[æ̃] etc	ant	lamp	man†

* does not occur in this position
† occurs in AAL and/or regional varieties of Continental U.S. English

Reference

Lanehart, Sonja. 2023. *Language in African American Communities*. London: Routledge.

Chapter 1

Talkin and Testifyin

Introduction: My Subjectivities and Positionalities

Welcome to Day One in learning about language in African American communities. While I am approaching this as something like an "Introduction to Language in African American Communities" class, I also see it as what I can contribute to your learning and understanding of how **we do language**. To do that, I need to tell you about myself and how I position myself in the world and the work (i.e., my subjectivities and positionalities) so you will know where I'm coming from and why this book will be a little different from your typical linguistics book.

This book is about my language and my people. While that is business for some because it is just another project or topic for the next sound bite or grant, it is not just business to me; it is personal.[1] It took me years to understand how personal it is to me. That journey has involved my use of Critical Race Theory (see Delgado and Stefancic 2017), Black Feminist Theory (see Collins 1990), Intersectionality (see Crenshaw 1989, 1991), and Critical Discourse Analysis (see Fairclough 1995) as lenses for how I view language and all those other things that are interwoven with the languages of our identities (Lanehart 1996).

---

1 This references a conversation in the 1988 film *You've Got Mail* which, in itself, is a reference to *The Godfather*.

On the first day of class, I normally introduce myself as Dr. Lanehart—and I ask that you do call me Dr.—because I am a Black woman from a working-class family in the South (Texas and Louisiana) who too often is seen on college campuses as a student at best and the help at worst—for nearly 30 years—and I do not want you to **get it twisted**. I have been made to feel like I did not **earn** a PhD and did not have the bona fides to speak my truth (impostor phenomenon, aka impostor syndrome,[2] is real). I have often been made invisible in a space I have inhabited for all my adult life or been silenced because no one can seemingly understand what I say unless a white male mansplains[3] it. So, yes, my language of identity is personal because I am reminded that it is not valued on a daily basis, which means my culture is not valued. I spent years trying to disassociate myself from the language of African Americans because I had been taught that it was deficient, bad, lazy, and in need of repair. But if my people's language needed repair, what about me? My people's language was never good enough, my people's culture was never good enough, my body was never good enough, I was never good enough in this sea of anti-Black racism that reminded me every day wherever I looked that my language and my body were not safe. I guess that is why I worked super hard to never be seen as the rule (e.g., "deficient") but as the exception (e.g., "articulate") in a world that would never value me for all I had to offer as my authentic self.

2 *Impostor phenomenon* was coined by Pauline Clance and Suzanne Imes in the 1970s. It means you (women and People of Color) don't think you're smart enough or good enough for the job that needs to be done. You tend to think everybody else is better than you and that you'll be found out at any minute to be a fraud. You believe this because you've been told or shown by society to believe that you are less than. Additionally, any success you've achieved you've been told it was not because of how smart you are but because of being given a break or, let me throw up a little in my mouth, quotas or affirmative action. Never mind all those white males who fail up (see Peter and Hull's [1969] *The Peter Principle*). See also Christina Whittaker's 2021 TED×AlpharettaWomen talk; Dr. Deena Brown's TEDxMartindaleBrightwood talk; and Elizabeth Cox's TED-Ed talk.

3 *Mansplaining* is when men explain or re-explain something to women or what was said by a woman in a condescending or patronizing way as if women are idiots and men are their saviors. Think 1950s television shows.

Working class was a step up for my parents as a family unit compared to how they grew up. My parents were part of the second wave of the Great Migration of courageous Black folks who left Louisiana to go anywhere but where they were. My family and many of their friends and compatriots landed in Texas (e.g., Houston and Dallas), California (e.g., Oakland and Los Angeles), Chicago, and New York in the 1960s. This was monumental for them given that, to this day, I have family in Louisiana who have never left the state, much less their hometown, even though the weight of anti-Black racism and oppression are, to me at least, palpable. Still, I have friends from Louisiana who steadfastly believe that there's something about the soil, the dirt, the air that makes them long for Louisiana and doesn't allow them to stay away for too long. Nevertheless, when I think of Louisiana and other Deep South places, whether by geography or mentality, I feel like I can't breathe because whiteness has its knee on our necks. My mom says that white children were taught that they could have or do anything while Black children were taught that they couldn't have or do anything. Everything was for white folks; nothing was for me. That is how I grew up.

My parents were determined to provide me with a better life than they had. When someone broke into our first home when I was a child, my dad decided it was time to move out of the predominantly Black MLK neighborhood in the city to the white suburbs. My mom put me in every social-educational program she could find to help me excel in a world hostile toward Black folks. Through these experiences, people recognized that I was smart. Everyone noticed it in me. I was often the teacher's pet. I lived to be the best. I was competitive. I wanted all-A grades—which I usually achieved. I was athletic. I wanted to win all the games. I loved playing sports, cards, and games, and I loved school. I made school rooms out of cardboard boxes so I could teach my friends in my garage—for fun. I always wanted to be a teacher—until it was time to decide on a college major. I let my parents know, which means they let the neighborhood know as well as my family. They were all against it because being a teacher just was not a big enough dream for me as far as they were all concerned. That is the first time I recall my parents openly speaking about my academics. They never had to before that point because I was doing things they had never done, thought of doing, or even had the opportunity to do. I had accomplished all sorts of things academically and in sports. They never needed to tell me to do my homework or practice (except for piano because those lessons were expensive and they needed to get their money's worth). I had all the intrinsic motivation I needed to get the job done. I was the perfectionist seeking approval. But being a teacher? That would not do for them because they wanted me to think beyond the confines they'd had: If you wanted to be successful in the South, you could be a teacher or preacher. Both are noble professions, but I needed to dream bigger. In their eyes, I was capable of more than what white folks said I could or couldn't be.

Black women of my family's background and social class in the South were expected to be domestics and cooks at least and preachers or teachers at best. But my parents, the neighborhood, and my family expected me to break that mold. I could be somebody beyond the limitations society historically imposed upon Black folks. I could get a business or engineering degree and go on to do great things and earn a living beyond just enough to get by. So, I changed my dream. Instead, I decided I would become a corporate lawyer and then work at Transco Tower in Houston's upscale Galleria Area after matriculating at the University of Texas at Austin (UT Austin) because it was the best school in Texas since Rice University, the prestigious private school, still had the stench, I mean legacy, of not admitting Blacks. That was the new dream. To this day when we visit Houston, I point out what used to be Transco Tower and tell my husband and son about how I was going to work as a corporate lawyer in Transco Tower, the tallest building in the area. They now tease me about it because they have heard it so many times.

As a typical undergraduate student, I changed my major many times. I was going to be a lawyer, an MBA, a speech pathologist (see Lanehart 2002), a mathematician, a polyglot, etc. I landed on a major in English language and linguistics. Being away from my mom, who was always my champion, meant that I had to learn to adult.[4] I developed common sense along the way, apparently. My

---

4 I laugh about this now because my son has complained about having to adult on many occasions since going off to college far away and then going to graduate school during COVID.

mom would always say I had book sense but no common sense (see Gloria Naylor's 1988 *Mama Day* for more insight about book learning vs. common sense in Black communities). By my junior year in college, she granted that I had learned common sense by being in school and on my own—much to her amazement. I credit her example for that as much as for being forced to grow up by not having my mom there to fight my battles.

I graduated from UT Austin with around a 3.75 GPA. I had wonderful mentors and sponsors who helped me get a Mellon Fellowship, a Ford Foundation Predoctoral Fellowship, and fellowship offers from several great schools, including Ivy Leagues schools.[5] I chose to go to the University of Michigan at Ann Arbor for graduate school because of its long history with and degree concentration in English language and linguistics. It was one of a few programs that would allow me to construct my degree the way I wanted. I was going to work at the Middle English Dictionary on my way to a degree in English language and linguistics with a specialization in medieval studies. I took my first airplane ride to do an in-person interview for the Mellon Fellowship at the DFW Airport hotel on my path to graduate school. Even when I went off to graduate school in Ann Arbor, Michigan, my parents and I drove there as usual. But I had finally traveled to another state besides Louisiana and my home state of Texas. I later realized that the same was mostly true for my parents. They had never traveled to those states along the way either.

For the first time ever, I was away from home and family—and with snow. My first year of graduate school so far away from my family and so far away from my then boyfriend/future husband was a lot to take in. I suffered through my first year living in Ann Arbor.

---

5 I was accepted to every graduate school I applied to except the University of Minnesota. Since my husband is from Minnesota, he often teases me about this. After having been a faculty member at several institutions and departments, I now console myself about being rejected from the University of Minnesota by believing that they thought I wasn't going to go to their school given all the other schools I applied to and the strong likelihood that I wouldn't accept their offer of admission no matter how they might try to sweeten the offer. I feel vindicated in some way, however, because our son was offered a full ride at the University of Minnesota—but he rejected their offer and the Ivy League schools. Karma.

I did not do my best in a couple of classes: I escaped with a B in my yearlong "Language and Uses of Literacy" proseminar and a B in an independent study on Old English. Both of those professors, though, later ended up serving on my dissertation committee despite the low grade.[6]

I smile now thinking of my growth because, with gaining my voice once I had gone off to college and then off to graduate school in a place even farther away, I started asking for what I wanted. When I wanted to pursue medieval studies and realized I preferred organized classes instead of independent studies, I rallied my fellow like-minded graduate students and petitioned the English Department Chair to have "Middle English" offered by one of my favorite professors—and it happened. Despite the wonderful experience I had in that class, something was not sitting right with me. You see, in undergrad at UT Austin, I wanted to be a speech pathologist so I could help Black people speak better and get better educations and better jobs and better pay. I was still naïve enough to believe it was about the language and that logic and research could solve the problem. I wanted to help Black people, my community, and my family. Being a lawyer meant I could make a lot of money and help my family financially. But I realized that being a medievalist was not going to help Black people. And even though I had long ago stopped thinking of the way Black people speak as a pathology or deficit or something that needed to be fixed, I was still strongly driven to work at something to make things better for Black people, my people, and my family.

But **what's the move**? At this point, I had completed my master's degree in English language and literature with an emphasis in medieval studies, and I had passed my comprehensive exams in "Language in African American Communities" and "History of the English Language" as well as my language exams in Latin and Old English. It was time for my dissertation proposal meeting. I proposed something about language and education that my committee just was not buying—and I was not doing a good job of selling. See,

---

6 Unlike in undergraduate school, a B is more like a C or C−, and a C is a failing grade in graduate school.

I thought doing a certain type of research was what I needed to do as part of the perfection expected of me in a system that said "real" research existed in a certain way.

The conversation I had with my dissertation committee chair, Richard W. Bailey, during the meeting changed my life: "What do you really want to do?" "What have you always wanted to do?" Wow. What did *I* want to do? What would bring me joy? We had a conversation about my family and language and my developing and changing identity and . . . the rest is history. My dissertation, titled *Peculiar to Your Mind* in reference to Alice Walker's *The Color Purple* where Celie says, "Look like to me only a fool would want you to talk in a way that feel peculiar to your mind," went on to become *Sista, Speak!: Black Women Kinfolk Talk about Language and Literacy* (Lanehart 2002), adorned on the cover with my maternal grandmother. *Sista, Speak!* launched my career in unimaginable ways. I was tenured and promoted at the University of Georgia in Athens based on *Sista, Speak!* and my other scholarship. However, I didn't get to bask in the glow of this success for long. Within a year, I was in a hospital in Albuquerque, New Mexico, while attending the National Academies of Sciences, Engineering, and Medicine's Ford Foundation Fellows conference. I had a DVT and pulmonary embolism as the result of a foot surgery from a tennis injury. I missed what, to this point, was my one and only invitation to be a plenary speaker at what was then one of my favorite conferences, NWAV: New Ways of Analyzing Variation. What made it worse was that it would have been at the place where I finished writing *Sista, Speak!* while on my Ford Foundation Postdoctoral Fellowship: Stanford University. And the invitation came from the beloved scholar and mentor John Rickford. Still, I won awards for *Sista, Speak!* That book has traveled the world, and in a way, I feel my grandmother went to places she could never have even dreamed of or imagined. I have traveled to many places, and I'm amazed at how many people from so many academic fields have read and been inspired by reading about the language and uses of literacy of the Black Southern women in my family in that book. It is my dearest work.

I left the University of Georgia after 11 years to become an endowed chair and full professor at the University of Texas at San Antonio (UTSA). There I had the funding and support to organize several major conferences on language in African American communities, all of which became edited books. Those conferences provided a space for Black scholars and those researching language, literacy, and education in African American communities to fellowship and let their voices be heard. All of that fellowship with my LinguistiSistas, the Black community of scholars, and all those researching in language, literacy, culture, and education in African American communities led to my crowning achievement: Editing *The Oxford Handbook of African American Language* (Lanehart 2015).[7] It takes a village, y'all.

And now we are here. After 13 years, I left my endowed chair at UTSA and became a Professor of Linguistics (College of Social and Behavioral Sciences) as well as Teaching, Learning, and Sociocultural Studies (College of Education), an Affiliate Faculty in Africana Studies (College of Humanities), and a Faculty Fellow for Mentoring and Retention of Under-represented and Minoritized Students in the Graduate College at the University of Arizona in Tucson. And what does here look like and why am I telling you all of this? Because I know who I am, I know how I got here, I know what brings me joy, and I know what I need and what I believe. I went from buying into seeing Black people as needing to be fixed, which conflicted with my love for them as my family and my people, to making sure that we are seen and heard. As Issa Rae said on the Red Carpet at the 2017 Emmys, "I'm rooting for everybody Black." That is **how we do**; that is how Black women do. One of my best friends got me a desk plate that says, "Black Feminist **AF**" (even though everyone who knows me knows that I don't cuss) because she knew and knows me.

I know Black women's prayers got me to where I am. I stand on their shoulders. I thank my ancestors and elders for their prayers and all those Black mothers, grandmothers, and great-grandmothers who saw and see us through. It is not my intention to diss Black men, but Black women are the mules of society, as Zora Neale Hurston

---

[7] Shout out to Lisa Green and Jennifer Bloomquist for all those summers working together at the University of Massachusetts Amherst and at Lisa's house to develop and prepare the handbook. Those collaborative sessions gave me life.

(1935) has said, and society rides us till we die. But the secret is that we are like Bébé's kids (see *Bébé's Kids*): We don't die; we multiply—our voices, our stories, our songs, our power. Linguists and academics broadly forget or just do not give enough **props** to the groundbreaking and life-giving work of Black women language and linguistics scholars like Geneva "Docta G" Smitherman, Beryl Bailey, Claudia Mitchell-Kernan, Gwendolyn Etter-Lewis, Michèle Foster, Marcyliena Morgan, Elaine "Docta E" Richardson, Margaret Lee, Mary Zeigler, and more. Just check people's references or bibliographies and see who you see—and don't see. But I know where I came from. So, in this book, when we investigate, describe, and just preach about the language of my people, this is where I am coming from: A place of love, respect, and mad props; a place of family and home. You will see this in how we talk about my language and my people. Black folks will **be all up in here**. This book will pay homage to Black scholars, critics, educators, authors, artists, musicians, creatives, and the like who have contributed so much to my living and being and understanding of Blackness, my language, my culture, my identity, and myself. So, "**Let's get it on**" (Marvin Gaye 1973).

Name a Thing a Thing: About Definitions and Naming

To start with, let's talk about definitions and naming. I will do this throughout the book because **calling a thing a thing** is important to make sure we are all on the same page. As you have already seen, I have used "Black" and "African American" interchangeably, but they are not synonymous. For me, *Black* is an umbrella term for native African ancestry peoples in the African Diaspora. Black people are those with native African heritage. That means, South Americans, Caribbeans, Mexicans, Middle Easterners, etc. can be Black. *African American* refers to those from the United States who are of native African heritage. As such, all African Americans are Black but not all Black people are African American. African Americans are only one particular group of Black folks in the African Diaspora.

White is a broad term as well but with a more complicated history because those who count as white fluctuate based on sociopolitics (e.g., Italians), religion (e.g., the Moors), ascribed skin color (e.g., Africans), colorism (e.g., Black folks and Latinx), hair texture (e.g., South Africa's pencil test,[8] laws (e.g., one-drop rule), and actual skin color (e.g., Japanese). However, one's Blackness is ever present and inescapable. These distinctions and definitions are important because words matter; a shared vocabulary matters.

I also just use "Black" sometimes because it makes me think of the 1960s civil rights movement and James Brown's 1968, "Say it loud: I'm Black and I'm proud." It just feels good. "Black" and "African American" and even *Black American* are used interchangeably in society because some folks (strongly) prefer one over the other to mean what I mean when I use "African American." That preference is mostly generational with older generations preferring "Black" or "Black American" and younger generations preferring "African American."

Another thing you will notice is that I capitalize "Black." In recently re-reading Crenshaw (1991), I came across her footnote on the subject:

> I use "Black" and "African American" interchangeably throughout this article. I capitalize "Black" because "Blacks, like Asians, Latinos, and other 'minorities,' constitute a specific group and, as such, require denotation as a proper noun." Crenshaw, supra note 3, at 1332 n.2 (citing Catharine MacKinnon, *Feminism, Marxism, Method, and the State: An Agenda for Theory*, 7 SIGNS 515, 516 (1982)). By the same token, I do not capitalize "white," which is not a proper noun, since whites do not constitute a specific cultural group. For the same reason I do not capitalize "women of color."
>
> (1244, note 6)

Many print media are now capitalizing "Black" and making public statements about doing so, which means I do not have to make that

---

8 These are complex issues that manifest in a variety of ways. If you'd like to explore these issues further, consult the online *Zinn Education Project* for general information; Baugh (2018, 131, note 9), regarding South Africa's hair test; Spears (2020) on colorism; and Spears (2021) on anti-Blackness.

argument myself anymore with editors and publishers. However, as Crenshaw (1991) notes above, that is not always the case with *white*. I do not consistently capitalize "white" in my writings because of the longstanding denial of whiteness and its random normalization as Crenshaw notes. Some of the same print media that moved to capitalizing "Black" did not do so for "white." I do, however, also capitalize *Women of Color* (WOC)—which I extend to *People of Color* (POC), *Students of Color* (SOC), *Faculty of Color* (FOC), and the like—because WOC, as coined by Loretta Ross in 1977 at the National Women's Conference, is political and meant to call out the collective marginalization of non-white women by white women who call themselves feminists but who do not work on behalf of non-white women and their issues that do not overlap with white women's. On this, then, I diverge from Crenshaw (1991) about the capitalization of WOC.

It is also important to name **a thing a thing**. It was difficult to come up with a title for this book. The title the publisher originally wanted was *Ebonics*. While I understand the appeal of that title since it is one that most people would be familiar with and connect to the content of this book, it is not the term linguists use. If linguists do not use it and this book is published in collaboration with the Linguistic Society of America, then it should focus on that space, right???

What to Expect

You should take note of titles, subtitles, phrases, and the like **in this font** that are direct quotations from or references to Black language, Black linguistics, Black music, Black literature, Black Twitter, the Traditional Black Church, Hip Hop, and Black social and cultural life. Of course, this has already started. For example, "Talkin and Testifyin" is a nod to Docta Emerita Geneva Smitherman's 1977 classic, *Talkin and Testifyin: The Language of Black America*. The objective is for this book to be **Blackity Black Black** so you, the reader, are steeped in Black language, linguistics, and life. As such, it requires you to do some work. Not everything will be handed to you. You will need to do some work on your part to figure out some things on your own or with the help of your instructor and classroom community. There are many resources available online and many people online who are willing to help—especially if they can see you have put in some genuine effort and interest. I use **Gill Sans** to highlight words and phrases that reference Black linguistic, language, social, and cultural life that you might not readily notice or understand. Sometimes I will explicitly call out their presence and their underlying meaning and use and sometimes I will just **use this font** and keep it moving. Please use these as opportunities to do a little digging to find out more about what you do not know or may not immediately understand. This approach will help you find ways to connect with and engage the materials in this book but also help me to **let it all hang out** so I can be my authentic self in a space that was not originally meant for me (as Black, as woman, as having working-class origins, as mother, etc.).

Each chapter will, of course, not only provide you with content but also moments for discussion, activities, and reflection. I want you to engage this material with your full self. You will need to be open and honest as well as vulnerable when it comes to sharing and exploring your beliefs, attitudes, ideologies, behavior, knowledge, learning, and understanding. You have enough information to see where I stand, my ideologies and beliefs, my attitudes and behavior, and my self-concept—without apology. When you finish this book, my expectation is that you will be better informed about language in African America by having read it.

In the next chapter, we dive right into attitudes, beliefs, ideologies, and identity. We have to deal with those before we can go further into examining language in African American communities. You need to know and acknowledge where you stand, what your subjectivities and positionalities are, and what lenses you will be using to engage this information and discussion even if you don't have the learned language to call them what they are (i.e., your theoretical positioning). We will not all start at the same place, so we will not all finish at the same place either, but you will have the information and knowledge you need to keep learning and growing—if you choose to accept this mission (again, lots of pop culture that sometimes shows my age since I still think of the original series for this phrase instead of the Tom Cruise franchise).

In Chapter 3, we go further into naming and defining this variety we are talking about. I must admit I have changed and grown so much in this area, and I am continuing to do so. I have changed in the years since completing *The Oxford Handbook of African American Language* (Lanehart 2015). Those changes will be reflected in this chapter, where I want to push you in your thinking about things and your precision as I do the same for myself. Naming and defining can be hard because, as Kelly Wright said in a talk at the University of Arizona on September 17, 2021, it's mindboggling to think that white people named "heaven" and "Earth" and everything in between. Deconstructing that and coming from a different perspective is hard, and it is not always as neat and tidy as we would like it to be. **Be ready** (see Tiffany Haddish 2019).

Chapter 4 delves into one of the most contested areas of this variety. We will be problematizing the origins and development of language in African American communities because I don't want you to **get it twisted**. There are Anglicists, Creolists, and more—oh my! This area is going to test your attitudes and beliefs, historical understandings, your language ideologies, and your views of the world. **Check yo self before you wreck yo self** (see Ice Cube 1993; and shout out to Pough 2004).

I use Chapter 5 to do my very best to provide a concise, descriptive, meta-grammar.[9] This descriptive meta-grammar reflects my worldview on language as a system, not a set of features, as Lisa Green has been telling us all for years. It is difficult to not fall back on listing features that we can all go "ooh and aah" over. I will use the International Phonetic Alphabet, or IPA (see Table 0.0), as well as modified spellings commonly used by others, to signify appropriate and precise pronunciation. Again, this is a space for you to do some work and exploration. **Get ready**.

In Chapter 6, we explore regional and geographic variation of language varieties of African Americans, especially the ways in which they are underexplored. Here we talk about online resources

---

9 There are two primary types of grammars: descriptive and prescriptive. Descriptive grammars describe languages as they are used. Prescriptive grammars tell people what they believe to be the "correct" or "right" or grammatical way to use language. My undergraduate honors thesis at UT Austin was about the history of English prescriptive grammar titled "Whose Right Is the Rule? A Three-Century Dilemma of the English Language Scholars" (Lanehart 1990). So, yeah, I got this.

available for exploration and ways in which linguists might get outside of their comfort zones. This section is not exhaustive, as is the case with most things in this book, but it is informative and a good start to doing the work.

In Chapter 7, we delve into a particular area of interest of mine: Social variation in general and gender and sexuality variation in particular. For years, I tried to encourage people to pursue this work, I looked for people doing this work, and I tried to support people with an interest in this work. I, myself, do some of this work with my interest in language use among African American women and their discourse practices. This chapter reflects what we have accomplished and how much further we must go to have heterogeneous and inclusive views of the language varieties of African Americans.

In Chapter 8, we dip our toes into looking at this variety in pop culture and social media. There is a lot to cover here because the language varieties of African Americans have exploded on the internet, especially with Black Twitter. Black folks have changed the game—again. TikTok is stealing Black creativity and not giving credit where credit is due, as is usual, and Black artists and creatives are feeling the pain. **Y'all ain't ready**.

Chapter 9 addresses the long-standing history, controversies, and existence of Black folks and Black languages in schooling and education. I cannot adequately cover all the details and nuances involved in educating African American children who acquire and use native, African American, home languages that conflict with white, school language. However, this is an important topic and why there are the most end-of-chapter questions. This matters. **Get ready**.

We will end with a chapter reflecting on the book's content and that problematizes where we are and where we need to go from here. You should be ready to do this. I hope you are ready to work because this work takes more than one village. **Let's do this thang. Let's turn this mutha out**.

Please be advised that there are instances of what some of you may deem as obscene language (e.g., profanity) in addition to use of the N-word in its various forms. Please see Spears (2001, 2022) for a linguistic discussion on obscenity.

Questions, Discussion, and Further Inquiry

1. What are your subjectivities and positionalities?
2. What have you thought about how language works (meta-linguistic thought)?
3. What is your linguistic autobiography?
4. How did you come to think about how you speak and are perceived in the world?
5. How has the way you show up linguistically in the world informed your work/life/school trajectory?
6. Whose "right" (i.e., language ideologies) is the rule?
7. How have you experienced imposter syndrome?

References

Baugh, John. 2018. *Linguistics in Pursuit of Justice*. Cambridge, UK: Cambridge University Press.

Clance, Pauline Rose, and Suzanne Ament Imes. 1978. The Impostor Phenomenon in High Achieving Women: Dynamics and Therapeutic Intervention. *Psychotherapy: Theory, Research, and Practice* 15.3: 241–247.

Collins, Patricia Hill. 1990. *Black Feminist Thought: Knowledge, Consciousness, and the Politics of Empowerment*. New York: Routledge.

Crenshaw, Kimberlé. 1989. Demarginalizing the Intersection of Race and Sex: A Black Feminist Critique of Antidiscrimination Doctrine, Feminist Theory and Antiracist Politics. *University of Chicago Legal Forum* 1.8: 139–167. [http://chicagounbound.uchicago.edu/uclf/vol1989/iss1/8]

Crenshaw, Kimberlé. 1991. Mapping the Margins: Intersectionality, Identity Politics, and Violence against Women of Color. *Stanford Law Review* 43.6: 1241–1299.

Delgado, Richard, and Jean Stefancic. 2017. *Critical Race Theory: An Introduction*, 3rd ed. New York: New York University Press.

Fairclough, Norman. 1995. *Critical Discourse Analysis: The Critical Study of Language*. London: Longman.

Hurston, Zora Neale. 1935. *Mules and Men*. Philadelphia: J.B. Lippincott.

Lanehart, Sonja L. 1990. *Whose Right Is the Rule? A Three-Century Dilemma of the English Language Scholars*. Undergraduate Honors Thesis. University of Texas at Austin.

Lanehart, Sonja L. 1996. The Language of Identity. *Journal of English Linguistics* 24.4: 322–331.

Lanehart, Sonja L. 2002. *Sista, Speak! Black Women Kinfolk Talk about Language and Literacy*. Austin, TX: University of Texas Press.

Lanehart, Sonja L. 2015. *The Oxford Handbook of African American Language*. Oxford: Oxford University Press.

MacKinnon, Catharine A. 1982. Feminism, Marxism, Method, and the State: An Agenda for Theory. *Signs: Journal of Women in Culture and Society* 7.3: 515–544.

Naylor, Gloria. 1988. *Mama Day*. New York: Ticknor & Fields.

Peter, Laurence J., and Raymond Hull. 1969. *The Peter Principle*, vol. 4. London: Souvenir Press.

Pough, Gwendolyn D. 2004. *Check It While I Wreck It: Black Womanhood, Hip-Hop Culture, and the Public Sphere*. Boston, MA: Northeastern University Press.

Smitherman, Geneva. 1977. *Talkin and Testifyin: The Language of Black America*. Boston: Houghton Mifflin.

Spears, Arthur K. 2001. Directness in the Use of African American English. In *Sociocultural and Historical Contexts of African American English*, edited by Sonja L. Lanehart, 239–259. Amsterdam: John Benjamins.

Spears, Arthur K. 2020. Racism, Colorism, and Language within Their Macro Contexts. In *The Oxford Handbook of Language and Race*, edited by H. Samy Alim, Angela Reyes, and Paul V. Kroskrity, 47–67. Oxford: Oxford University Press.

Spears, Arthur K. 2021. White Supremacy and Antiblackness: Theory and Lived Experience. *Journal of Linguistic Anthropology* 31.2: 157–179.

Spears, Arthur K. 2022. African-American Language Use: Ideology and So-Called Obscenity. In *African-American English: Structure, History, and Use*, Classic Edition, edited by Salikoko S. Mufwene, John R. Rickford, Guy Bailey, and John Baugh, 249–276. London: Routledge.

Walker, Alice. 1982. *The Color Purple*. New York: Harcourt Brace Jovanovich.

Williams, Robert L, ed. 1975. *Ebonics: The True Language of Black Folks*. St. Louis: The Institute of Black Studies.

Wright, Kelly. 2021. "You Have to Be Better": Confronting Inequitable Linguistic Experiences with Experimental Sociolinguistics. Paper presented at the University of Arizona Fall Linguistics Colloquium, Tucson, AZ, September 2021.

Filmography

Coppola, Francis Ford, director. 1972. *The Godfather*. Paramount Pictures. 175 minutes.

Ephron, Nora, director. 1998. *You've Got Mail*. Warner Bros. 119 minutes.
Haddish, Tiffany. 2019. *They Ready*. Netflix.
Harris, Robin, creator. 1992. *Bébé's Kids*. Paramount Pictures.

Discography

Brown, James. 1968. Say It Loud—I'm Black and I'm Proud. Track 7 on *A Soulful Christmas*. King.
Gaye, Marvin. 1973. Let's Get It On. Track 1 on *Let's Get It On*. Tamla.
Ice Cube. 1993. Check Yo Self. Track 13 on *The Predator*. Lench Mob and Priority.

Digital Media

Brown, Deena. 2021. TED^{x}MartindaleBrightwood's Imposter Syndrome: Facing Unconscious Bias in the Workplace. YouTube, uploaded by Ted^{x}MartindaleBrightwood.
Cox, Elizabeth. 2021. What Is Imposter Syndrome and How Can You Combat It? YouTube, uploaded by TED-Ed. https://youtu.be/ZQUxL4Jm1Lo
Whittaker, Christina. 2021. TED^{x}AlpharettaWomen's One Thing No One Told You about the Imposter Syndrome. YouTube, uploaded by TED^x Talks. https://youtu.be/OMzoyiAS878
Zinn Education Project. www.zinnedproject.org/materials/

Chapter 2

A Seat at the Table

What Are You Bringing to the Table Before We Even Get Started?

Introduction: Real Talk

Before we get started **for real for real**, we need to talk about your attitudes, beliefs, ideologies, subjectivities, and possibly some baggage. One of the biggest things I deal with in addressing language variation are the stereotypes, biases, pre-judgements, and language ideologies people have. There has been a lot of research in Folk/Perceptual Linguistics as well as Community Linguistics that tries to get at what people really believe and know about language and language variation. Much of it reveals that white people feel good about their variety and then less so about all other varieties, or they think highly of a couple of other varieties and not so much about others or less about their own and more about certain others. Usually, Southerners are a bit insecure and Midwesterners are more secure in their varieties. In fact, Southerners are, as would be expected, not high on most people's lists. Folk/perceptual linguistics research mostly deals with asking white people about white people's varieties. When you ask people about how they feel about the language varieties of African Americans, the consensus is that it is bad English, improper, slang, incorrect, informal. Occasionally, people see it as what the cool kids use. More disconcerting is what some Black folks think about it.

So, what do you think? Do you have any African American friends you hang out with (e.g., do they come to your home, break bread with you, know your family)? What do you think about their language? Do they sound like what you expect African Americans to sound like? Do they sound just like you? Do you like the way your language variety sounds to you? When you hear African Americans talking, do you think they sound cool, hip, **ignant**, ghetto, normal, uneducated, country, **ratchet**? Do you clutch your proverbial pearls? Do you cross the street and hope it does not rub off on you or your children or your grandchildren? Do you want to talk like them—at least with your friends but maybe not around your parents or family or workplace? Do you want to be around them? Do you want to be like them (not in a Rachel Dolezal way, though)? Do you change the channel? Keep in mind that I am asking these questions of all readers—not just white readers. Let's unravel this.

I am going to rely on some of my earlier work as a point of reference here because we need to discuss language ideologies, language attitudes and beliefs, and language and identity, which I have discussed previously (see Lanehart 1996, 1998). We also need to talk about definitions of some words and concepts that you may not know or that linguists use differently than you might use or that you are not understanding satisfactorily, like "language," "variety," "slang," "register," "dialect," etc. We will do this in this chapter and chapters to come. After you have thought about what you think language in African American communities is, we can then talk about what it actually is and how we are going to talk about it here.

Linguistic Prejudice

> In response to the Oakland school board's December 18, 1996, resolution to recognize "Ebonics" as the primary language of African American students in that California district, poet Maya Angelou told the *Wichita Eagle* that she was "incensed" and found the idea "very threatening." NAACP president Kweisi Mfume denounced the measure as "a cruel joke," and although he later adopted a friendlier stance, the Reverend Jesse Jackson on national television initially called it "an unacceptable surrender, borderlining on disgrace."
>
> (Rickford and Rickford 2000, 5)

This protest against language in African American communities was not new. Dr. Benjamin H. Alexander, a former, short-term president of the University of the District of Columbia in 1983, said the following in a speech delivered to the Fellows of the American Council on Education in South Bend, Indiana, September 23, 1979, in response to the verdict in the *Martin Luther King, Jr., Elementary School Children v. Ann Arbor School District*, 473 F. Supp. 1371 (E.D. Michigan 1979), aka the Ann Arbor "Black English" Trial:

> I will not accept the legitimacy of Black English or any other kind of non-standard English. . . . If people cannot communicate in Standard English and have not developed their talents and skills—then who wants them? . . . I consider it a cheap insult to see educational standards lowered in Ann Arbor schools— solely for [B]lack students. How can we justify recognition of their non-standard broken English and then ask teachers to learn it?
>
> (Alexander 1980, 437–438)

The Oakland Ebonics controversy was not new. It was a repeat of history that we are sure to see again because the issues have not been adequately resolved or addressed historically, socially, educationally, legally, politically, or equitably. These differing opinions among African Americans represent a history of contradictions that I do not foresee an end to anytime soon. What is disconcerting is the outright linguistic prejudice shown toward language varieties in African American communities by African Americans. This internalized hatred is heartbreaking. It is bad enough when non-Blacks hate our language because we should expect that. That's **just another Tuesday**. It is another matter altogether to have to fight your own to hold what is yours. Think Sofia in Alice Walker's *The Color Purple* telling off Celie for advising Harpo to beat his wife, Sofia; i.e., "all my life I had to fight"—or Kendrick Lamar (2015); Dave Chappelle's Clayton Bigsby (i.e., the character Dave Chappelle created for *Chappelle's Show*), who is the world's only Black white supremacist but who does not know he himself is Black because he is blind; Stephen's (i.e., the character played by Samuel L. Jackson in *Django Unchained,* Tarantino 2012) "**Massa, we sick?**" (Malcolm

X 1963) character; Uncle Ruckus from *The Boondocks* (who the aforementioned Stephen actually looks like) who both hates Black folks and spews his hate using his native language born in African American communities; and the like who, throughout the history of Black people in America, denigrate and deny their own language and their own people.

In the case of Dr. Alexander and those like him—highly educated Black people who want to save Black people from themselves and whitewash them of their Blackness—they say it is out of love for Black people (think Kanye West). But Alexander is as misguided as and more dangerous than Clayton Bigsby. Dr. Alexander is the upper crust, the **Talented Tenth** (DuBois 1903b), the one rubbing shoulders with white people in their service to make Black people respectable (think the fictional Dr. Gleason Golightly in Derrick Bell's [1992] "Space Traders"). You know, the **House Negro**. When Dr. Alexander, the so-called educated, Black face of the white savior says,

> The achievement of academic excellence is not possible without first mastering Standard English. . . . In one basic phase of that excellence, I am a traditionalist. I refuse to recognize that the achievement of excellence is possible without mastery of Standard English. . . . The non-traditional student, as well as the traditional student, cannot succeed unless he [sic] has been trained from the beginning in Standard English. Standard English—not Black English or Brown English or White English—is the only foundation for effective reading, speaking, writing, and learning.
> (Alexander 1980, 437, 439–440)

I am going to go, instead—after throwing up a little in my mouth from Alexander—with the other educated Black man, Uncle Jimmy, or better known to some as James Baldwin, who wrote this famous article for the July 29, 1979, edition of the *New York Times* in his response to the Ann Arbor "Black English" Trial: "The brutal truth is that the bulk of white people in America never had any interest in educating [B]lack people, except as this could serve white purposes."[1] To paraphrase the rest, a child cannot be taught by anyone who demands they repudiate their experience and enter a limbo where they will no longer be Black and know they can never become white (Baldwin 1979). Paulo Freire (1970) was right when he said the oppressed become the oppressors. In this case, that means Black people were taught to hate themselves and everything about themselves. You have Black **edumacated** folk **dissing** where they came from and who their people are because it does not coincide with their ideals of respectability and the white gaze.[2] **Respectability politics** did not save Martin Luther King Jr. from being assassinated while wearing a suit and tie. It's not the clothes, **it's not the shoes**, it's not the language. It's because you Black. And trying to change yourself to be white doesn't make you white. Using your white voice[3] won't make you white. At best, you are "the exception"; you know, the one not like the other ones (think *Sesame Street*). The one who is "articulate" or "clean" or that one Black friend. You are Aldis Hodge playing the famed running-back-turned-actor Jim Brown in *One Night in Miami* (King 2020) when Mr. Carlton, the elderly, white, Southern gentleman character played by Beau Bridges, is praising Jim Brown about his football prowess and accolades and how he is a **credit to his race**, yada, yada, yada, and then tells him, "You know we don't let [nɪgɚz][4] in the house," after Brown had offered to help him move a large, heavy piece of furniture for him and his daughter. Brown was acceptable enough to be invited to sit and drink lemonade on the front porch with Mr. Carlton after performing outdoor manual labor, but not good enough to enter his home with his white daughter

---

1 Uncle Jimmy was speaking Critical Race Theory before it even had a name.
2 See the retired Black woman English teacher's conversation with Steve Harvey on *The Steve Harvey Show* where he refuses to succumb to her idea of "correct" American English (https://youtu.be/kmPYyk8OX50).
3 See *Sorry to Bother You* by Boots Riley and his interview with *CBS Morning* on "the white voice."
4 N.B.: I will not be discussing "The N-word" in this book, but it does appear in this book. There is a forthcoming book with a linguistic history and analysis of the N-word by Hiram Smith with Georgetown University Press titled *Nigga: Facts, Myths, and Misunderstandings about a Controversial Word*. Instances of racial slurs and profanity will usually be written using the IPA to minimize sensitivities.

inside. Any racial slurs come to mind here that are turned on their head? Just in case, it is [pɔrtʃ mʌŋki]. See the irony and feel the discomfort? That is the history of Black people in the Americas.

And then there are those African Americans who financially profit from the language and culture of African Americans while simultaneously **dissing** them. Bill Cosby's 1970s career with *Fat Albert and the Cosby Kids* (1972), *Uptown Saturday Night* (1974), *Let's Do It Again* (1975), and *A Piece of the Action* (1977) were built on Black people, Black language, and Black culture. Jesse Jackson's charisma is built on the Black Church. Maya Angelou's groove was built on her use of language and culture of African America. They all use language varieties acquired, nurtured, and developed in their African American communities and yet denied their own people for the sake of respectability. *Et tu*?

Linguistic Shame and Denial

Well, you might ask, "Where were 'regular' Black folk during these crises since the Black elite were **acting a fool**?" They too were denying the legitimacy of their language, culture, and history. Black folks are some of the most vehement and vocal critics against their own language and educational interventions. In Mufwene's "What Is African American English?" he relates the following incident that exemplifies the contradiction:

> A young man in a congregation to which I was explaining the situation said in reference to Ebonics, perceived as the speech of "the ignorant" and gang members, "Ain't nobody here talk like that." His focus may not have been so much on those features in his own statement that make it obvious to a linguist that he speaks AAVE but on the kinds of words and communicative exchanges which are contained in several examples that linguists and the media have provided of what AAVE or Ebonics is.
>
> (Mufwene 2001, 35)

In a separate incident and as further evidence, the following conversation occurred between my mother (G), my sister (D), and me

(S). Both my mother and sister strongly identify with their Southern Black language, culture, and communities:

G: I see they took Patti LaBelle's show off.
D: I know. I likeded that show.
G: Now what you sayin that fuh?
S: It's supposed to be on next week.
G: That's <undecipherable> talking bout I likeded that show.
D: I say I likeded that show.
G: I liked. L—I—K—E—D.
S: It's coming on today.
G: Don't you go down there changing—acting—changing yo uh speech. That's two things—cause something else you said. Those tesses. Better be trying to tell them (Lanehart 2002, 178).

Again, if African American communities cannot and will not accept their language varieties publicly and proudly, without prejudice, then who will or should?

For most of my life, I have served as the arbiter of good English in my family. When I was a child, I relished the role as one who wanted to fix the way Black people talk (hence, my initial, misguided intention to be a speech pathologist). When I became an adult and learned better while taking English language and linguistics classes as an undergraduate, I cringed at the role I had embraced most of my life at that point. I spent years afterwards trying to shed myself of that role and all it signified to me: The time in my life when I thought we (i.e., Black people, Black language, Black culture) were the problem. Yes, indeed, **how does it feel to be a problem** (DuBois 1903a)? As I tried to shed the role of the prescriptivist language authority, I passionately tried to instill confidence in family members, and my mom in particular. One day my mom said to me, "You can tell me it doesn't matter and to just write or say what I want how I want because you know how to say it right. I don't." That hit me like a ton of bricks. In other words, I had the luxury of telling my mom to use her language, be proud of it, and to not overthink it because my linguistic repertoire was larger than hers and included ways of talking and writing that reflected my acquiescence—I mean, acquisition—of white ways of speaking and writing that white people found acceptable and Black people found respectable. I am the one who is told, "**You are so articulate**" (see Alim and Smitherman 2012), not my mom. Our language of identity **is complicated like that**.

Linguistic Pride and Acceptance

Fortunately, other African Americans are saying very different things about their language. Some realize the language and the people are inextricably linked, as evidenced in the work of Geneva Smitherman (e.g., Smitherman 2000) and attested by Toni Morrison during an interview in response to the question, "What do you think is distinctive about your fiction? What makes it good?"

> **The language, only the language** [emphasis added]. . . . It is the thing that [B]lack people love so much. . . . The worst of all possible things that could happen would be to lose that language. There are certain things I cannot say without recourse to my language. It's terrible to think that a child with five different present tenses comes to school to be faced with those books that are less than his [sic] own language. And then to be told things about his [sic] language, which is him [sic], that are sometimes permanently damaging. He [sic] may never know the etymology of Africanisms in his [sic] language, not even know that "hip" is a real word or that "the dozens" meant something.
> (LeClair 1981, 27)

This is why we love Toni Morrison. She centered Black people. She told Black stories without apology. She loved Black language, her people, her culture, her communities. She was **rooting for everybody Black** even when they were not. African Americans like Toni Morrison, Robert Williams, and James Baldwin valued the language varieties of their African American communities because they **understood the assignment** (i.e., the controversies, the internalized hatred, the backlash against the language was never about the language). I'll also add Ossie Davis (2003) to the list for his article, "The English Language Is My Enemy!" where he laments that there are so many positive or neutral synonyms for white and none for "black/Black" in the English language. And that's the language we're supposed to use? Yeah, we most definitely **understand the assignment**.

Contradictions and All

An irony in these contradictions of beliefs and practices is the fact that the language of African Americans has existed and thrived for hundreds of years. While some Black folks deny their language, they continue to use it—at home with family and friends, at church, at beauty and barber shops, at family reunions, at **the cookout**, in literature and song eloquently and without excuse, and, yes, at school—because of its *covert prestige* (Baugh 1999). Still, most will not publicly accept it as a legitimate form of communication and expression outside of their community other than to refer to it as slang, incorrect, substandard, or just bad (but not in the good way). Clearly, there is an issue of covert prestige involved because no matter how much some African Americans denigrate their language varieties and say that it is bad English, they continue to use it. For some African Americans, it is the only language they know. This contradictory stance presents a conundrum in a day and time when non-Black folks and business and industry continue to appropriate elements of Blackness and Black culture as if they are **bad (but in the good way; you know, like Michael Jackson)**, for the purpose of making money, selling African American culture to the highest bidders and the hungriest consumers of our culture (see Lee 1999). The message seems to be that it is permissible to act Black or fake-speak Black, but it is not acceptable to actually be Black and do Black Talk (Smitherman 1994). It may be cool to do so in certain circumstances, but it is certainly not "professional." But this is nothing new. Black folks are used to being robbed and **dissed**:

> I do not know what white Americans would sound like if there had never been any [B]lack people in the [U.S.], but they would not sound the way they sound. . . . [I]t is late in the day to attempt to penalize [B]lack people for having created a language . . . of reality.
>
> (Baldwin 1979, A19)

Yes, what would language in the U.S. look like without the language of Black Americans to steal from? No, really, what do you think? This is a good thought experiment to incorporate not only language variation and change, but also rethinking sociocultural and historical contexts of the U.S. and subsequent globalization.

What You're Not Going to Do: Definitions, Naming, and Pet Peeves

I have some pet peeves about language just like everyone else. When I say pet peeves, I do not mean that I think some language varieties are better or worse than others. However, keep in mind that I did start off my life as a prescriptivist who was going to be all about fixing (Black) people's languages as a speech pathologist and eventually evolved into a descriptivist who was more interested in understanding how people actually use language as opposed to telling them how they should. My biggest pet peeve is when people refer to language varieties of African Americans as slang. **That's what you're not going to do here**. In order to show you why, we need to spend some time with definitions.

Let's start with *slang* since that is the big one for me. Slang exists in all varieties; it is not specific to Black folks. Slang only refers to vocabulary, words and phrases, or expressions; temporary aspects of the lexicon that closely tie to identity, stance, routine, micro-groups, etc. As such, the language of Black folks can't be called slang. Slang is fleeting. It is about being hip and cool or in-the-know now. It is the catchy phrase or the latest song hook. Some slang outlasts its fleeting title, like *bad* meaning "good, cool." Some of that depends on how hip and in-the-know now you are, your age or generation, locale, etc. What is slang and hip for me as a 50-something-year-old **Blackademic** mother and wife with Texas and Louisiana roots married to a white, male, rural, Minnesotan is different for my 20-something biracial musician and gamer son with Georgia and Texas roots with a teensy bit of Louisiana and Minnesota thrown in the mix. My son laughs and shakes his head at me all the time with a look that says, "Mom, just stop," when I think I **got it goin on**. That is slang: A 50-something woman trying to sound cool with some words she heard in a popular Beyoncé,

Megan Thee Stallion, Lizzo, or Cardi B song or voting for the American Dialect Society's Word of the Year. *WAP*, *and I oop*, *hot girl summer*, *woke*, *on fleek*, **YOLO (à la Drake 2012)**. That is slang. Language varieties of Black folks do not constitute as slang since languages are not a bunch of cool words strung together to make cool sentences. These varieties *use* slang like all varieties do, but **slang is not synonymous with language**. Slang is vocabulary. It is part of the lexicon. You know, how **24/7** became hip on *CNN Headline News* (I was alive to witness it) or how the late Stuart Scott, a host on ESPN's *SportsCenter*, was the envy of white dudes for his Black expressions they tried to imitate as if they were *as cool as the other side of the pillow*.

To HEL—or HEC—and Back: The Messiness of Having the Army and the Navy

Now things get a little messy because language, in addition to being social and communal, is political. Linguists tend to define *language* as a structured system of communication that is mutually unintelligible from other systems. Swahili is a language. It is mutually unintelligible from Korean or Portuguese. English is a language, and it is mutually unintelligible from Arabic or Chinese. Chinese, however, is complicated. Most people tend to think of Chinese as one language because that's what the Chinese government wants everyone to believe. In actuality, it is several different languages. For political reasons, the Chinese government prefers to have us all believe that Chinese is one language with several dialects. *Dialects* are mutually intelligible forms of language that are used by different regional, ethnic, or social (demographic) groups, making up one big happy family of a language. However, roughly ten Chinese "dialects" are actually separate Chinese languages; i.e., they are not mutually intelligible. Mandarin is the most widely spoken and what people often mean when they refer to "Chinese" because it is the official language of the Chinese government and considered to be standard Chinese. You may also be familiar with Cantonese, which is the official Chinese language in Hong Kong. Chinese languages use a common writing system that allows for ease of communication across the languages and some shared understanding when in writing (see "How the Chinese Language Got Modernized" [Buruma 2022]).

Since you brought it up, my next pet peeve is how the term "standard" American English (SAmE) is often misused and misperceived. I feel like a *Doctor Who* "wibbly wobbly, timey wimey stuff"[5] explanation is due here. People think of SAmE as the be all, end all and, therefore, what we should all strive for. It is the King's/Queen's English. It is what is in grammar books. It is the **King James Version of the real deal in language (where my big white** *Bible* **African Americans at?)**. People also think that if they use this thing called "SAmE," they will have success, they will do well in life, they will have lots of opportunities, they will have it all because SAmE is equated with **all those things and a bag of chips** (or should I say "crisps" since we are still sort of in the British thing right now with *Doctor Who*?). If only the smart, educated, successful, good people use SAmE, then I can learn and use it and be all those things or have all those things too. These are examples of ideologies people have about SAmE (see Lanehart 2002).

People believe there is only one standard that reigns supreme (e.g., SAmE) in their language and everything else is lacking. They like to say things like, "If it is not in the dictionary, then it is not acceptable," or "If the grammar book says it is incorrect, then it is bad English." **Shut yo mouf!** Those are the same people who have no idea of what they are talking about. I'm sorry if that is you, but

---

5 For those of you who don't know, *Doctor Who* is a British sci-fi television show whose main character is known as The Doctor. The television show premiered in 1963, the day after President John F. Kennedy was assassinated. It is still ongoing. The main character is a Time Lord who travels through time and space in a machine called the TARDIS (Time and Relative Dimension in Space). Because the first Doctor was an elderly white man with serious health issues, the creators of the show decided that upon a Doctor's death, they could regenerate into a new Doctor; i.e., same person of sorts but different body. That way, if the actor playing The Doctor died, as was the concern about William Hartnell, the First Doctor, they could recast the role. The original idea was that a Time Lord could only regenerate ten times. However, they had to adjust that as the show is still in production today and now on the Thirteenth Doctor and soon to be Fourteenth. You should know that David Tennant as the Tenth Doctor is my all-time favorite and this line comes from one of the best *Doctor Who* episodes, "Blink."

you do not have to stay that way. There is no *one* dictionary. There is no *one* prescriptive grammar book. There is no *one* SAmE. Those are myths you have been sold, I mean told. Back in my undergraduate days, I spent a lot of time reading grammars and reading about the evolution of SAmE for my honors thesis. **I'm going to school you** here so you will not continue to spout ignorance or be held prisoner to feeling as though you are not good enough or telling someone they are not good enough because of how they speak.

Let's start with Rule #1 (my son has known this very well since he was little and throws it back at me when he can): All language is made up. That's right. It's made up. There is no reason why "dog" refers to the animal we know it as or why "hiss" refers to the sound of a snake in English. "Dog" is "chien" in French, "mbwa" in Swahili, and "txakurra" in Basque. Is every other language wrong that does not use "dog" for the four-legged animal being referred to in English? Of course not. In fact, I did not even use certain language examples because not all languages even use a Latin alphabetic orthographic (writing) system (e.g., Japanese is logographic and syllabic). Just because all language is made up, however, does not mean languages are not structured, systematic, or rule-governed. Remember the definition for language: A structured system of communication that is mutually unintelligible from other systems. Just because Swahili, French, and Basque are different from English—and each other—does not mean those differences are good or bad; they are just different.

Because I studied grammar books and the history of the English language (aka HEL or HOTEL) for fun when I was younger (undergrad and grad school), I also know that English grammar is based on Latin. That's right. All those crazy rules that were put in early grammar books were based on Latin grammar. That is why you are told things like, "Do not end a sentence with a preposition" or "Do not split an infinitive." Those things are not possible in Latin. It is literally not possible to split an infinitive in Latin because the infinitive is one word only and it, therefore, cannot be separated. Latin cannot help that English uses *to* to mark the infinitive (see, that's one there, that "to mark"). Also, grammars were written by various white men from different locales and backgrounds and prejudices. Some used their favorite authors as examples for SAmE in addition to using

Latin. Different white men admired a variety of other white men. **Whew, chile!** Some of these white men liked certain white poets better so they used them. As you can imagine, their grammars of what SAmE was varied not only because they valued different other white men but also because even the white men they valued did not consistently use language in the way their white male admirers liked or wanted to acknowledge. For example, many writers—and people—back in the Middle Ages used multiple negation (e.g., "There ain't no sense in this"). Of course, I cannot move on without also using "ask" as an example since even Oprah Winfrey had to tackle this when she had her talk show. Way **back in the day**, there were two versions of what we write as "ask": [æsk] and [æks]. At some point, someone's grammar that believed "ask" was the best spelling and [æsk] the best pronunciation won out over "aks" [æks], so there you have it. All of this is based on some people's *ipse dixit* opinions about what they preferred and not on anything scientific, logical, or even consistent. Hence, all language is made up.

Even today, grammars and grammarians do not agree on even best usage or best practices. I grew up going to Houston, Texas, schools and our grammar books versus others (and Microsoft Word's spellcheck and Dictonary.com) do not even endorse the same word spellings—in the United States of America. I grew up using the spelling "judgement," but others grew up using "judgment." That's right; different states use different textbooks, and those different textbooks tell you different things. While this could be a whole other thing, let's just stick with grammar books—and dictionaries. Not all dictionaries have the same words or definitions or acceptability judgements. If grammar "correctness" is based on the ordinary and often flawed or varied *ipse dixit* opinions of some old, dead white men, why are you getting your panties in a bunch over saying your variety is better than some other variety? Why believe that your variety is not good? There is no such thing as SAmE in that there is no one, all-powerful, all-encompassing best way to speak American English. SAmE is an ideal that was created for you to think horrible things about others and/or yourself. Stop it. Just stop it. In the words of Maya Angelou, **"When you know better, do better."** Well, now you know.

Did I hear someone say something about *variety*? In linguistics, we use the term "variety" when referring to a linguistic system. That means variety can be used to refer to language, dialect, vernacular, etc. That also provides a non-judgmental way to talk about human communication and expression. That is how I can refer to language use in African American communities without the judgement that goes along with saying whether it is a language or dialect or even creolized. We can refer to its vernacular varieties, though, since *vernacular* simply means the everyday, home, community, "informal" way of speaking your native variety as an ordinary, everyday person. Vernacular is used to refer to much of the language varieties of African Americans, and I want to push back on that. We all have a vernacular way of speaking because it is home for us. No judgement. As long as by now you know that language use in African American communities is *not* slang, then we are good. Speaking of slang, I should add that it is not *jargon* either since jargon, like slang, is only vocabulary, but specific to particular domains that are often technical in nature, like computerese, business, law, banking, gaming, technology, etc. It is vocabulary that insiders use with one another and that if you heard it you would likely just be hearing the Charlie Brown teacher sound effect "wah, wah, wah" because it does not make sense to you, an outsider of the specialized niche. Another example would be listening to **Blerds** (i.e., Black nerds) talk about technical things in sci-fi or video games. Wah, wah, wah.

Accent is another term you should know. *Accent* refers only to pronunciation. An accent is the way different people pronounce words. People from New Orleans, Louisiana, have a different accent, or way of pronouncing words, than people from Caledonia, Minnesota, or Oakland, California. Accents may be associated with particular dialects, but they are not *the* dialect—just the word pronunciations associated with the dialect. Just like "slang" is not a language, accent is not a language. For example, received pronunciation, better known as RP, is an accent used in British journalism media to reflect a certain type of learned speech. It is not a language; it is an accent that was contrived to reflect an ideal.

This time I know I am the one who brought up "creoles" because I noted that I use the term "variety" as a way to not commit to something when it is in question for some people. *Creole* is a hotly contested concept mainly because of the racial undertones (or overtones?) that seem to be connected to its history and use.

The racialization around creoles as a description for the creation or emergence of language is that it is often used to refer to the emergence of language by non-white folks: Gullah Geechee, Haitian Creole, Jamaican Creole, Hawaiian Creole, Guyanese Creole, etc. Notice anything? However, there is little if anything that differentiates the linguistic emergence of these creoles from that of the English language. Remember, I started off my studies in language as a medievalist. The English language is a creolization of the languages of the Angles, Saxons, and Jutes that formed the country that we now call England and the language that we call English. Show me how I am wrong if you do not believe it. I know this is a very condensed version of the history of the English language (HEL)—or should I say the history of the English creole (HEC)? Wait, still a language. That is funny because the former is often abbreviated as HEL (or HOTEL) and this latter one could be abbreviated as HEC, as in "heck." Get it? Word nerd humor. Be that as it may, the point is, let's **call a spade a spade**. We'll talk more about this in Chapter 4.

What I want you to see in all of this is that there are not really clean, clear ways we talk about or understand human communication and expression because we are combining ideologies, attitudes and beliefs, politics, and more. Even though all language is made up, it is made up by those who hold varying ideas and beliefs and have particular ways of knowing and understanding that are built into the DNA of our languages of identity (see Lanehart 1996). Okay, we are done for now—as long as you are all good with these terms and what they are and are not.

While we are on the subject, I should note Rule #2: Language changes. If a language is not changing, it is dying or dead. Think Latin. The "English" that the Angles, Saxons, and Jutes created did not look or sound the same as English 700 years later. That 700 hundred years later version did not look or sound the same as the 1,000 years later version. And none of it looks or sounds the same as English does today. You would absolutely not comprehend English from its humble beginnings or a thousand years ago. The only reason we have any semblance of what we know as English today is because of Caxton's printing press that was used to codify English spelling. The printing press was named the most significant invention of the millennium (i.e., 1000–1999) for a reason. The ability to print books for the masses and codify spelling was a marvel. Even though people pronounced the words printed on the page differently, they had shared meaning and understanding (remember the discussion about Chinese?). It is no mystery why the Gutenberg Bible was the first thing printed (think colonization and missionaries). Bringing books to the masses meant being able to share knowledge more quickly and expansively—but it also meant the narrative could be controlled by those with the army and the navy,[6] literally and figuratively.

The printing press aided the rise of the middle class. Social media is the 21st-century expansion of the impact of the printing press. In other words, the printing press allowed for everyday folks to learn to read and write in their native language, share their learning and understanding, and move above their station in societies that had a firm grasp on social hierarchy. What the printing press could not do is stop language change. So, while it was codifying spelling (which was not instantaneous, of course) and trying to do the same with grammar, it could not stunt language change and variation. While you may be able to comprehend some Middle English, which is the variety of English in use at the time of the invention of the printing press, the printing press did not halt the emergence of Early Modern English and now Modern, or Present-day, English. All languages change or they will die. Language is human communication and expression that serves the purposes and needs of humans. Humans are both individuals and groups (i.e., cultural and social). The former acquires and creates language that impacts the language of the latter and vice versa. Language is a living entity that grows and evolves. Forces outside of the individual impact the maintenance and development of language.

Here is where identity and racism come into play. This calls for a definition break. I am using the definitions provided by Merriam-Webster

---

[6] The expression, "a language is a dialect with an army and a navy," was attributed to Max Weinreich (1945), a Yiddish scholar. It means that definitions and use around "language" and "dialect" are arbitrary and depend more on social and political power.

online and endorsed by the renowned Michael Harriot of *The Root* (www.theroot.com/is-credit-racist-1847571502): *Racism* is defined as

(1) a belief that race is a fundamental determinant of human traits and capacities and that racial differences produce an inherent superiority of a particular race; (2a) the systemic oppression of a racial group to the social, economic, and political advantage of another; and (2b) a political or social system founded on racism and designed to execute its principles (www.merriam-webster.com/dictionary/racism).

Donnor (2019, 21) defines *white racism* as:

1 The culturally sanctioned, accepted, and enforced beliefs that regardless of intent defend and advance the historically derived political, legal, social, and material advantages white people have accrued at the expense of the collective advancement of African Americans (Wellman 1993); and
2 How white people use society's governing institutions (i.e., education, law, and public policy) to entrench the aforementioned advantages and subordinate Black people.

Racism is embedded in language because language reflects our identities, ideologies, attitudes, and more. With the increase in the availability of books came the onset of higher rates of literacy. With literacy came the need for mass education because society could not have everyone reading and writing without there being some control over what that looked like. They could not have just anyone sharing their ideas with the masses. They had to establish what ideas were worth sharing. It was okay to have some education for the masses, but it was not okay to have quality, extensive learning and growing, and exploration. Just check out what state constitutions say about education or the *Brown v. Board of Education of Topeka* (1954, 1955) decisions (yes, there were two decisions). Equality was never the plan. Did I also mention my background in the history of literacy and education in the U.S. and Canada? I can stop here because, as we all know, this does not apply to Black people in the history of North America. Literacy and education were denied to them for hundreds of years in this land they were herded to because, as W.E.B. DuBois said in *The Souls of Black Folks*,

> The South believed an educated Negro to be a dangerous Negro. And the South was not wholly wrong; for education among all kinds of men [sic] always has had, and always will have, an element of danger and revolution, of dissatisfaction and discontent. Nevertheless, men [sic] strive to know.
>
> (1903a, 61)

All those people who are anti-education, anti-CRT (Critical Race Theory), anti-Ethnic Studies, anti-Blackness, anti-everything that challenges the white status quo should take notice of the words of W.E.B. DuBois and the impetus behind this pseudo activism.

There is a connection between the codification of written language and literacy. If Black people were denied education and literacy, what of their language was being codified from its oral status and by whom?

Before we move on, I want to take your pulse on your attitudes and beliefs. You each came to this **feeling some kinda way** about language varieties in African American communities. I cannot instantly change those feelings with a few words, but I do hope you confront those feelings, especially if they are negative. To have negative feelings about the language varieties of African Americans is to have negative feelings about the people. You cannot separate the two; you just can't. So, ask yourself: What is it that you really do not like about Black people's use of their language? What does it evoke in you when you hear a Black person speak? Is the reaction to the language or the person? Set-up question: What ideologies, attitudes, and behavior arise when you hear a Black person even say, "Hello?" (Purnell, Idsardi, and Baugh 1999). At the very least, let's be honest with each other—and ourselves. Regardless, I implore you to remember that I, too, am America (Langston Hughes 1926).

Questions, Discussion, and Further Inquiry

1 What language and linguistic attitudes, beliefs, ideologies, and subjectivities are you bringing to the table of this classroom?

2   What is your vernacular language?
3   Do you have any African American friends you hang out with (e.g., do they come to your home, break bread with you, know your family)? What do you think about their language? Do they sound like what you expect African Americans to sound like? Do they sound just like you? Do you like the way your language variety sounds to you? When you hear African Americans talking, do you think they sound cool, hip, **ignant**, ghetto, normal, uneducated, country, **ratchet**? Do you clutch your proverbial pearls? Do you cross the street and hope it does not rub off on you or your children or your grandchildren? Do you want to talk like them—at least with your friends but maybe not around your parents or family or workplace? Do you want to be around them? Do you want to be like them (not in a Rachel Dolezal way, though)? Do you change the channel?
4   What does DuBois mean by asking, "How does it feel to be a problem?"
5   What are some examples of how linguistic prejudice shows up in the media you consume and the people you spend time with?
6   Why do you think SAmE ideology is so pervasive? Do you believe one has to be competent in SAmE to exhibit intelligence and achieve academic, personal, and career success?
7   What makes one language or variety better than another?
8   How is racism embedded in language; i.e., how is language racialized?
9   If Black people were denied education and literacy, what of their language was being codified from its oral status?
10 So, ask yourself: What is it that you really do or do not like about Black people's use of their language? What does it evoke in you when you hear a Black person speak? Is the reaction to the language or the person?
11 What are your earliest memories of what was correct and what was wrong linguistically?
12 Where have you seen the language varieties of African Americans influencing American linguistic culture more broadly?
13 What would language in the U.S. look like without the language of Black Americans? Would Hip Hop exist?

14 Considering Baldwin (1979), what is the correlation between access to education and societal respect? If we deny a population education, how does that affect the attitudes toward that population? That population's attitudes toward themselves?
15 What are some "contradictions" surrounding your language and identity? Where do you experience cognitive dissonance?

References

Alexander, Benjamin H. 1980. Standard English: The Hell with Anything Else. *Vital Speeches of the Day* 46.14: 437–440.

Alim, H. Samy, and Geneva Smitherman. 2012. *Articulate While Black: Barack Obama, Language, and Race in the U.S*. Oxford and New York: Oxford University Press.

Baldwin, James. 1979. If Black English Isn't a Language, Then Tell Me, What Is? *The New York Times*. July 29: E19. https://archive.nytimes.com/www.nytimes.com/books/98/03/29/specials/baldwin-english.html?_r=1&oref=slogin

Baugh, John. 1999. *Out of the Mouths of Slaves: African American Language and Educational Malpractice*. Austin, TX: University of Texas Press.

Bell, Derrick. 1992. Space Traders. In *Faces at the Bottom of the Well: The Permanence of Racism*. New York: Basic Books.

Brown v. Board of Education of Topeka, 347 U.S. 483 (1954).

Brown v. Board of Education of Topeka, 349 U.S. 294 (1955).

Davis, Ossie. 2003. The English Language Is My Enemy! Association for the Study of African-American Life and History and ProQuest Information and Learning Company.

Donnor, Jamel K. 2019. Understanding the Why of Whiteness: Negrophobia, Segregation, and the Legacy of White Resistance to Black Education in Mississippi. In *Understanding Critical Race Research Methods and Methodologies: Lessons from the Field*, edited by Jessica T. DeCuir-Gunby, Thandeka K. Chapman, and Paul A. Schutz, 13–23. New York and London: Routledge.

DuBois, W.E. Burghardt. 1903a. *The Souls of Black Folk: Essays and Sketches*. Chicago: A.C. McClurg & Co.

DuBois, W.E. Burghardt. 1903b. The Talented Tenth. In *The Negro Problem: A Series of Articles by Representative Negroes of Today*, edited by Booker T. Washington. New York: James Pott & Company.

Freire, Paulo. 1970. *Pedagogy of the Oppressed*. Translated by Myra Ramos. New York: Seabury Press.

Hughes, Langston. 1926/2015. I, Too. In *The Weary Blues*. New York: Alfred A. Knopf.

Lanehart, Sonja. 1996. The Language of Identity. *Journal of English Linguistics* 24.4: 322–331.

Lanehart, Sonja. 1998. African American Vernacular English in Education: The Dynamics of Pedagogy, Ideology, and Identity. *Journal of English Linguistics* 26.2: 122–136.

Lanehart, Sonja. 2002. *Sista, Speak! Black Women Kinfolk Talk about Language and Literacy*. Austin, TX: University of Texas Press.

LeClair, Thomas. 1981. The Language Must Not Sweat: A Conversation with Toni Morrison. *New Republic*, March 21. https://newrepublic.com/article/95923/the-language-must-not-sweat.

Lee, Margaret G. 1999. Out of the Hood and into the New: Borrowed Black Verbal Expressions in a Mainstream Newspaper. *American Speech* 74.4: 369–388.

Malcolm X. 1963. *The Race Problem. Recorded at African Students Association and NAACP Campus Chapter*. East Lansing: Michigan State University.

Martin Luther King, Jr., Elementary School Children v. Ann Arbor School District, 473 F. Supp. 1371 (E.D. Michigan 1979).

Mufwene, Salikoko S. 2001. What Is African American English? In *Sociocultural and Historical Contexts of African American English*, edited by Sonja Lanehart, 21–51. Amsterdam: John Benjamins.

Purnell, Thomas, William Idsardi, and John Baugh. 1999. Perceptual and Phonetic Experiments on American English Dialect Identification. *Journal of Language and Social Psychology* 18.1: 10–30.

Rickford, John Russell, and Russell John Rickford. 2000. *Spoken Soul: The Story of Black English*. New York: John Wiley and Sons.

Smith, Hiram. Forthcoming. *Nigga: Facts, Myths, and Misunderstandings about a Controversial Word*. Washington, DC: Georgetown University Press.

Smitherman, Geneva. 1994. *Black Talk: Words and Phrases from the Hood to the Amen Corner*. Boston: Houghton Mifflin.

Smitherman, Geneva. 2000. *Talkin that Talk: Language, Culture, and Education in African America*. London: Routledge.

Walker, Alice. 1982. *The Color Purple*. New York: Harcourt.

Weinreich, Max. 1945. *YIVO Bleter* 25.1–3.

Wellman, David T. 1993. *Portraits of White Racism*, 2nd ed. Cambridge: Cambridge University Press.

Filmography

Chappelle, Dave, and Neal Brennan. 2003. *Chappelle's Show*. Season 1, Episode 1. Hollywood, CA: Comedy Central.

Cosby, Bill. 1972–1984. *Fat Albert and the Cosby Kids*. New York: CBS Studios. 110 episodes.

King, Regina, director. 2020. *One Night in Miami*. Amazon Studios. www.amazon.com/Night-Miami-Leslie-Kingsley-Ben-Adir/dp/B08NLFDCXZ

McGruder, Aaron, creator. 2005–2014. *The Boondocks*. Culver City, CA: Sony Pictures Television. 55 episodes.

Moffat, Steven, writer. 2007. *Doctor Who: Blink*. Series 3, Episode 10. BBC.

Newman, Sydney, C. E. Webber, Donald Wilson, creators. 1963–present. *Doctor Who*. BBC Studios.

Poitier, Sidney, director. 1974. *Uptown Saturday Night*. Warner Bros.

Poitier, Sidney, director. 1975. *Let's Do It Again*. Warner Bros.

Poitier, Sidney, director. 1977. *A Piece of the Action*. Warner Bros.

Riley, Boots, writer and director. 2018. *Sorry to Bother You*. Mirror Releasing, Focus Features, and Universal Pictures. 112 minutes.

Tarantino, Quentin, director. 2012. *Django Unchained*. Sony Pictures Home Entertainment. 165 minutes.

Discography

Drake. 2012. The Motto. Track 19 on *Take Care*. Cash Money Records.

Jackson, Michael. 1987. Bad. Track 1 on *Bad*. Epic.

Lamar, Kendrick. 2015. Alright. Track 7 on *To Pimp a Butterfly*. Aftermath/Interscope Records.

Digital Media

Ask Steve: Don't Correct Me! 2017. *YouTube*, uploaded by Steve TV Show, April 11. https://youtu.be/kmPYyk8OX50

Buruma, Ian. 2022. How the Chinese Language Got Modernized. *New Yorker Magazine*. www.newyorker.com/magazine/2022/01/17/how-the-chinese-language-got-modernized

Director Boots Riley on the "Mythical White Voice" in *Sorry to Bother You*. *YouTube*, uploaded by *CBS Mornings*, July 16, 2018. https://youtu.be/Q00Dl8UHvPU

Harriot, Michael. Is Credit Racist? 2021. *The Root*. September 2. www.theroot.com/is-credit-racist-1847571502

Racism. www.merriam-webster.com/dictionary/racism

Chapter 3

"*Put Some Respeck on My Name!*"

Language and Uses of Identity in African American Communities

Introduction: *How We Gon Play This?*

I hope **we straight** on what you're bringing to the table in this journey. I cannot say the same when it comes to naming. Up until now, I have not given a name to the language we are talking about beyond language in African American communities. However, that has become even more difficult for me. I taught a graduate course on this topic in Spring 2021 at the University of Arizona with a small but amazing group of linguistics doctoral students. We had some of the best discussions I have had about language in African American communities, about naming, origins and development, and variation. We brought in noted language and linguistics scholars during the second half of the course to discuss various topics and go down the rabbit hole with us as we worked our way through the nearly 1,000 pages of *The Oxford Handbook of African American Language* (Lanehart 2015, which I will rely on for a bit here in this initial discussion). There, I said it: African American Language.

I have been using the term *African American Language* as an umbrella term to refer to all varieties of language use in African American communities for several years, recognizing that there are many varieties within the umbrella term, which include Gullah Geechee and vernacular varieties, as well as varieties that reflect differences in age/generation, sex, gender and gender identity, sexuality, social and socioeconomic class, dis/ability, region, education, religion, and other identities that intersect with one's ethnicity/race and being and belonging. My preference to use African

DOI: 10.4324/9781003204756-3

American *Language* (AAL) as opposed to African American *English* (AAE) has been to bypass some of the problematic implications of "English" within the socioculture and history of enslaved Africans in the United States and the contested connections of their language varieties to the motherland and colonized varieties in the U.S. that encompass rhetorical and pragmatic strategies that might not be associated with English. "AAE" is fraught with connotations and assumptions that preclude certain discussions. While "AAL" can instigate contentious discussions as well, at least they have the potential to be new ones. And, in this case, it was African American linguists who originated the term. Also, "language" is less restrictive or limiting than "English" in this situation. Its use allows me to lessen the focus on the origins of AAL and increase the focus on the social and cultural lives of those who created and continue to evolve AAL. In other words, the use of the term "AAL" is more neutral and, therefore, less marked but also more unifying. If only it were that simple.

The existence of Gullah Geechee and the perspective of its speakers (i.e., Gullah Geechee speakers say they speak English) is a complicating factor, but how complicating depends on how you define AAL. I choose to define AAL in agreement with Mufwene as the variety "spoken by or among African Americans" because "[a] language variety is typically associated with a community of speakers and, in many communities, a language means no more than the particular way its members speak" (Mufwene 2001, 21). For example, if we look up "Italian" on Dictionary.com, it is defined as "of or pertaining to Italy, its people, or their language; a native or inhabitant of Italy, or a person of Italian descent." Mufwene is saying that we can define AAL in the same way: of or pertaining to African Americans; a person of African American descent. Given this definition, AAL is the umbrella term for all ways of language use of African Americans—including Gullah Geechee, Louisiana French Creole, and African American Vernacular Language (AAVL). In my classes, I describe AAL as the umbrella covering all its varieties across the U.S. where African Americans are. That means it covers West Coast AAL, East Coast AAL, Southern AAL, Louisiana French Creole, Afro-Seminole, Gullah Geechee, AAVL, and everything in between.

Who Do People Say That I Am?[1]

"Research" on language use in African American communities began as early as the 1920s with a few preliminary investigations into the variety (see, for example, Krapp 1924). However, Lorenzo Dow Turner's *Africanisms in the Gullah Dialect* was the earliest, most influential (real) research on AAL. Research did not truly escalate until the 1960s and early 1970s with the civil rights movement, school desegregation, and integration and the subsequent work of mostly white linguists, such as Robbins Burling (1973), Joey L. Dillard (1972, 1977), Ralph Fasold (1972), William Labov and colleagues (1968, 1972), William Stewart (1967), and Walt Wolfram (1969), and some Black linguists, such as Claudia Mitchell-Kernan (1971, 1972a, 1972b, 1973), Geneva Smitherman (1968, 1972, 1973a, 1973b, 1974), and Orlando Taylor (1972, 1973). As the body of work developed, three very broad categories emerged: linguistic structure and description, origins and development, and language use and attitudes—especially in education.

From the mid- to late-1960s, the initial period of heightened interest in language use in African American communities, to the present, many different labels have been used to refer to the language varieties, and the label has often been related to the social climate (see Baugh 1991; Smitherman 1991). To some extent, the labels have been used to link the variety to those who speak it. For example, when African Americans were referred to as "Negroes," the varieties were called "Negro English" and "Negro dialect." When African Americans were referred to as "Black," the varieties were called "Black English" and "Black Vernacular English," or "Black English Vernacular." As such, the terms of self-reference and linguistic labels have changed over the years, spanning a range from use of "Colored" to "Negro" to "Black" to "African American" and other less flattering terms. The varied labels for AAL are: *Negro Dialect, Nonstandard Negro English, Substandard Negro English, Negro English, American Negro Speech, Black Dialect, Black Communication, Black Folk Speech, Black Street Speech* (by Baugh 1983), *Black English, Black*

---

[1] See Matthew 16.

English Vernacular (BEV), *Black Vernacular English* (BVE), *Vernacular Black English* (VBE), *Black Language* (BL, which is back in style à la Baker-Bell 2020), *Afro-American English, Ebonics* (Robert Williams 1975), *African American English, African American Vernacular English* (AAVE), *Spoken Soul* (Rickford and Rickford 2000), *African American Language*, and *African American Vernacular Language* (AAVL). How AAL is named is, in part, based on who is defining it and how it is defined and who is doing the naming. With the various labels and the varied definitions, some definitions refer more broadly to ways of speaking among some African Americans, and others refer to more narrow components of grammar used by those who are members of particular speech communities. The point is that researchers use these terms but with little consensus or clarification as to what or whom their term is referring to specifically.

Still, regardless of which term(s) researchers use—AAE or AAL, AAVE or AAVL—they all refer to language varieties that have systematic, rule-governed phonological (system of sounds), morphological (system of structure of words and relationship among words), syntactic (system of sentence structure), semantic (system of meaning), and lexical (structural organization of vocabulary items and other information) patterns. So, when speakers know AAL, they know sounds, word and sentence structure, meaning and structural organization of vocabulary items, and other linguistic, metalinguistic, and paralinguistic systems about their language, such as pragmatic rules and the social function of AAL. Indeed, the linguistic variety also includes slang linked to popular culture, drag queen ballroom culture, Hip Hop culture, Black Twitter, etc. However, as we have noted, AAL is not slang, "broken English," or "bad English" because those terms and ideas do not characterize the variety of those who speak AAL, or any language variety. Such labels only serve to diminish the language and its speakers and say more about the person using those labels than the people referred to by the labels. Keep remembering that.

A Word on Ebonics

Remember from Chapter 1 when I questioned what I should title this book because the term the publisher wanted—Ebonics—was not the term linguists use? I asked, "If linguists do not use it and this book is published in collaboration with the Linguistic Society of America, then it should focus on that space, right??? **Well** ... Dr. Robert Williams coined the term *Ebonics* in 1973 at a psychology conference of Black scholars. In his 1975 introduction to *Ebonics: The True Language of Black Folks*, Williams states:

> **Ebonics** [emphasis added] may be defined as "the linguistic and paralinguistic features which on a concentric continuum represents the communicative competence of the West African, Caribbean, and United States slave descendant of African origin. It includes the various idioms, patois, argots, idiolects, and social dialects of Black people," especially those who have been forced to adapt to colonial circumstances. **Ebonics** [emphasis added] derives its form from ebony (black) and phonics (sound, the study of sound) and refers to the study of the language of Black people in all its cultural uniqueness.
>
> (1975, vi)

The view of Williams and other Black scholars at the conference was that the language of Black people had its roots in Africa's Niger-Congo languages. By definition, Ebonics is larger than the scope of this book since we will only be discussing African Americans and their language in the United States. Here we have Black scholars giving my language a name. No, they weren't linguists, but they were Black, educated, scholars who were psychologists who were part of the Black Psychology movement. We need to give **props** to them for what they did, not ridicule.

Ebonics became a household term during the 1996–1997 Oakland School Board Ebonics Controversy and thereafter. In my opinion, that was one of the best things that came out of the national conversation because, finally, it gave a name to what many non-linguists usually referred to as "bad language" or no language at all—including those who spoke it. So, getting to "Ebonics" from "bad language" or "broken English" was at least a step in a better direction. However, questions about its validity and characterization in relation to what to call it and what it actually is have been both politically and ideologically fraught. Unfortunately, in spite of this increased focus on the most studied language variety in the U.S., it is also still quite misunderstood by the general public and still in search of a shared meaning and vocabulary. In order to narrow the communication gap between the lay public, non-linguists, and linguists, it is imperative that linguists do a better job presenting themselves and their research and raising the level of conversation. We need to have a shared vocabulary and understanding about language use in African American communities and linguistics in general. To start, we need to clarify what we mean when we refer to the language used by those in African American communities and how we talk about it.

What Does It Feel Like to Be a Problem?

It feels like everything about being Black in this world is to make us feel and believe that we are the problem—even naming our language varieties. My grappling with this even more of late is connected to the evolution of Blackness in the Americas as we demand more but also as we see the global struggle of our **brothas and sistas**. And I am fully aware that not everyone who is Black wants to claim it. For example, Afro-Latinx are Black. Middle Easterners are Black (the Middle East, after all, is in Africa). Southeast Asians are Black. That does not mean they cannot be both-and, but at least **call a spade a spade**. And all of this is complicated because, as I say, the African Diaspora is larger than many want to acknowledge. I know identity matters, sociocultural and historical contexts matter, but also, importantly, I recognize that race is a social construct that was meant to divide us for nefarious purposes and serves as a partner in crime with racism. You cannot have racism without race (see Wilkerson 2020).

The British Black Music/Black Music Congress (https://twitter.com/BBMBMC) held an online conference in 2020 on terms of self-reference and identity. They tackled the issue of naming in the U.K. and globally, especially Mother Africa. Africans and Africanists were in the room in addition to "Black" Brits. I was one of only a few Americans in the conference. I did not realize the level of conflict around the "Black vs. African vs. something else (the question seems to be a permanent point of discussion in the various emails I still receive from the organization). Those in the motherland called themselves "African" as a "race" but their tribal/ethnic/

"Put Some Respeck on My Name!" 47

language community as their primary ethnic identity. Those in the U.K. wanted either "African" or "Black" or something else. Right now, they are in the midst of a naming controversy in the U.K. over *BAME* (*Black, Asian, and Minority Ethnic*) and *BME* (*Black and Minority Ethnic*)—terms the (white) media chose to refer to Black folks—because they are considered inappropriate or offensive labels that Black Brits reject.[2] Really, people, don't **call me outta my name**!

I began my naming journey when I read Toni Morrison's "Unspeakable Things Unspoken" (1989) in graduate school at the University of Michigan. I had not yet arrived at the University of Michigan when Toni Morrison delivered the Tanner Lectures on Human Values on October 7, 1988. When I did discover it several years later, I felt abuzz with affirmation that I could look at things differently (while also confirming my *Go Blue!* allegiance). I did not have to view my life, my language, my culture, my people through a white gaze. Toni Morrison freed me.

> One has the feeling that nights are becoming sleepless in some quarters, and it seems to me obvious that the recoil of traditional "humanists" and some post-modern theorists to this particular aspect of the debate, the "race" aspect, is as severe as it is because the claims for attention come from that segment of scholarly and artistic labor in which the mention of "race" is either inevitable or elaborately, painstakingly masked; and if all of the ramifications that the term demands are taken seriously, the bases of Western civilization will require re-thinking. Thus, in spite of its implicit and explicit acknowledgment, "race" is still a virtually unspeakable thing, as can be seen in the apologies, notes of "special use" and circumscribed definitions that accompany it—not least of which is my own deference in surrounding it with quotation marks. Suddenly (for our purposes, suddenly) "race" does not exist. For three hundred years [B]lack Americans insisted that "race" was no usefully distinguishing factor in human relationships. During those same three

2 See https://civilservice.blog.gov.uk/2019/07/08/please-dont-call-me-bame-or-bme

centuries every academic discipline, including theology, history, and natural science, insisted "race" was *the* determining factor in human development. When [B]lacks discovered they had shaped or become a culturally formed race, and that it had specific and revered difference, suddenly they were told there is no such thing as "race," biological or cultural, that matters and that genuinely intellectual exchange cannot accommodate it. In trying to come to some terms about "race" and writing, I am tempted to throw my hands up. It always seemed to me that the people who invented the hierarchy of "race" when it was convenient for them ought not to be the ones to explain it away, now that it does not suit their purposes for it to exist.

(Morrison 1989, 3)

This was **all the things**. If Twitter existed back then, this would have been a hashtag: #UnspeakableThingsUnspoken along with #ImBlackAndProud, or something to that effect, to show that naming race in this racist system is important. And if we are going to connect the naming of my language to race, then the naming of my language is important too.

That was back then. What about now? Still, Toni Morrison. In a 1998 interview with Charlie Rose in which he asked about her thoughts regarding critiques on how her books fail to center white characters and worlds, she responds with a memorable Black woman's, "**Child, don't play with me today**" or "**Nah, Bruh**, I don't think so. Not today" expression that is now legend in GIFs as she eviscerates any critiques regarding race in her writings (see minutes 25:00 to 29:00 at https://charlierose.com/videos/17664). Next is a snippet of Morrison's interview response so you can see why the GIF is so powerful:

28:08

But, if I can say, when are you going to write about Black people to a white writer—if that's a legitimate question to a white writer, then it is a legitimate question to me. I just don't think it is. You know, the glove has to be pulled inside out. If— it's not a literary question. It has nothing to do with a literary imagination. It's a sociological question that should not be put to me. I couldn't ask that of any writer. You know, I wouldn't ask it of a Black writer, "When are you going to write about white people?" Now, maybe I'm wrong. You can tell me, now or later, if I've blown it up all out of proportion. I don't think so. I just don't know what the question means, except what I think it means. You think it may just be a little question, a little curious, you know, small incidental question. "When are you gonna?" Maybe I'm responding because I have had reviews in the past that have accused me of not writing about white people. I remember a review of *Sula* in which the reviewer said, "This is all well and good, but one day she"—meaning me—"will have to face up to her real responsibilities and get mature and write about the real confrontation for Black people, which is white people." As though our lives have no meaning and no depth without the white gaze. And I've spent my entire writing life trying to make sure that the white gaze was not the dominant one in any of my books.

Ooh, chile! That is a **mic-drop** moment and why this interview and Morrison's look during the interview when Rose asks the question became GIF worthy. But it is also why Toni Morrison is the **GOAT** as a writer and scholar. She released me from believing that the only way to talk about the language varieties of Black people is by talking about and comparing or juxtaposing them to white people's. In other words, I/we can examine, study, research, and engage the language varieties of Black folks without **studn bout** white folks. This may seem like an easy thing to say, but I have had fallouts with white folks over this because they wanted students to compare their research on Black people's language to that of white people's because somehow that made it legitimate in their eyes. Black people do not need or want the gaze of white people!

This issue of naming (both a racial group and its language varieties) and race go even deeper. I have used and capitalized "Black" throughout this book and my writing, and I will continue to do so for terms that refer to my people. However, my concern is with who gets to name me. Not all Black people we call Black call themselves Black or see themselves as such. Although this includes some Blacks who detest the term because of its connotations (i.e., black = bad), it also includes those who do not believe you can use a crayon color to delineate who they are (see Lanehart and Malik 2018). How many Black folks are actually black? How many white folks are actually white? And what "Asian" folks are yellow and Native Americans red? There is a Supreme Court case by an Asian person who disputed the segregation they were suffering under the Naturalization Act of 1790 (see *Ozawa v. United States*, 260 U.S. 178, 1922). Since the law limited citizenship to "any alien being a free white person" (among other things), then they should be eligible since their skin was whiter than most white people's. Of course, they lost the case. The Supreme Court ruled, essentially, that whiteness is a construct (of course, they didn't say it like that but that was the message) and, therefore, not really about actual "white" skin. Really?!!

In the 2011 documentary *Dark Girls*, there is a little girl who is darker than her brothers and mother, and she is tormented by that. She refuses to be called "Black" because she says she is not. In reality, her skin is not black—but she is a Black body. The distinction is important. Though her brothers and mother are of a lighter skin complexion, they are Black bodies as well. That is why the *one-drop rule* and names like *octoroon* (one-eighth Black ancestry/blood), *mulatto* (a person having one-half Black ancestry/blood), *quadroon* (a person having one-quarter Black ancestry/blood), and *good hair* do not let one escape the marginalization of the Black body and what goes with the narrative that has been constructed: You are still Black even if you are not black/Black or have one drop of black/Black blood so long as society says you are. Hence, Barack Obama is called our first Black president even though he is biracial. So, I capitalize "Black" because it is so much more than a color, just like hair in the Black community is not just hair (see Jacobs-Huey 2006; Chris Rock's 2009 *Good Hair*; and the 2018 Netflix movie *Nappily Ever After*). As James Sledd noted more than 50 years ago, even "compassionate, liberal educators, knowing the ways of society [i.e., the narrative society has constructed about Blackness], will change the color of their student's vowels because they cannot change the color of their students' skins" (1969, 1312). (See Lanehart 2015 for more discussion.)

"Put Some Respeck on My Name!" 51

My point is, this crayon list of races is a problem for the content of this book because, in part, every time there is a new term of self-reference that tries to get away from the white gaze, it is either not accepted in the white scholar community or it aligns with one group of African American or Black folks but not others. A look at the history of the names of the language variety of African Americans is a stroll down memory lane of where and **who we were when**—as a nation and as a people. That stroll is not a nostalgic one; it is a painful memory of **what it feels like to be a problem**. It is also a reminder that our name changes and the official name of our language variety changes, but the ways of white folks do not because they named everything. We never stood a chance. So, in the end, you still black/Black.

When we talk about the language variety of African Americans, we make it seem exotic—like it was "discovered"—using the white gaze. How do we escape that gaze? We name ourselves. However, when Robert Williams and other Black psychologists met to name it themselves, their term, Ebonics ([B]/black + sounds), was ridiculed and rejected (see Rickford and Rickford 2000; Scott 1998). Why? I know I have spelled out that Ebonics is larger than the language variety of African Americans in the U.S. However, Dr. Geneva Smitherman, aka Docta G (1998a, 1998b), proposed and uses *U.S. Ebonics* (*USEB*) as an alternative that was also rejected by linguists. Interestingly, Ebonics caught on with the public, I believe, not only because of the Ebonics Controversy but also because of the simplicity of it. It did so in a way linguists' terms for the language varieties of African Americans never did. I, myself, have not used Ebonics or U.S. Ebonics as a term of reference for the language variety of Black Americans when Docta G told us to use it because I wasn't ready.[3] I was too particular about the definition of Ebonics vs. what USEB could mean and do. I was still clinging to respectability in the same way I was trained to do so by the (white) academy even though my academic advisor, Dr. Richard Bailey, had tried to set me free all those years ago. So, where does that leave us?

---

3 "For what it's worth, I use 'Ebonics' when talking to lay audiences. And I tell them linguists use AAE or AAL nowadays AND that when I use 'Ebonics,' and when other linguists use it, we use it in a sense different from that of Williams, et al." (Arthur Spears, personal communication, December 2021).

Say My Name!

What's it going to be here: AAE, AAL, Ebonics, USEB, Black Language, or something else entirely? I think this is connected to the people and their language varieties and their right to name. Do we want a term that is connected to the changing terms of self-reference (e.g., Black Language vs. African American Language), or do we want a term that is connected to a language variety separate from changing terms of self-reference (e.g., U.S. Ebonics)? Doing the former means we will continue to have changing names for ethnic/racial language varieties as they change in society and communities. Doing the former means negotiating with a white gaze. Doing the latter means we can just do what we do on our own terms.

We have some options. We can take a page from Geneva Smitherman and use "U.S. Ebonics." While the public might not use the "U.S." part of it, linguists will know what people are talking about and they would be using something from Black scholars. If we follow Dr. April Baker-Bell (2020), we would use "Black Language" in contrast to "White Language." There would be no "Mainstream American English" or "General American English" or other things that try to obscure that those names are not meant to include Black people and surely are meant to mark/unmark white people. [That's why I liked Docta G's "Language of Wider (often mistaken for 'whiter') Communication."] More fundamentally, it is about the power wielders in the U.S., who are white. This is, in part, why we have had such trouble with things like bidialectalism, codeswitching, contrastive analysis, and the like in schools and society (see Chapter 9): They ask us to change our language and, therefore, change who we are as African Americans knowing that neither is possible epistemologically **because racism**.[4]

I think my best bet is to go with Toni Morrison (1989) and say that I cannot let the discomfort of white people deter me from speaking

---

4 Read or watch Derrick Bell's (1992) *Space Traders* for a deeper understanding and representation for what I am saying about the social construction of race and racism as seen through a Critical Race Theory, CRT, lens using a central CRT tenet, counter-storytelling, or counter-narrative. You can view *Space Traders* at https://youtu.be/2cfvbr62NBw.

and reclaiming Blackness into the life I give it (think *Afrofuturism*) instead of the death white people made for it (i.e., *Afropessimism*). And keeping in line with how I use and see "African American" and "Black," there may not be just one thing unless we use USEB. I am ready to embrace using USEB (thanks, Docta G), AAL (Docta G and me), Black Language (Dr. April Baker-Bell 2020), and John Russell Rickford and Russell John Rickford's *Spoken Soul* (Rickford and Rickford 2000), with a revised and adapted definition from Williams (1975):

> The linguistic, metalinguistic, and paralinguistic systems which on a concentric continuum represents the communicative and linguistic competence of the United States slave descendant of West African and Caribbean origin that includes the various dialects of generations of African Americans who have been forced to adapt to colonial circumstances, systems, and racism. It refers to and is the study of the language of African Americans in all their sociocultural and historical uniqueness.

That means USEB, AAL, Black Language, and Spoken Soul include regional variation (e.g., Pittsburghese, Louisiana French Creole, and Gullah Geechee); age/generation variation (e.g., children, youth, elders); dis/ability (e.g., Black American Sign Language, deafblind, deaf African American children in hearing families; see Stapleton 2015); gender (e.g., African American Women's Language); gender identity (e.g., genderqueer, nonbinary, transgender); sexuality (e.g., homosexual, pansexual, heterosexual); locale (e.g., urban, rural, suburban, exurban); Hip Hop Nation Language; repertoire (vernacular, "standard," codeswitching); family (e.g., Black children in adoptive white families, Black children of mixed-race families); and so much more because identity is complex, fluid, performed, constructed, and perceived through language, individuals, social networks, communities, societies, politics, etc. So, in this space at least, you can call it U.S. Ebonics/USEB, African American Language/AAL, Black Language/BL, or Spoken Soul—and **put some respeck on it!** I'll be using AAL and/or USEB moving forward. Just **don't call me outta my name**.

Questions, Discussion, and Further Inquiry

1. What labels have you used to describe different types of English varieties?
2. In your own words, why do you think nomenclature (i.e., naming) and definitions are important?
3. Should names used for race be connected to "Crayola colors" even though people are not really those colors?
4. Should "Crayola color" names for race be capitalized?
5. How do terms of self-reference complicate or elucidate naming linguistic/language varieties connected to peoples (e.g., ethnolects) and identities (e.g., sociolects)?
6. How might you name the variety centered in this discussion? Which name do you prefer?
7. What is African American Language? What is Black Language? What is Ebonics? What is U.S. Ebonics? What is Spoken Soul? Are they all exactly the same, or do they have some shades of difference?
8. How did the civil rights movement impact research on AAL/USEB?
9. Why was it insulting for Charlie Rose to ask Toni Morrison, "Can you imagine writing a novel that's not centered about race?" What did that question mean? Do you believe Morrison was "importing too much into the question"?
10. How might African Americans escape the white gaze?
11. Where have you seen examples of AAL/USEB in social media, readings, movies, TV, etc., and how has AAL/USEB been portrayed?
12. What are the consequences of speaking (i.e., using language) when the speech comes from a person with a Black body?
13. Why do you think "Ebonics" (or "U.S. Ebonics") was ridiculed and not embraced by linguists but was in broader society during and after the Ebonics Controversy?

References

Baker-Bell, April. 2020. *Linguistic Justice: Black Language, Literacy, Identity, and Pedagogy*. New York: NCTE-Routledge Research Series.

Baugh, John. 1983. *Black Street Speech: Its History, Structure, and Survival*. Austin: University of Texas Press.

Baugh, John. 1991. The Politicization of Changing Terms of Self-Reference among American Slave Descendants. *American Speech* 66.2: 133–46.

Bell, Derrick. 1992. Space Traders. In *Faces at the Bottom of the Well: The Permanence of Racism*. New York: Basic Books.

Burling, Robbins. 1973. *English in Black and White*. New York: Hold, Rinehart, and Winston.

Dillard, Joey L. 1972. *Black English: Its History and Usage in the United States*. New York: Vintage House.

Dillard, Joey L. 1977. *Lexicon of Black English*. New York: Seabury.

Fasold, Ralph. 1972. *Tense Marking in Black English*. Arlington, VA: Center for Applied Linguistics.

Jacobs-Huey, Lanita. 2006. *From the Kitchen to the Parlor: Language and African American Women's Hair Care*. Oxford: Oxford University Press.

Krapp, George P. 1924. The English of the Negro. *American Mercury* 2.5: 190–195.

Labov, William. 1972. *Language in the Inner City: Studies in the Black English Vernacular*. Philadelphia: University of Pennsylvania Press.

Labov, William, Paul Cohen, Clarence Robbins, and John Lewis. 1968. *A Study of Non-Standard English of Negro and Puerto Rican Speakers in New York City*, 2 vols. Philadelphia: US Regional Survey.

Lanehart, Sonja. 2015. African American Language and Identity: Contradictions and Conundrums. In *The Oxford Handbook of African American Language*, edited by Sonja Lanehart, 863–880. Oxford: Oxford University Press.

Lanehart, Sonja L., and Ayesha M. Malik. 2018. Black Is, Black Isn't: Perceptions of Language and Blackness. In *Language Variety in the New South: Contemporary Perspectives on Change and Variation*, edited by Jeffrey Reaser, Eric Wilbanks, Karissa Wojcik, and Walt Wolfram, 203–222. Chapel Hill: University of North Carolina Press.

Mitchell-Kernan, Claudia. 1971. Language Behavior in a Black Urban Community. Working Paper 23, No. 2. Berkeley, CA: Language Behavior Research Laboratory.

Mitchell-Kernan, Claudia. 1972a. On the Status of Black English for Native Speakers: An Assessment of Attitudes and Values. In *Functions of Language in the Classroom*, edited by Courtney B. Cazden, Vera P. John, and Dell Hymes, 195–210. New York: Teachers College Press.

Mitchell-Kernan, Claudia. 1972b. Signifying, Loud-talking, and Marking. In *Rappin' and Stylin' Out: Communication in Urban Black America*, edited by Thomas Kochman, 315–335. Urbana, IL: University of Illinois Press.

Mitchell-Kernan, Claudia. 1973. Signifying. In *Mother Wit from the Laughing Barrel: Readings in the Interpretation of Afro-American Folklore*, edited by Alan Dundes, 310–329. Englewood Hills, NJ: Prentice-Hall.

Morrison, Toni. 1989. Unspeakable Things Unspoken: The Afro-American Presence in American Literature. *Michigan Quarterly Review* 28.1: 1–34.

Mufwene, Salikoko. 2001. What Is African American English? In *Sociocultural and Historical Contexts of African American English*, edited by Sonja L. Lanehart, 21–51. Amsterdam: John Benjamins.

Ozawa v. United States, 260 U.S. 178 (1922).

Rickford, John Russell, and Russell John Rickford. 2000. *Spoken Soul: The Story of Black English*. New York: John Wiley and Sons.

Scott, Jerrie C. 1998. The Serious Side of Ebonics Humor. *Journal of English Linguistics* 26.2: 137–155.

Sledd, James. 1969. Bi-dialectalism: The Linguistics of White Supremacy. *English Journal* 58.9: 1307–1329.

Smitherman, Geneva. 1968. Continuity and Change in American Negro Dialects. *The Florida FL Reporter* 6.1: 3–4.

Smitherman, Geneva. 1972. Black Power is Black Language. In *Black Culture: Reading and Writing Black*, edited by Gloria M. Simmons and Helene D. Hutchinson, 85–91. New York: Holt McDougal.

Smitherman, Geneva. 1973a. Grammar and Goodness. *English Journal* 62.5: 774–778.

Smitherman, Geneva. 1973b. White English in Blackface, or Who Do I Be? *The Black Scholar* 4.8–9: 32–39.

Smitherman, Geneva. 1974. Soul'n Style (series). *The English Journal* 63.2–5.

Smitherman, Geneva. 1991. What Is Africa to Me?: Language, Ideology, and African American. *American Speech* 66:2: 115–132.

Smitherman, Geneva. 1998a. "Dat Teacher Be Hollin at Us:" What Is Ebonics? *TESOL Quarterly* 32.1: 139–143.

Smitherman, Geneva. 1998b. Ebonics, King, and Oakland: Some Folk Don't Believe Fat Meat Is Greasy. *Journal of English Linguistics* 26.2: 97–107.

Stapleton, Lissa. 2015. When Being Deaf is Centered: d/Deaf Women of Color's Experiences with Racial/Ethnic and d/Deaf Identities in College. *Journal of College Student Development* 56.6: 570–586.

Stewart, William. 1967. Sociolinguistic Factors in the History of American Negro Dialects. *Florida Foreign Language Reporter* 5: 1–7.

Taylor, Orlando. 1972. An Introduction to the Historical Development of Black English: Some Implications for American Education. *Language, Speech, and Hearing Services in Schools* 3.4: 5–15.

Taylor, Orlando. 1973. Teachers' Attitudes toward Black and Nonstandard English as Measured by the Language Attitude Scale. In *Language Attitudes: Current Trends and Prospects*, edited by Roger Shuy and Ralph Fasold, 174–201. Washington, DC: Georgetown University Press.

Turner, Lorenzo Dow. 1949. *Africanisms in the Gullah Dialect*. Ann Arbor: University of Michigan Press.

Wilkerson, Isabel. 2020. *Caste: The Origins of Our Discontents*. New York: Random House.

Williams, Robert L. ed. 1975. *Ebonics: The True Language of Black Folks*. St. Louis: The Institute of Black Studies.

Wolfram, Walt. 1969. *A Linguistic Description of Detroit Negro Speech*. Washington, DC: Center for Applied Linguistics.

Filmography

Al-Mansour, Haifaa, director. 2018. *Nappily Every After*. Netflix. 98 mins.

Berry, D. Channsin, and Bill Duke, directors. 2011. *Dark Girls*. Urban Winter Entertainment. 75 mins.

Rock, Chris, narrator. 2009. *Good Hair*. HBO Films/Chris Rock Productions. 96 mins.

Rose, Charlie, talk show host and executive producer. *The Charlie Rose Show*. PBS. Episode https://charlierose.com/videos/17664

Digital Media

Bunglawala, Zamila. 2019. Please, Don't Call Me BAME or BME! Civil Service (blog). July 8. https://civilservice.blog.gov.uk/2019/07/08/please-dont-call-me-bame-or-bme/

Space Traders by Derrick Bell. *YouTube* video, uploaded by Linetta Alexander Islam, October 29, 2021. https://youtu.be/2cfvbr62NBw.

Chapter 4

"Where Your People From?"
Problematizing Origins and Development

Introduction: Controversial History, Development, and Contested Origins

Here, I rely on previous publications of mine (Lanehart 2007, 2018) for the meat of this discussion because this debate has gone on long before my career even started and will likely continue long after. I have said what I said about it. My tone may be a little different from the other chapters as a result, but I also hope you feel the fatigue of a debate that will not die given so many other important things linguists could work on in AAL/USEB research and use their powers for good. So, let's get to it.

In examining the origins of AAL/USEB, linguists have taken a number of different approaches to explain how it has developed historically, including considerations of (Neo-)Anglicist and Dialectologist origins (Labov 1972; Poplack 2000; Poplack and Tagliamonte 2001; Schneider 1989; Wolfram and Thomas 2002), (Neo-)Creolist origins (Dillard 1972; Rickford 1999, 2022; Rickford and Rickford 2000; Smitherman 1977, 2000; Weldon 2003, 2007), Substratist connections (Dalby 1972; DeBose and Faraclas 1993; Dunn 1976), Ecological and Restructuralist factors (Mufwene 2000; Winford 1997, 1998), and Divergence/Convergence hypotheses (Labov and Harris 1986). Proponents of monolithic origins hypotheses (e.g., Anglicist, Creolist, and Substratist) have compared morphosyntactic and syntactic processes in creoles, early varieties of English, and (to a limited extent) African languages to those in AAL/USEB as a means of determining the origins, development, and classification of AAL. Restructuralist and Ecological theorists have also considered factors such as second language learning, social dynamics, and contact effects. We will explain and discuss all of this shortly. However, there is another position that, in spite of evidence to the contrary, persists: Deficit Hypothesis. It has been pernicious and difficult to dismiss in the minds of some, including certain scholars, who continue to believe that African Americans are inferior to white people and, as such, their language and culture must be as well.

The Deficit Hypothesis

The Deficit Hypothesis emerged in the 19th century and is based on the idea that Blacks are genetically inferior to whites. Although it is not strictly about the origins of AAL/USEB, it is about the nature of African Americans and their language. This position posits that Africans in America were, at most, capable of imperfectly learning American English (though, at the time, scholars were initially focused on comparisons to SAmE), and that imperfection is what accounts for the differences between AAL/USEB and varieties of American English spoken by white people. Since the native languages of the enslaved, from the Deficit Hypothesis, were inferior and uncivilized (despite existing long before English was a language and England was a country), enslaved Africans did the best they were capable of doing in learning English—as is seen in their "imperfect" language use (hear this as a baby voice speaking 👶. Some even referred to AAL/USEB as "baby talk").

This position endures till this day for the cultural and linguistic practices of African Americans and reached a climax in these debates with the research of Carl Bereiter and Siegfried Engelmann in 1966 in complicity with other educational psychologists in the 1960s. The publication of William Labov's polemical and seminal article, "The Logic of Nonstandard English," in 1972 was meant to quash, or stomp, the ethnocentric and racist perspectives espoused by those who used language differences as social, cultural, and linguistic (i.e., human) deficit. What made this worse was the use of so-called empirical evidence to support deficit beliefs (e.g., standardized tests),[1] which has continued for decades since. It is ironic that at the same time the Black Power movement and the civil rights movement was taking place, some white scholars were working to discredit the intelligence and cultures of those seeking the rights granted to them under the U.S. Constitution.

The persistence of the Deficit Hypothesis in the late 20th century continued with the publication of Eleanor Wilson Orr's *Twice as Less: Black English and the Performance of Black Students in Mathematics and Science* in 1987 (as well as many others, even as recently as just a couple of years ago, that like in *Harry Potter*, I will not name them). Orr was the co-founder of the Hawthorne School in Washington, DC. Her observations of the Black, low-income, scholarship students she admitted led her to believe that Blacks had cultural deficits that did not allow them to understand math and science in a way necessary for abstract thinking and learning (again, despite the fact that African language and culture had existed long before English was a language and England was a country). These views of deficit or cultural poverty get re-packaged with code words like "at risk," "low income," "urban," "under-privileged," or even "minority" (which is why I used the term "minoritized," in the spirit of Malcom X's "We didn't land on Plymouth Rock; Plymouth Rock landed on us"). Though Labov (1972) and John Baugh's review of *Twice as Less* in 1988 provide substantive rebuttal of Deficit Hypotheses, both cultural and linguistic, the belief just will not die.

More recently, these claims are being linked to the debates in the U.S. about teacher and student accountability in this age of standardized testing. It is believed by some people that low-income, at-risk, urban students and their teachers cannot be held accountable for their poor performance because, through no fault of the children, their families are poor and deficient in providing what their children need to be successful and to be taught ☜. Yes, poverty is horrific and has a devastating generational effect on families and society as demonstrated by the Occupy Wall Street movement started in

---

[1] Psychologist Robert Williams created an intelligence test in 1972 that was based on Black language and culture that was called the *Black Intelligence Test of Cultural Homogeneity*, also known as the BITCH-100 Test.

Zuccotti Park in New York City in September 2011, the 2011 advertising campaign by Bono where he purports that "famine" is the new f-word, and the Black Lives Matter movement that started in 2013 after the acquittal of the murderer of **Trayvon Martin**. However, society can't just throw up its hands and say our children aren't worthy. It's not OK to say that our families and our languages are deficient and, therefore, Black children and their families are the problem. That is not conscionable, and it defies logic, science, compassion, equality, equity, and humanity. **Nah, Bruh**.

(Neo-)Anglicist and (Neo-)Creolist Origins Hypotheses

The dominant sociolinguistic perspectives about the history and development of AAL/USEB have been held by two distinctive groups: (1) Neo-Anglicists (English origins), mostly white scholars who spend much of their time and energy trying to support their claim that AAL/USEB is a dialect of British English and that Africans in America who created AAL/USEB forgot (**in the CeeLo Green sense**) their native cultures and languages upon arrival in America; and (2) Neo-Creolists (African origins), mostly Black scholars who spend much of their time and energy arguing for and trying to support their belief that AAL/USEB derived from language contact between Blacks and whites and the cultures and languages they brought to their contact situation evolved in a similar way as, say, English (remember Angles, Saxons, and Jutes). In other words, the latter group believes Africans in America maintained aspects of their languages and cultures in adapting to their oppressive and inhumane environment while the former group believes Africans in America either did not value their cultures and languages enough to preserve them as part of their identities or they did not have the capacity to do so.

The Creolist Hypothesis regarding the origins and development of AAL/USEB, which emerged in the 1960s in response to the Anglicist position, purports that AAL/USEB evolved from a prior U.S. creole developed by enslaved Africans in America that was widespread across the colonies and slave-holding areas. Neo-Creolists no longer believe there was a widespread African English-lexifier creole in the U.S. because there is no evidence to support such, but they do believe Caribbean and African languages' influence is real and reflected in the history and development of AAL/USEB. The Southeastern U.S. is considered the cradle of AAL/USEB, given the large number of plantations and the Southeast's strong support of slavery and the slave trade through the Middle Passage. The economic interest in slavery increased with the dependence on cotton and other crops.

Neo-Creolists tend to use morphosyntactic, phonological, and lexical features to support their perspective on the history and development of AAL/USEB. The most contentious linguistic feature used to support the Creolist position involves the *copula*, or the verb "to be," because this particular feature has not been found to exist in English varieties. Specifically, it involves the "zero, or Ø, copula," or constructions in British English where one would use the copula (e.g., "she is not here") but where in AAL/USEB, like many languages, the copula is not required and, therefore, not always used (e.g., "she Ø not here"). This is not to say that AAL/USEB never uses a copula but only refers to AAL/USEB grammatical constructions that do not require a copula where one is required in English. So, for example, a copula is required in both English and AAL/USEB for something like, "I went to the store" or "she was compelled to leave" or "I am not amused." However, because many African languages, Gullah Geechee, and other Caribbean creoles—in addition to other languages in the world such as Bengali, Japanese, Hungarian, Ukrainian, and some Native American/Indigenous languages—either do not have a copula or do not require a copula, zero copula in certain grammatical constructions in AAL/USEB has been used as a primary connection to creoles.

Until the 21st century, there had been no documented evidence of the existence of zero copula in British English varieties cited in the literature. However, Poplack (2000) and Poplack and Tagliamonte (2001) make the claim that zero copula is also present in an obscure dialect of British English. While that claim is contested, I should point out that both Creolists and Anglicists rely heavily on linguistic features or constructions without any oral recordings to support their positions for the language of Africans in America at their inception in the Americas because they do not exist. While Caribbean creoles are still recognizable as creoles in present-day use, that is not the case for varieties of AAL/USEB—with the exception of Gullah Geechee and Louisiana French Creole. There is no dispute, for example, that Gullah Geechee is a creole; but its existence as being widespread in the U.S. is not supported. Gullah Geechee is historically found in the Lowcountry region of the U.S. starting in Cape Fear, North Carolina, down the coasts of Georgia and South Carolina, and down to Jacksonville, Florida. Its use is receding due to economic and ecological conditions. While Gullah Geechee's persistence in the South Carolina Sea Islands seems to be better than in the Georgia Sea Islands due to infrastructure and economic supports in South Carolina that are not as prevalent in Georgia, many of the Gullah Geechee people have to leave in order to survive. But, again, remember that Gullah Geechee people say they speak English. And continue to remember what a creole is: a language; a language just like English, Panjabi, or Turkish.

I also want to acknowledge that "Gullah" is the name given to Geechee people by white settlers (you know, because white people named everything). The people of these regions of the U.S. do not refer to themselves or their language simply as "Gullah" but instead as "Geechee" or "Gullah Geechee." Since we have talked a lot about naming and self-reference, I think we should bear this in mind. A lot of what we talk about in linguistics revolves around white settler-colonial practices, including naming, and BIPOC[2] scholars are doing their best to disrupt the history and trauma of those practices that tended to exclude voices of oppressed Scholars

---

2 *BIPOC* can either be used for "Black, Indigenous, and People of Color" or "Black and Indigenous People of Color." I use the latter because, as I discussed in Chapter 3 around who is included in "Black" for me in the U.S., this term then includes Afro-Latinx, Afro-Indigenous, Indigenous Mexicans, and other Afro-X peoples. And, since some people tryna claim POC (People of Color) aren't under-represented and minoritized folk and don't have a continuous history of oppression in the U.S. (certainly not like unique circumstances of African Americans and Indigenous folks), I prefer the latter use. N.B.: I'm not tryna get into an Oppression Olympics here and I realize other groups, such as Chinese, Japanese, and Jews, have been oppressed in this country. However, the histories of Africans brought to America is even unique in its origins and brutality compared to Native Americans and unique still from all other groups in the U.S.

of Color and their epistemologies and ideologies that are often at odds with ideas like "tradition" and "canon." We should bear that in mind when we even talk about "Africa," "Asia," and other spaces and places in which the peoples themselves do not necessarily claim the names and identities imposed on them by colonial, imperial, or antiquated histories that misrepresent them. For example, how often do people continue to think of Africa as a country? 😒, or better still, remember that Toni Morrison GIF from the interview with Charlie Rose (see minutes 25–29 at https://charlierose.com/videos/17664) that I mentioned in Chapter 3? Yeah, that's the one.

And speaking of creoles, let me get back to that bone I started picking in Chapter 2. A traditional, colonialist, hegemonic Creolist view is that a *creole* is a contact language that emerges when two or more language groups come in contact, often over trade—including human trafficking, like slavery—but also imperialism, colonization, war, intermarriage, and the like that arises out of the necessity for communication. However, none of the languages involved are known to the others, so there is no *lingua franca*[3] that can be used. As a result, a language of communication and necessity is created that includes aspects of the contact languages. One language might provide a lot of vocabulary (*substrate*[4]) and another might provide much of the syntax (*superstrate*[5]). As children acquire this new language as their native or primary language, which, traditionally, has been called a *pidgin*, the grammar expands for all aspects of language use, expression, and identity and is now magically a creole.

According to Baptista's non-hegemonic perspective,

> Creole languages typically emerge in multilingual settings and result from the multiple, complex social factors and linguistic processes that participate in language emergence, development,

---

3 A *lingua franca* is a language in common amongst a group of speakers. The language need not be the native language of any of the speakers—only one that they all have in common with likely differing levels of competence.
4 A *substrate* is a language spoken by people who held a socially subordinate position in the contact that produced them (often the grammatical language).
5 A *superstrate* is a language spoken by people who held a socially dominant position in the contact that produced them (often the lexifier language).

and change. Their emergence is driven by the complex interactions between their lexifier (language contributing to a great majority of their lexicon) and speakers' first languages (commonly labeled substrates or adstrates[6]) contributing to a great part of the Creole grammar.

(2021, slide 3)

Again, because it bears repeating: this is how languages, in general, develop, so why do we have a special term for certain languages? This is not a rhetorical question.

Hegemonic linguistic perspectives use the term "creole" in very racialized ways and lean into things like *Creole Exceptionalism*. Creole Exceptionalism includes hegemonic linguistic perspectives that believe creoles are "a special class of languages apart from 'normal'/'regular' languages"; "structurally inadequate"; "expressively inadequate because of intrinsic structural deficiencies"; "living linguistic fossils"; and "special hybrids with exceptional genealogy" (see DeGraff 2003 for these quotes on Creole Exceptionalism as cited on slide 7 of Baptista 2021). From a non-hegemonic, non-colonialist, non-white supremacy perspective, creoles are just languages—just like any other language. Given a "just language and language contact" perspective, the development of the English language or Romance languages should be recognizable as the development of a creole if that is how you wanna play it. If you know anything at all about English, you know that it came to be from the interaction of the Angles, Saxons, and Jutes in 449. What emerged from their language contact situation was English. Add to that, in 1066 with the Norman Invasion and the subsequent Romanizing of English through the language contact of English and Norman French, how is that not the same thing as the emergence and development of a creole? It is! But the term "creole" has been reserved mostly for communities made up of non-Europeans and Indo-European languages. Once again, it's white people deciding that they discovered

---

6 Another language involved that's neither in a dominant nor a subordinate situation (often one that came into contact after the initial situation applied, such as Spanish in Haitian Creoles).

something and they get to name it. White people didn't discover language; they just put themselves in a position to name it. In this sense, creoles are racialized in ways to mark non-Europeans as "The Other." So, again, given the definitions we have discussed thus far, languages are creoles and creoles are languages! And, riffing off of Syndrome in the Pixar movie *The Incredibles*, "If all languages are creoles, then none of them are," because we then do not need a separate word for them—unless you want to overtly come from up under the hood and mark creoles as racialized languages and everything else as, well, just language—just a different hegemonic provenance.[7] Hmmm.

Moving on. The Anglicist Hypothesis purports that Africans in America learned regional varieties of British English dialects from British overseers with little to no influence from their own native languages and cultures. This hypothesis emerged in the mid-20th century and is in opposition to the Creolist Hypothesis. Anglicists use ex-slave recordings and texts (see Bailey, Maynor, and Cukor-Avila 1991) as well as comparisons to other historical texts, British varieties, and slave resettlement in the Americas to support their position. More current is the Neo-Anglicist Hypothesis that non-standard varieties of British English are the precursors of AAL/USEB as opposed to standard ones since the whites who had the most contact with enslaved Africans would have spoken non-standard varieties of British English instead of standard varieties and, in some cases, were not native English speakers themselves. Neo-Anglicists now also acknowledge that, of course, there are aspects of AAL/USEB grammar that come from African languages in the origins of AAL/USEB. (Is that so?) Neo-Anglicists, like Neo-Creolists, believe they have accounted for all salient linguistic structures in some past or

---

[7] I strongly recommend watching Michel DeGraff's 2022 Linguistic Society of America plenary address, "*On Impure Linguistics for Self-Purification and Direct Action*," which he delivered in Haitian Creole (Kreyòl). He provided a redux on February 18, 2022, that is available to the public at https://youtu.be/N6QPJ-lBciY. Also, if possible, watch the Princeton Linguistics Lecture by Salikoko Mufwene entitled "How Food and Sex Delayed or Prevented the Emergence of Pidgins" (March 2, 2022).

current variety of British English, including zero copula. According to Mufwene,

> to resolve the creolist-dialectologist debate, what is needed is convincing information regarding different kinds of plantations, their settlement history, and the patterns of Anglo-African interaction on them. Although history argues against the creole-origin hypothesis, the literature against it has done a poor job in attempting to refute it.
>
> (2001, 315)

He goes on to say that Poplack (2000) had done a better job of this but that there are still contradictions in evidence even with her collection of essays, such as Samaná, a variety of English used in the Spanish-speaking Dominican Republic by African Americans who sailed from Philadelphia in the 1820s (Mufwene 2001). While Poplack finds Samaná to be closer to AAL/USEB than to Caribbean English creoles, Hannah (1997), for example, finds that not to be the case. However, like Baptista and DeGraff, Mufwene also supports a non-hegemonic view of the term "creole" and even supports eliminating it as a result (see Mufwene 2022).

Consensus Hypotheses: Substratist, Restructuralist, and Ecological

Though the first two hypotheses take up most of the air in the room, there is a third grouping of hypotheses that are referred to as Consensus Hypotheses. Substratists purport that distinctive patterns of AAL/USEB are those that also occur in Niger-Congo languages, such as Kikongo, Mande, and Kwa. In effect, the view is that AAL/USEB is structurally related to West African languages and bears only superficial similarities to White American English, or WAmE (Green 2002, 8–9). It (i.e., substratist) is so named because it is argued that the West African or substrate languages influenced the sentence and sound structures of AAL/USEB (Green 2002, 9). As Goodman (1993, 65) notes, one characteristic of a *substratum* "is the subordinate social or cultural status of its speakers vis-à-vis those of the reference language [i.e., English]" (as quoted in Green 2002, 9).

Restructuralists and Ecological theorists acknowledge the difficulty of knowing the origins of AAL/USEB but propose that we can say something useful about Earlier AAL//USEB as opposed to nascent AAL/USEB given settlement and migration patterns as well as socio-ecological issues. Mufwene (2000, 234) purports:

1   The socioeconomic history of the United States does not support the hypothesis that AAE developed from an erstwhile creole, either American or Caribbean.
2   However, this position does not preclude influence . . . from Caribbean English varieties imported with slaves in the seventeenth and eighteenth centuries on the restructuring of colonial English that produced AAE.
3   Nor does the recognition of possible Caribbean influence entail that AAE could not have developed into what it is now without it.
4   Closer examination of sources of the direct origins of slaves during the eighteenth century suggests that influence from African languages was perhaps more determinative than that from the Caribbean.
5   By no means should anyone overlook or downplay the nature of colonial English as spoken by both the English and the non-English in the seventeenth and eighteenth centuries, nor its central role as the target language during the development of AAL, (especially Gullah Geechee), and their Caribbean kin.

Restructuralists and Ecologists are closer to Neo-Anglicist positions in some ways and Neo-Creolist positions in others. As noted by language ecologist and creole syntactician Salikoko Mufwene, "Creolists' recognition of some merits in assuming that AAVE had an independent development; i.e., it did not originate as a creole nor does it simply represent "the transfer and acquisition by Africans and African Americans of English dialects spoken by British and other white immigrants to America in earlier times" (2000, 254–255). In other words, AAL/USEB likely did not originate from or as a creole (using hegemonic definitions), but that absence does not then preclude the influence of native African languages in the subsequent emerging language varieties of Africans in America.

Restructuralists, such as Wolfram and Thomas (2002) and Bailey and Thomas (2022), focus more on settlement patterns of European Americans in relation to settlements (i.e., enslavement) of Africans in America and their subsequent resettlements through "freedom" and migration. While no one can go back to the beginning, using these patterns provides a picture of interaction and languages in contact. Over the history of America, Europeans have settled differing areas and brought their different varieties of English and their native languages with them. "Language Variation 101," or Rule #3, says that separation from native language speakers and their homeland results in language variation (i.e., variation via physical separation). While the expatriate British English speakers were undergoing linguistic changes, so were the languages of the involuntary immigrants (i.e., enslaved Africans; see Ogbu 1978)—but with a larger pool of varieties that were in contact because, as Mufwene (2000, 255) states, "all varieties of English in North America are contact-based and developed concurrently."

Also, the conditions of contact changed over time, as well as the interaction of language varieties. As such, these Restructuralists and Ecologists believe that the language of Africans in America was different when compared to the 18th, 19th, 20th, and 21st centuries because the social, political, and economic realities of those times differed in ways that greatly influenced language. So, for example, moving from colonial indentured servitude to colonial enslavement to Southern/Southeastern plantation enslavement to Southern sharecroppers to Northern industrialist workers to national migrants (i.e., the Great Migration) to civil rights activists to #BlackLivesMatter—all the while with ideas of identity and culture waxing and waning—influenced the language of these involuntary immigrants so that the comparison is more about these factors in relation to one another than about the origins of AAL/USEB.

The Divergence/Convergence Hypothesis

The Divergence/Convergence Hypothesis emerged in the 1980s with the work of William Labov and others.[8] According to Labov

---

8 See Butters (1989) for a critique of the Divergence/Convergence Hypothesis.

and Harris (1986), divergence from white varieties has more recently shaped AAL/USEB. That is, AAL/USEB more recently diverged from varieties of American English due to racism, segregation, and inequality. As a result, African Americans are actually forming new speech communities with innovative forms, especially with a growth in urbanization. According to Labov, "the more contact [B]lacks have with whites, the more they move away from the vernacular side, and the more contact whites have with [B]lacks, the more we observe borrowings [appropriation for profit] of [B]lack forms" (Fasold et al. 1987, 10). What they are saying is, when there are increases in inequities and inequalities in society, AAL/USEB diverges from WAmE and when inequities and inequalities in society subside and there is more contact between African Americans and whites, AAL/USEB converges toward WAmE. Too bad the same logic is not used with the Anglicists since the Divergence/Convergence Hypothesis, by extension, implies that when people/society treat you badly you are less inclined to want to associate with or identify with them compared to when people/society treat you humanely, thereby fostering more of an inclination to mix and mingle. However, persistent racial segregation, and its concomitant social and educational issues that the politics and policies that support it, greatly contribute to AAL/USEB becoming more divergent instead of convergent with WAmE despite so-called desegregation in the 1960s to the present (although studies tend to show the U.S. is resegregating in communities and schools). In other words, "I don't need you when **I can do bad all by myself**" (see Blige 2009).

My Conclusion: *Periodt!*

Regardless of the origins of AAL/USEB, the current state of it reflects the historical ills of inequities in the U.S. toward African Americans and their response to maintain their own distinct cultural, language, and linguistic practices. My position is that the origins and development of AAL/USEB is that of a language, just like any other language. We don't need to talk about pidgins, creoles, dialects, and the like. It's just language. **Periodt!**

Questions, Discussion, and Further Inquiry

1. How had you considered the origins and development of American Englishes before reading this chapter or this book?
2. Why is it problematic that people continue to conflate Africa as a continent with Africa as a country? What does it imply?
3. If this longstanding debate around the origins and development of AAL/USEB were resolved today, what would it matter? Would we be closer to helping AAL/USEB-speaking children learn to read and write? Would we be closer to helping AAL/USEB-speaking children learn critical thinking and literacy skills? Would we be closer to helping AAL/USEB-speaking children have better schools with better facilities and better funding and better opportunities? Would it collapse the school-to-prison pipeline in the prison industrial complex? Would it save one child from being gunned down in the street/in the car/while jogging/while birding/while walking/while just living life?
4. Do you think you would recognize Gullah Geechee if you heard it? Try it.
5. What is your understanding of *language* and *creole* after reading this chapter?
6. Would you consider English or Romance languages as creoles now, given the definition and examples used in the book thus far? What are the implications of saying so?
7. Do you think only white people use or speak White American English (WAmE)? What other varieties of American English do you suppose white people speak?
8. Do only African Americans use or speak AAL/USEB? What varieties of American English do you suppose African Americans speak?
9. What evidence is there to confirm or disconfirm that Black and White vernaculars are diverging or converging?

References

Bailey, Guy, Natalie Maynor, and Patricia Cukor-Avila. 1991. *The Emergence of Black English: Text and Commentary*. Amsterdam: John Benjamins.

Bailey, Guy, and Erik Thomas. 2022. Some Aspects of African-American Vernacular English Phonology. In *African-American English: Structure, History, and Use*, Classic Edition, edited by Salikoko S. Mufwene, John R. Rickford, Guy Bailey, and John Baugh, 93–118. London: Routledge.

Baptista, Marlyse. 2021. Out of Many Voices, One Language. Plenary address delivered at NWAV49, Austin, TX, October 23.

Baugh, John. 1988. Review of *Twice as Less: Black English and the Performance of Black Students in Mathematics and Science* by Eleanor Wilson Orr. *Harvard Educational Review* 58.3: 395–403.

Bereiter, Carl, and Siegfried Engelmann. 1966. *Teaching Disadvantaged Children in the Preschool*. Englewood Cliffs, NJ: Prentice-Hall.

Butters, Ronald. 1989. *The Death of Black English: Divergence and Convergence in Black and White Vernaculars*. Frankfurt am Main: Peter Lang Verlag.

Dalby, David. 1972. The African Element in American English. In *Rappin' and Stylin' Out: Communication in Urban Black America*, edited by Thomas Kochman, 170–188. Chicago: University of Illinois Press.

DeBose, Charles, and Nicholas Faraclas. 1993. An Africanist Approach to the Linguistic Study of Black English: Getting to the Roots of the Tense-Aspect-Modality and Copula Systems in Afro-American. In *Africanisms in Afro-American Language Varieties*, edited by Salikoko Mufwene, 364–387. Athens, GA: University of Georgia Press.

DeGraff, Michel. 2003. Against Creole Exceptionalism. *Language* 79.2: 391–410.

DeGraff, Michel. 2022. *On Impure Linguistics for Self-Purification and Direct Action*. Plenary address delivered at the Annual Meeting of the Linguistic Society of America. https://youtu.be/N6QPJ-lBciY

Dillard, Joey. 1972. *Black English*. New York: Random House.

Dunn, Ernest F. 1976. The Black-Southern White Dialect Controversy. In *Black English: A Seminar*, edited by Deborah S. Harrison and Tom Trabasso, 105–122. Hillsdale, NJ: Lawrence Erlbaum.

Fasold, Ralph W., William Labov, Fay Boyd Vaughn-Cooke, Guy Bailey, Walt Wolfram, Arthur K. Spears, and John Rickford. 1987. Are Black and White Vernaculars Diverging? Papers from the NWAVE XIV Panel Discussion. *American Speech* 62.1: 3–80.

Goodman, Morris. 1993. African Substratum: Some Cautionary Words. In *Africanisms in Afro-American Language Varieties*, edited by Salikoko S. Mufwene, 64–73. Athens, GA: University of Georgia Press.

Green, Lisa J. 2002. *African American English: A Linguistic Introduction*. Cambridge: Cambridge University Press.

Hannah, Dawn. 1997. Copula Absence in Samaná English: Implications for Research on the Linguistic History of African-American Vernacular English. *American Speech* 72:4: 339–372.

Labov, William. 1972. The Logic of Nonstandard English. In *Language and the Inner City: Studies in the Black English Vernacular*, edited William Labov, 201–240. Philadelphia: University of Pennsylvania Press.

Labov, William, and Wendell A. Harris. 1986. De Facto Segregation of Black and White Vernaculars. In *Diversity and Diachrony*, edited by David Sankoff, 33–44. Amsterdam: John Benjamins.

Lanehart, Sonja. 2007. If Our Children Are Our Future, Why Are We Stuck in the Past?: Beyond the Anglicists and the Creolists, and Toward Social Change. In *Talkin' Black Talk: Language, Education, and Social Change*, edited by H. Samy Alim and John Baugh, 132–141. New York: Teachers College Press.

Lanehart, Sonja. 2018. Can You Hear (and See) Me Now? Race-ing American Language Variationist/Change and Sociolinguistic Research Methodologies. In *Understanding Critical Race Research Methods and Methodologies: Lessons from the Fields*, edited by Jessica T. DeCuir-Gunby, Thandeka K. Chapman, and Paul A. Schutz, 34–47. London: Routledge.

Mufwene, Salikoko S. 2000. Creolization Is a Social, Not a Structural, Process. In *Degrees of Restructuring in Creole Languages*, edited by Ingrid Neumann-Holzschuh and Edgar W. Schneider, 65–84. Amsterdam: John Benjamins

Mufwene, Salikoko S. 2001. Some Sociohistorical Inferences about the Development of African American English. In *The English History of African American English*, edited by Shana Poplack, 233–263. Malden, MA: Blackwell.

Mufwene, Salikoko. 2022. How Food and Sex Delayed or Prevented the Emergence of Pidgins. Princeton Linguistics Lecture Series, March 2.

Ogbu, John U. 1978. *Minority Education and Caste: The American System in Cross-Cultural Perspective*. New York: Academic Press.

Orr, Eleanor Wilson. 1987. *Twice as Less: Black English and the Performance of Black Students in Mathematics and Science*. New York: W.W. Norton.

Poplack, Shana. 2000. *The English History of African American English*. Malden, MA: Blackwell.

Poplack, Shana, and Sali Tagliamonte. 2001. *African American English in the Diaspora*. Malden, MA: Blackwell.

Rickford, John R. 1999. *African American Vernacular English: Features, Evolution, Educational Implications*. Malden, MA: Blackwell.

Rickford, John R. 2022. The Creole Origins of African-American Vernacular English: Evidence from Copula Absence. In *African-American English: Structure, History, and Use*, Classic Edition, edited by Salikoko S. Mufwene, John R. Rickford, Guy Bailey, and John Baugh, 169–220. Oxford: Routledge.

Rickford, John R., and Russell John Rickford. 2000. *Spoken Soul: The Story of Black English*. New York: John Wiley and Sons.

Schneider, Edgar W. 1989. *American Earlier Black English: Morphological and Syntactic Variables*. Tuscaloosa, AL: University of Alabama Press.

Smitherman, Geneva. 1977. *Talkin and Testifyin: The Language of Black America*. Boston: Houghton Mifflin.

Smitherman, Geneva. 2000. *Talkin that Talk: Language, Culture, and Education in African America*. London: Routledge.

Weldon, Tracey. 2003. Revisiting the Creolist Hypothesis: Copula Variability in Gullah and Southern Rural AAVE. *American Speech* 78.2: 171–191.

Weldon, Tracey. 2007. Gullah Negation: A Variable Analysis. *American Speech* 82.4: 341–366.

Williams, Robert L. 1972. The BITCH-100: A Culture-Specific Test. St. Louis: Washington University at St. Louis. https://eric.ed.gov/?id=ED070799

Winford, Donald. 1997. On the Origins of African American Vernacular English—A Creolist Perspective. Part I: The Sociohistorical Background. *Diachronica* 14.2: 305–344.

Winford, Donald. 1998. On the Origins of African American Vernacular English—A Creolist Perspective. Part II: The Linguistic Features. *Diachronica* 15.1: 99–154.

Wolfram, Walt, and Erik Thomas. 2002. *The Development of African American English*. Malden, MA: Blackwell.

Filmography

Bird, Brad, director. 2004. *The Incredibles*. Walt Disney/Pixar.

Rose, Charlie, talk show host and executive producer. *The Charlie Rose Show*. PBS. Episode https://charlierose.com/videos/17664

Discography

Blige, Mary J. 2009. I Can Do Bad All by Myself. Track 6 on *I Can Do Bad All by Myself*. EMI.

Chapter 5

What's Good?[1]
A Concise Descriptivist Meta-Grammar of Language Use in African American Communities

Introduction: *We Bout to Ride Up on This Elephant*

This is one of the most difficult chapters for me, in part because of my personal relationship with AAL/USEB and how linguists often talk about it and approach it. As I indicated in Chapter 1, I had a journey to self-actualization of an AAL/USEB identity. For those of you unfamiliar with social psychology research on racial identity development—and this includes POC, mixed-race folks, and white folks—there are several stages, according to Tatum (1992), that are not necessarily linear or static. In my case, I have gone through all the stages, and I am firmly in the Internalization-Commitment stage. Others have done this work, but I find comfort in its alignment with an Afrofuturistic perspective that time is not linear in the same way that our lives and identities are not linear because they are in constant conversation.

Be that as it may, given where I came from to where I am now, talking about AAL/USEB as if it only comprises discrete features instead of intertwined systems of meaning-making is difficult for me because my language—just like everyone else's language—is so much more than the sum of its parts. As I have said earlier, you will not acquire a language from reading a grammar book. Besides

---

1 This title references Nicki Minaj's signfiying on Miley Cyrus at the 2015 VMAs (Video Music Awards). And shout out to LaToya Sawyer for introducing me to Nicki Minaj's work in her presentations and dissertation.

the obvious, grammar books do not cover all aspects of a language—linguistics or paralinguistics—and they will not because that is not really their purpose. Grammar books cannot include everything that makes a language a language or how the speakers of that language give life to a personal entity used for communication and expression. This is an epistemological issue for me; i.e., it is about my understanding and knowing when it comes to language. I used to use Crystal (1988) in my "Introduction to English Language Studies" course at the University of Georgia. He talked about the difference between *knowing* grammar and knowing *about* grammar. "Knowing grammar" means acquiring it and using it with little thought or effort, something we do naturally as native speakers of a language. "Knowing about grammar" means knowing and being able to articulate the technical aspects of what grammar is, something that is not natural and what we do in classes with grammar textbooks or research. Native speakers tend to know a language and how to use its grammar, but they don't often know about the grammar. They would have to take grammar classes for that—or a foreign language class. That is why you often find that fluent non-native speakers of a language know more about the language's technical grammar than native speakers (and they often make great copy editors). They had to learn both—knowing and knowing about—if they learned it in school where they were taught about lexical categories, phrase structure, and the like. I learned more about grammar when taking Spanish in high school than I did in any English class. But those uses of "know" are about awareness. I am making fine distinctions between knowing and cognition, which is a broader category that encompasses knowing/knowledge, sort of like AAL/USEB is a broader concept that encompasses AAVL/VUSEB.

Time for a definition break here beyond the granular distinctions between knowing and knowing about. When I use *grammar* in this way—which is mostly how I use it anyway—it is to refer to the body of a language's system of structures, patterns, and rules. In this way, grammar means all the systems, patterns, structures, and rules that make up the language. As such, it is not synonymous with *syntax* in this usage. A common usage of grammar, and the one that you are most likely familiar with, is the one where it is synonymous with syntax, or the study of sentence, phrase, and clause structure. I use the former definition (grammar as language system) as opposed to the latter (grammar as syntax) unless indicated otherwise.

On another side note, grammar books are either, and more likely, *prescriptive* grammars (i.e., existing to tell people to use their language in a "correct" or "educated" way or, in the case of American English, in a very Classicist, as in Latinate, way), or they are *descriptive* grammars (i.e., existing to provide people with the observations of how their language actually works or is used as opposed to telling someone how they should use their language). In either case, they are prescribing or describing based on models of language study that tend to focus on particular aspects of language that are often related more to language analysis and study than expression, identity, or community. For example, if you ask a biologist or biochemist what makes you "you," they will characterize you by your chemical and anatomical makeup. If you ask a psychologist or psychiatrist, they will characterize you by your mind, psyche, and spirit. If you ask a cultural anthropologist, they will characterize you by culture and community. If you ask a theoretical linguist (e.g., someone who studies morphology, syntax, semantics), they will characterize you by language, of course, from their slice of the study of language. We describe the elephant based on what we know, but we don't know the whole thing.[2]

So, in this chapter, the goal is not to be comprehensive since neither this book nor this chapter is meant to be a grammar about AAL/USEB that you can then use to say you are an expert or proficient user. That is just not gon happen here. However, I also want to note that the other issue I have is writing something that believes it could do that. What I can do is give you a glimpse of looking at AAL/USEB in the same way we look at and write about any language's grammar because at least that is better than how we have looked at AAL/USEB traditionally. This book—not just this one chapter—is meant to get you beyond the idea of looking at AAL/USEB as an anomaly of ("standard") American English and, instead, as a variety

---

[2] See James Baldwin's telling of the "Blind Men and the Elephant" at https://americanliterature.com/author/james-baldwin/short-story/the-blind-men-and-the-elephant.

that is so much more synergistic. See this chapter as a taste of something different because **what we not gon do** is compare AAL/USEB to SAmE or WAmE varieties.

Why Y'all so Interested in Language Use in African American Communities?

Let's think about two questions: (1) Why is AAL/USEB so intriguing to linguists and non-linguists? and (2) What is really different about AAL/USEB grammar? The meta-grammar aspect of this chapter is my approach to how others think about AAL/USEB grammar: Features and systems. The meta-grammar, meaning "thinking about grammar," is me processing these two ways of how researchers think about AAL/USEB and represent their cognition and epistemology in their research and talk about AAL/USEB grammar and lexicon. To address the first question, some early descriptions of AAL/USEB were motivated by questions about its legitimacy and the extent to which it was different from or similar to varieties of WAmE. This can/should be read as seeking to find the "exoticism" of AAL/USEB. When it comes to languages (and people), the word "exotic" needs to die, especially when used in that very white colonial, white supremacy, white gaze sort of way (is there any other way?). It gives me an unsettled feeling. This perspective is also used to continue to marginalize Black people who want to study AAL/USEB but who are then told they can only do so by comparing it to WAmE varieties. If I have said it once, I have said it a thousand times: **You do not need to study AAL/USEB through a white gaze!** AAL/USEB stands on its own and does not require comparison to varieties of WAmE in the same way we do not have to compare Italian to Spanish to make it "legitimate." And if Labov (1969) did not put this need for legitimacy to rest with "The Logic of Nonstandard English," then you just don't want to learn. But then, as Smitherman (1998) has reminded us, **some folk don't believe fat meat is greasy**.

One approach to describing AAL/USEB was to highlight surface features that were maximally different from grammatical structures in SAmE, a mythical ideal, or later "nonstandard" varieties of WAmE. I even spent years myself compiling AAL/USEB features lists that I would add to my ever-growing list of AAL/USEB features and present to my classes. I finally included my list of compiled features in a chapter I wrote (Lanehart 2012/2018) to illustrate how problematic such lists are. I kindly provide lists of salient linguistic features of AAL/USEB here from the research literature.

Some Lexical and Slang Terms

24/7	dope	Miss Ann
ace-boon-coon	dozens/snaps/joning	Miss Thang
amen corner	fell out	nappy
ashy	forty acres	nitty gritty
bad	fresh	old school
bad-mouth	funky	on the DL
baller	G/OG	phat
Benjamins	game	player/playa
big-boned	get down	po-po
big time	get over	posse
bling	girl	run tell that
bogard	GOAT	saddity/seddity
boo coo	got their nose wide open	shade
bougie	healthy	shorty/shawty
break it down	HNIC	slay
chillin	homie/homes	suck-teeth
color struck	hoopty	trash talk
cool	hot comb	trippin
CP time	hype	Uncle Tom/Tom
crunk	illin	whack
cut-eye	kinfolk	woofin
diss	kitchen (hair)	yelluh/high yelluh
dog/dawg	mannish/womanish	

Phonological Features (adapted from Bailey and Thomas 2022; Green 2002; Rickford 1999 unless otherwise stated)

1 Final consonant cluster reduction (loss of 2nd consonant)

    a   bold → [boʊl]
    b   land → [læn]
    c   acting → [ækɪn]

2 Unstressed syllable deletion (initial and medial syllables)

    a   about → bout [baʊt]
    b   government → guhment [gʌmɪnt]

3 Ø final consonant (especially affects nasals)

    a   give → [gɪː]
    b   mean → [miː]

4 Reduction of final nasal to vowel nasality

    a   man → [mæ̃]
    b   bram → [bɹæ̃]

5 Ø /b/, /d/, /g/ as the first consonant in certain tense-aspect markers or auxiliary verbs (Rickford 1999, 5; Morgan 2001)

    a   "I don't know" → *Ah 'on know.*
    b   "I'm going to do it" → *Ah'ma do it.*
    c   "He didn't do it" → *He ain't do it.*

6 Haplology (deletion of reduplicated syllable)

    a   Mississippi → [mɪsɪpɪ]
    b   general → [dʒɪnɹəɫ]

7 Final stop devoicing (without shortening of preceding segment)

    a   bad → [bæt]
    b   tag → [tæk]

8 Coarticulated glottal stop with devoiced final stop

    a   bad → [bætʔ]
    b   jib → [dʒɪpʔ]

9 Labialization of interdental fricatives ([θ → f] in final position and [ð → v] in medial position)

    a   birthday → [bɝfde]
    b   fifth → [fɪf]

    c   with → [wɪf]
    d   baths → [bævz]
    e   brother → [bɹʌvə]

10 Syllable-initial fricative stopping (especially with voiced fricatives)

    a   those → [doʊz]
    b   these → [diz]
    c   them → [dɪm]

11 Stopping of voiceless interdental fricatives (especially contiguous to nasals)

    a   tenth → [tɪnt]
    b   with → [wɪt]
    c   month → [mʌnt]

12 Vocalization (pronunciation of a weak neutral vowel) or Ø postvocalic /l/

    a   toll → [toʊɤ]
    b   pull → [pʊɤ]
    c   help → [hɛp]
    d   he'll → [hiə] or [hiɤ]

13 Ø /r/ after consonants (after /θ/ and in unstressed syllables)

    a   throwdown → [θoʊdaʊn]
    b   professor → [pəfɛsə]

14 Vocalization or loss of intersyllabic /r/

    a   hurry → [hʌi]
    b   furrow → [fʌə]
    c   story → [stoi]

15 Vocalization of stressed syllabic /r/

    a   bird → [bɜd]
    b   burr → [bɜ]

16 Vocalization of postvocalic -*r*

    a   four → [foə] or [foʊ]
    b   ford → [foəd]

17 Vocalization of unstressed syllabic /r/

   a   father → [faðə]
   b   never → [nɛvə]

18 [ŋ → n] in gerunds (word-final position)

   a   going → [goɪn]
   b   walking → [wɔkɪn]

19 /k/ for /t/ in /str/ clusters

   a   street → [skɹit]
   b   stream → [skɹim]

20 Merger of /e/ and /ɪ/ before nasals

   a   pen → [pɪn]
   b   Wednesday → [wɪnzdi]

21 Merger of tense and lax front vowels before /l/ → [ɫ]

   a   bale → [bɛəɫ]
   b   feel → [fɪəɫ]

22 Diphthong /oɪ/ for "oa" spellings (Green 2002, 123)

   a   roach → [ɹoɪtʃ]
   b   road → [ɹoɪd]

23 Forestressing, or front stressing, of initial syllables

   a   police → ['poʊlis]
   b   Detroit → ['dɪtɹɔt]
   c   McDonald's → ['mækdanəlz]
   d   hotel → ['hotɛl]

24 Metathesis of final /s/ + stop

   a   ask → [æks]
   b   grasp → [gɹæps]

25 Fricative stopping before nasals

   a   isn't → [ɪdn]
   b   wasn't → [wʌdn]

26 [v → b] in word-medial position

    a   heaven → [hebən]
    b   jiving → [dʒaɪbɪn]

27 Ø /j/ after consonants

    a   computer → [kəmpuɾə]
    b   Houston → [hustən]

28 Glide reduction of /aɪ/ [aɪ → aː] before voiced obstruents and finally

    a   tied → [taːd]
    b   buy → [baː]

29 Glide reduction of /ɔɪ/ [ɔɪ → ɔə] before /l/ → [ɫ]

    a   oil → [ɔəɫ]
    b   coil → [kɔəɫ]
    c   boy → [bɔə]

30 [ɪ + ŋ] → [æŋ]

    a   thing → [θæŋ]
    b   think → [θæŋk]
    c   drink → [dɹæŋk]

31 Raising of /æ/ to /e/ before a nasal

    a   can't → [kent]
    b   dance → [dens]
    c   man → [men]

32 Miscellaneous words

    a   drop → [dɹæp] and dropped → [dɹæp] or [dɹæpt]
    b   sister → [sʊstə]
    c   sink → [zæŋk]
    d   shut → [ʃɛt]

***Morphological, Morphosyntactic, and Syntactic Features* (adapted from Lanehart 2002, 2018, or added from recent data by Lanehart unless noted otherwise)**

Preverbal Markers (i.e., Auxiliaries/Auxiliary Verbs) of Tense, Mood, and Aspect

33 Zero copula (aka copula deletion or copula variation)

    a   He Ø up in there talking that now.
    b   They Ø not here.
    c   You Ø the one who brought me through.
    d   She know she Ø doin wrong.

34 Habitual iterative auxiliary invariant *be* (Spears 2020, term)

    a   He *be* walking. (Spears 2020, 80)
    b   It *bees* dat way sometime. (Smitherman 1977)
    c   There don't *be* nothing in church now but sinners. (Bailey and Maynor 1985, 209)
    d   *Do* he *be* walking every day? (Spears 2020, 80)
    e   She *don't be* sick, *do* she? (Spears 2020, 80)

35 Invariant future *be* resulting from *will/would* deletion due to phonological rule

    a   He *be* here tomorrow. (Rickford 1999, 6)
    b   I *be* 82 on the 29th. (Bailey and Maynor 1987, 451)
    c   He *be* in in a few minutes.

36.1 Habitual iterative invariant *be* (*be* + verb +-*ing*), or be_2

    a   Those boys *be messin* with me. (Cukor-Avila 2001, 105)
    b   Do they *be playing* all day every day?
    c   I don't *be eatin* that stuff.
    d   You *be tellin* people all yo business.

36.2 Approximative habitual durative copula invariant *be* (Spears 2020, 82)

    a   He *be* about six feet tall. (Spears 2020, 82)
    b   She be about nine years old.

36.3 Equative habitual durative copula invariant *be*, or be_3 (Alim 2004; Spears 2020)

    a   I *be* the truth. (Alim 2006, 76)
    b   Leo *be* the one to tell it like it is. (Baugh 1983, 88)

c　We *be* them Bay boys. (Alim 2006, 77)
d　They *be* some weak-minded muthafuckas! (Alim 2015, 857)

37　Unstressed, or completive, *been/bin*

a　It *been* raining ever since y'all came here.
b　It *been* so long.
c　I *been* paid that bill last week (Spears 2020, 83)
d　I *been* to see about Mama.

38　Stressed *BIN* to mark remote past (i.e., an action happened or a state came into being long ago). It is not always stressed.

a　I *BIN* drinking coffee.
b　I *BIN* been knowing Russell. (Baugh 1983, 95)
c　They *BIN* left. (Dayton 1996)

39　Completive, or perfective, *done*

a　He *done* sold all that.
b　I knew you was foolin cause I *done* waited on you before. (Shoney's waitress, Athens, GA, February 2002)
c　He *been done* gone. (Rickford 1999, 6)

40.1　Resultative, disapproval marker *be done$_1$*

a　You do that again, I *be done* whip your little behind so fast you won't know what happened to you. (Spears 2020, 84)
b　If the police shoot anybody again, we *be done* had a riot up in here. (Spears 2020, 84)

40.2　Future or conditional perfect *be done$_2$*

a　He *be done* left by the time we get there.
b　I'a *be done* fixed it myself by then.

40.3　Habitual perfect *be done$_3$*

a　. . . they were all raggedy, and they buttons *be done* fell off. (Spears 2020, 85)
b　Every time I see him [dog], he *be done* dug up something. (Spears 2020, 84)
c　After you get there and get all settled in next week, you'll see—every time you run into him he *be done* spent all his money again. (Spears 2020, 84)

41 Aspectual *steady*

    a   They *steady* be laughing.
    b   Ricky Bell be *steady* stepping in them number nines. (Baugh 1983, 86)

42 *Come* of indignation (disapproval marking [semi-]auxiliary)

    a   He *come* walkin in here like he owned the damn place. (Spears 1982, 852)
    b   He *come* askin me my phone number.
    c   Don't *come* actin like you don't know what happened. (Green 2002, 73)
    d   Fool come being all stuck-up with everybody just cause he was driving a Ferrari. (Spears 2020, 85)
    e   He *come* coming in here raising all kind of hell. (Spears 2020, 84)

43.1 *Gon* ("going to")

    a   I'm *gon* fix some grits.
    b   We *gon* go back home and keep workin.
    c   We *gon* be alright.

43.2 Disapproval marking auxiliary *gone* (or *go*) as a (Spears 2020, 86)

    a   Now why he *gon* act like that? (Spears 2020, 86)
    b   And he gone raise the damn window! (Spears 2020, 86)

43.3 Disapproval marking "double" auxiliary *gone-come* (Spears 2020, 86)

    a   He *gone-come* telling me I had to change my whole transmission [instead of just doing a simple repair]. (Spears 2020, 86)
    b   Jane said he *gone-come* asking her if I could steal one for him. (Spears 2020, 86)

44 Auxiliary stressed *STAY* (Spears 2000, 2017), which is habitual iterative frequentative in aspect and expresses an event comprising subevents that recur frequently. It is not always stressed. (Spears 2020, 86)

a She *STAY* talkin on the phone. (Spears 2020, 86)
b He *STAYS* at Gramma house. (Spears 2020, 86)
c I'm glad he left town; he *stayed* [without stress] over here. (Spears 2020, 87)

45 Future *finna* or *fitna* (derived from "fixing to") to mark the immediate future

a He *finna* go. (Rickford 1999, 6)
b I'm *fitna* do it now.

46 Counterfactual *call*

a She *call* herself dancing.
b He *call* hisself threatening me.

47 *Had* + simple past

a Today I *had went* to work. (Cukor-Avila 2001, 105)
b See, what *had happened* . . .

48 Multiple, or double, modals (e.g., *may can, might can, might could, must don't*)

a He *might could* do the work. (Martin and Wolfram 2022, 35)
b They *might should oughta* do it. (Martin and Wolfram 2022, 35)
c They *must don't* know any better. (Rickford 1999, 6)

49 Quasi modals *liketa* and *poseta*

a I *liketa* drowned. (Rickford 1999, 7)
b You don't *poseta* do it that way. (Rickford 1999, 7)

Other Aspects of Verbal Tense Marking

50 Zero past tense or past participle suffix -*ed* (contextual signals)

a I probably woulda *endØ* up keeping it.
b I like *big-boneØ* women.
c That's when *light-skinØ* brothas was in style.
d You a *two-faceØ* ([fes]) fool.

51 Use of past tense or preterite form (V-ed) as past participle (V-en)

   a   She has *ran*. (Rickford 1999, 7)
   b   He had *bit*. (Rickford 1999, 7)

52 Use of past participle form (V-*en*) as past tense or preterite form (V-*ed*)

   a   She *seen* him yesterday. (Rickford 1999, 7)
   b   *He gone* to see him.

53 Use of verb stem (V) as past tense or preterite form (V-*ed*)

   a   *He come* down here yesterday. (Rickford 1999, 7)
   b   She turnØ the TV off when the *news come* on last night.
   c   *I'm a broke* person inside.

54 Reduplicated, or analogic, extension of past tense or past participle suffix -*ed* (primarily with *liked*, *looked*, and *skinned*, according to Green 2002)

   a   I *likeded* ([laɪkdɪd])/*like*Ø ([laɪk]) that show.
   b   He *lookeded* ([lʊkdɪd])/*look*Ø ([lʊk]) at you a little too funny.
   c   Dark-*skinneded* ([skɪndɪd])/*skin*Ø ([skɪn]) brothas are in style.
   d   I like *big-boneded* ([bondɪd]) women.
   e   You a *two-faceded* ([festɪd])/*two-face*Ø ([fes]) fool.

55 Generalization of *is* and *was*

   a   *You was* determined.
   b   Some *people is* worser than me.
   c   I knew *you was* foolin cause I done waited on you before. (Shoney's waitress in Athens, GA, February 2002)

56 Zero third-person singular present tense suffix -*s*

   a   At least he *know*Ø you have a phone.
   b   She *see*Ø me.
   c   She *know*Ø she doin wrong.

57 Aspectual verb -*s* suffix

   a   I don't let it tempt me; *I tempts* it.
   b   *I takes* what I want.
   c   That's the way *it bees* sometime.

Nouns and Pronouns

58 Zero plural suffix -*s* (contextual signals)

    a   That man done changed car places since then *two or three timeØ*.
    b   This *five poundØ* of shrimp.

59 Reduplicated, or reinterpretation of, suffix -*s*

    a   I went and took my *tests* ([tɛsɪz])/*testØ* ([tɛs]) at the school.
    b   We having a lot of *contestses* ([kantɛsɪz])/*contestØ* ([kantɛs]) at work. (Green 2002, 114)

60 Associative plural *nem* or *and (th)em*

    a   Larry *nem* lef already when I got here.
    b   That's Natalia *nem* right there.
    c   Bay *and nem* didn't play that back then.

61 Zero possessive suffix -*s* (contextual signals)

    a   I ain't never seen nobody don't know they *wifeØ phone number*.
    b   This *KathyØ boy*.

62 *They* and *y'all* possessive

    a   Who want to put on *they good clothes* looking like that?
    b   I ain't never seen nobody don't know *they wife* phone number.
    c   They had *they own* area.
    d   It's *y'all ball*. (Rickford 1999, 7)

63 Pronominal apposition, or pleonastic pronouns (aka double subject)

    a   *That sausage, it's* nice and hot.
    b   *That man, he* ain't no good.

64 Use of object pronouns (e.g., me, him, her) after a verb as personal datives (e.g., myself, himself)

    a   Ahma git *me* a gig. (Rickford 1999, 8)
    b   She gon get *her* some of that.

65 Bare subject relative clause

   a That's the man come Ø here. (Rickford 1999, 8)
   b He the man Ø got all the old records. (Martin and Wolfram 2022, 35)

66 Less differentiated personal pronouns (pronouns can serve as subject and object form)

   a They should do it *theyselves*.
   b *Them people* terrible.

Negation

67 Use of *ain't* as a general preverbal negator (includes *ain't* for *didn't*)

   a He ain' here. (Rickford 1999, 8)
   b He ain' do it. (Rickford 1999, 8)

68 Negative concord, or multiple negation

   a I *don't let* myself get in *no* more habit than I want to get in.
   b He *don'* do *nothin*. (Rickford 1999, 8)
   c You *ain't makin no* excuse for how you useta act.

69 Negative inversion of auxiliary and indefinite pronoun subject

   a *Cain't nobody* say nothin roun here.
   b *Ain't nobody* got nothin to say.

70 *But* negative (use of *ain't but* and *don't but* for "only")

   a He *ain't but* fourteen years old. (Rickford 1999, 8)
   b They didn't take *but* three dollars. (Rickford 1999, 8)

Questions

71 Formation of direct questions without inversion of the subject and auxiliary verb (usually with rising intonation)

   a Why *I can't* play? (Rickford 1999, 8)
   b Who that is? (Martin and Wolfram 2022, 32)
   c Why she took that? (Martin and Wolfram 2022, 32)

72 Auxiliary verb inversion in embedded questions (without *if* or *whether*)

   a   I asked him Ø *could he* go with me. (Rickford 1999, 8)
   b   I meant to ask her Ø *did she* like it.

Existential, Locative, Complementizer, Quotative, and Other Constructions

73 Existential *it* instead of "there"

   a   *It's a lot* of it in there.
   b   *It's a school* up there. (Rickford 1999, 8)

74 Existential *they got* (as a plural equivalent of singular "it is," instead of "there are")

   a   *They got* some angry women here. (Nina Simone song, Rickford 1999, 9)
   b   *They got* a lotta people up in here.

75 Use of *here go* . . . or *there go* . . . as a static locative or presentational form

   a   *There go* Mister beatin Celie again. (Maia Morris, Spring 2002 AAL class)
   b   *Here go* my own. (Rickford 1999, 39)

76 *Tell say* construction or complementizer/quotative *say*

   a   They *told* me *say* they couldn't go. (Rickford 1999, 9)
   b   They *tell* him *say*, "You better not go there." (Martin and Wolfram 2022, 15)

77 Inceptive *get/got to*

   a   I *got to* thinking about that. (Cukor-Avila 2001, 105)
   b   I *got to* studying his every move after that.

Discourse Features

78 Signifying

   Signifying, one form of smart talk, is a game of verbal wit. Smitherman (1977) defines signifying as an indirect form of ritualized insult in which "a speaker puts down, talks about, needles—signifies on—the listener" (118). Rodgers (1969, 14) defines signifying as a way of saying the truth that hurts with a laugh, a way of capping on someone (as cited in Rambsy and Whiteside 2015, 713). As cited in Rambsy and Whiteside (2015, 713–714),

a   The speaker of Ishmael Reed's (1976/1989) poem "Flight to Canada" cleverly signifies throughout a letter to his former master. At one point, he informs Massa Swille that he stole the owner's money but says,

> Don't worry
> Your employees won't miss
> It & I accept it as a
> Down payment on my back
> Wages (5)

Of course, those "employees" are slaves, and "back wages" refers to funds owed as well as the crushing weight of slave labor.

b   **Grace:** After I had my little boy, I swore I was not having any more babies. I thought four kids was a nice-sized family. But it didn't turn out that way. I was a little bit disgusted and didn't tell anybody when I discovered I was pregnant. My sister came over one day; I had started to show by that time.
Rochelle: Girl, you sure od need to join the Metrecal for lunch bunch.
Grace: (non-committally) Yea, I guess I am putting on a little weight.
Rochelle: Now look here, girl, we both standing here soaking wet and you still trying to tell me it ain't raining (cited in Green 2002, 140; from Mitchell-Kernan 1972, 323).

Instead of saying outright that Grace was, in no uncertain terms, pregnant, Rochelle signifies and gets the intended message across just the same.

79 Directness

  a **Man**: "So I guess you're one of the students in the course, learning all about black culture, hunh?"

  Woman student (fully aware of the remark's intent): "Yes, I came with my boyfriend, over there; he's in the course too." (For all practical purposes, she has told him to get lost, but he cannot drop the issue because others are present and have witnessed the exchange; he would lose face.)

  Man: So, what do you do with your spare time, when you're not studying and carrying on?

  Woman student (falling into the trap; her speech and behavior strongly suggest that culturally she is not African-American or only slightly so): A lot of things.

  Man: Like what?

  Woman: Ummm, I like to cook.

  Man (sharply): Cook! Well, you need to study that some more. It looks like you damn near burned that casserole thing you brought.

  (The woman tries to defend her casserole, but the scene has basically ended. The man has saved face, and he is ready to move on.) (Spears 2001, 248)

  b **Sheila** (perky, in her 30s, wearing her new Christmas gift, a green warmup suit): Oh, I l-o-o-o-ve this, it's so nifty, don't you love it. Look!

  Gloria (Sheila's sister, 40s, unimpressed): You look like a damn frog.

  (Sheila continues merrily on; no one reacts except for a few faint chuckles.) (Spears 2001, 248)

80 Indirectness

  AAL/USEB discourse genre in which the speaker targets a certain individual but does so indirectly (Morgan 2022).

   I saw a woman the other day in a pair of stretch pants, she must have weighed 300 pounds. If she knew how she looked she would burn those things. (Mitchell-Kernan 1972, 167) [Said about someone present who is overweight.]

81 Pointed indirectness

> When a speaker means to say something to a mock receiver that is intended for someone else and is so recognized, or when a speaker refers to local knowledge to target someone else; when a speaker attributes a feature to a target that is true (Morgan 2022, 284).
>
> *W:* "I like a man with a warm smile and deep dimples."
> (Unfortunately, the man, the mock target, responded with a flattered and beaming dimple-less smile.)
> *M:* "Thank you."
>
> *This caused everyone, including the intended target, to laugh at the mock target. Morgan 2022, 285)*

82 Baited indirectness

> The speaker focuses on negative attributes of an unspecified target rather than mock receivers. The speaker focuses on (usually negative) attributes or characteristics while in the target's presence, without directly addressing the target (Morgan 1996, 408–409).
>
>> An example of baited indirection, which resulted in controversy, occurred when a rapper, Ice T, recorded a rap song entitled "Cop Killer." It seems that the police did not first determine whether they fit Ice T's description of brutal cops before criticizing his rap song. Instead, they seemed to believe that Ice T referred to them. Ice T explains his position: At the very beginning of "Cop Killer," I dedicate it to the LAPD and to police chief Daryl Gates. The lyrics are blatant and very specific: the chorus explains what the record's about:
>>
>> COP KILLER, it's better you than me.
>> COP KILLER, fuck police brutality!
>> COP KILLER, I know you family's grievin'
>> Fuck 'em!
>> COP KILLER, but tonight we get even.
>
>> Better you than me. If it's gonna be me, then better you. My anger is clearly aimed at brutal police. The song was

created to be a protest record—a warning, not a threat—to authority that says, "Yo, police: We're human beings. Treat us accordingly" (Ice T and Siegmund 1994, 168–169; as cited in Morgan 2022, 288).

N.B.: The difference between pointed indirectness and baited indirectness, according to Morgan (1996, 409), is that the former has a mock target they are signifying on and the latter focuses on (negative) attributes in the target's presence while signifying.

83 Semantic license

Father: Go to bed!
Little boy: Aw, Daddy, we're playing dominoes.
Father: I'm gonna domino your ass if you don't go to bed now (Spears 2001, 248).

Semiotic Resources for Conversation Signifying

84 Reading

Reading occurs when someone verbally denigrates another person to their face in front of other people because of some inappropriate action or words or, according to Smitherman (1994, 192), "to tell someone off in no uncertain terms and in a verbally elaborate manner." "It is not unusual to get read for acting out class privileges, failing to greet friends, pretending to have beliefs that are not actually held, etc." (Morgan 1996, 410). Morgan (1996, 410) shares the following example:

While doing field work in Chicago, I was falsely read in a crowded waiting area of a fried chicken joint by one of the cooks (I swear I never saw him before that day!) who yelled, so everyone heard him, "See! Yeah! You speak to me when there's nobody around and we're all alone! But in front of people you're too good to speak!" The other customers waiting for their fried chicken either looked at me in disgust (shaking their heads), or didn't look at me at all. The point here is not that a reader is correct or incorrect, but that the reader is willing to jeopardize his or her own face (as well as that of the target) by disclosing what the reader believes to be the target's attempt to camouflage his or her beliefs, attitudes, etc.

85 Reading dialect (Smitherman and Troutman-Robinson 1988, 65)

A common way of reading dialect, among African American women, is through use of the expression, "Miss Thang." During a conversation, one speaker may want to "read" another person due to the latter's inappropriate behavior. In order to communicate dissatisfaction, then, the first person may refer to the targeted receiver as "Miss Thang": "We were doing alright until *Miss Thang* decided she didn't want to go along with the program." In this instance, the first person "reads dialect" using AAL/USEB, communicating a negative point about the targeted receiver. The expression "Miss Thang" within AAWL is a direct put down of a targeted receiver. The broader African American speech community, as well as the African American women's speech community, interprets *thang* negatively since a thing is an object, lacking an identity and other human qualities.

86 Marking

Marking is when a speaker dramatically imitates, or mimics, the words and perhaps the actions of a person and makes some comment about them in the process (Green 2002, 136). Mitchell-Kernan (1972, 332–333) notes that the "marker" reproduces "the words of the individual actors" and "affects the voice and mannerisms of the speaker" (Green 2002, 136). See Harvey (1997) in his stand-up show where he describes the difference between how a white person responds to being fired compared to a Black person.

87 Loud-talking

Loud-talking is when a speaker says something that was intended for someone else that's loud enough for people outside of the conversation to hear. According to Mitchell-Kernan (1972,

329), loud-talking is used to refer "to a speaker's utterance which by virtue of its volume permits hearers other than the addressee, and is objectionable because of this."

Speaker B, a 33-year-old Black male, kept asking Speaker A, a 32-year-old Black woman, where they should have dinner that night, but A didn't have any suggestions. After some time had elapsed, A and B had the following conversation.

A: I figured it out. Let's go to that place where I had that good veggie burger.

B: Oh yeah, American Café! That's a great idea.
A, B, and others get ready to go to dinner.

A: (*A walks over to B and delivers the line quietly with discretion and with hands on her hips.*) I know I have great ideas, but it takes time for me to come up with them, so don't rush me.

B: (*B looks at A and delivers the line so that the other four people in the room can hear him.*) Now see, see what I have to go through!

A retreats to the door, out of sight, and waits for the others.

She running to the door. She shame now. Dən told me off, now she wanna go in the dark.

Everyone laughs. (Green 2002, 141)

88 Ratchet, or emphasis, clap (prevalent on social media)

Just👏 don't👏 do👏 it👏!

Discourse Features in African American Women's Language

89 Reported speech

"Etter-Lewis explains this occurrence of reported speech as a result of highly regarded mentor relationships established between women narrators and their mentor, usually fathers/men but can include mothers/women. Also, reported speech of men, according to Etter-Lewis (1993), occurred as a result of women being socialized to 'talk like a lady' (1993, 84) and 'to listen to men' (1993, 84), thus giving deference to men's words" (Troutman 2001, 214).

My father said, "Now you're ready to go to school" (Etter-Lewis 1993, 83).

90 Cooperative, or collaborative, speech

Q: And the grandparents on your father's side?
A: My grandfather was a coachman for a very wealthy family in the north. My grandmother did not work. And there is a very interesting story about them too. You want me to relate that?
Q: Yes.
A: Well, the story as my paternal aunt told me . . .
Q: That was a wonderful story.
A: I thought I would like to write about it someday.
Q: Yes, please do. What was her maiden name? (Etter-Lewis 1993, 140)

Collaboration occurs when Speaker A asks for permission to share a story about her grandparents and Speaker Q (Etter-Lewis) gives permission for the sharing of the story. Etter-Lewis cooperates with the interviewee's request, although it is not part of the prepared interviewer questions. The interviewee, according to Etter-Lewis, cooperates by offering to tell a story since she is aware of Etter-Lewis' aim. As a result of Etter-Lewis' collaborative action, Speaker A shares a rich story, embellishing Etter-Lewis' data collection on oral narratives.

(Troutman 2001, 214)

91 *Little* usage

And that *little* case was written up in the newspapers and I got a *little* publicity and I was really very happy over that one. . . . It may have been the early part of '34. Yes, I liked that case. I've kept a *little* scrapbook and that's one of my favorites.

(Etter-Lewis 1993, 200)

92 Culturally-toned diminutives

A diminutive may refer to suffixes in English (e.g., *-let, -ling, -ette*), words used with suffixes (e.g., *piglet, dinette*), or words which express familiarity (e.g., *Gracie, Tommy*). Within the African American women's speech community, culturally-toned diminutives express solidarity. Examples include *girl, sistah, sistah friend, honey, honey child, child, baby, baby girl, precious, muh'dear*.

(Troutman 2001, 217)

93 Performance

Performance is "a special kind of communicative event in which there is a particular relationship among stylized material, performer, and audience" (Foster 1995, 333).

- *T:* You have a master plan to beat this economic system?
- *S:* No, not yet. (laughs)
- *T:* Well, that's what a budget is.
- *S:* I was referring to budgeting money to for payin the bills, runnin my house . . .
- *T:* Unhuh, that's a budget. . . . Somebody else who wanna share their ideas about a budget? I want to make sure everybody understands what a budget is before we go on. Yes, Miss Goins . . . (Troutman 2001, 218)

94 Latching

Latching is a turn-taking mechanism that occurs at the end of a conversational partner's speaking turn, avoiding an interruption or overlapping of a conversational partner's speech. Next is an example from an exchange between U.S. Senator Arlen Specter (AS) and Anita Hill (AH) during the Anita Hill-Clarence Thomas Senate Judiciary Hearing in October 1991 ("=" indicates latching; i.e., where one utterance ends and another begins without any perceptible pause).

- *AS:* His words are that you said quote the most laudatory comments unquote.
- *AH:* = I have no response to that because I don't know exactly what he is saying.

Hill does not hesitate, pause, or back-channel in taking her speaking turn nor does she interrupt Specter. She responds without missing a beat in the ABAB conversational pattern. . . . Her latch exudes assertiveness; she takes her turn readily (essentially, she asserts her turn).

(Troutman 2001, 219–220)

95 Capping

Capping is "setting the record straight" in a conversational exchange and is a type of assertiveness.

AS: Well, (.) I'll repeat the question again. Was there any substance in Ms. Berry's **flat** statement that (.) quote (.) Ms. Hill was disappointed and frustrated that Mr. Thomas did not show any sexual interest in her?

AH: No (.) there is not. There is no substance to that. He did show interest and I've explained to you how he did show that interest. (.) Now (.) she was not aware of that. If you're asking me (.) Could she have made that statement. (.) She could have made the statement if she wasn't aware of it. (.) But she wasn't aware of everything that happened. (Troutman 2001, 219–220)

96 Smart talk

Smart talk, a type of assertiveness, is a style of combative language in AAWL that is used to defend one's respectability.

YM: Mama, you sho is fine.
MK: That ain't no way to talk to your mother.
TM: (Laughter)
YM: You married?
MK: Um hm.
YM: Is your husband married?
TM: (Laughter) (Troutman 2001, 222–223)

97 Talking that talk

"*Talking that talk* is a referential phrase meaning that a particular speaker knows how to use language extremely well.

Such a speaker knows how to cap or win conversational exchanges through the use of signifying" (Smitherman 1977; Mitchell-Kernan 1972), loud talking, marking (Mitchell-Kernan 1972), rhyming, joking, reading dialect (Morgan 1996), and a variety of other verbal strategies ranging from the prosodic to the discursive. It appears to be an overarching rubric under which smart talk and other verbal strategies fit and which is available to the African American speech community at large, females and males, as exemplified in Troutman (2001, 223–224):

A: Baby, you a real scholar. I can tell you want to learn. Now if you'll just cooperate a lil bit, I'll show you what a good teacher I am. But first we got to get into my area of expertise.

B: I may be wrong but seems to me we already in your area of expertise.

A: You ain't so bad yourself, girl. I ain't heard you stutter yet. You a lil fixated on your subject though. I want to help a sweet thang like you all I can. I figure all that book learning you got must mean you been neglecting other areas of your education.

C: Talk that talk!

I supplied these lists of AAL/USEB features to provide that moment of a high of believing that if you have the lists, then you're good, you got it. Memorize the lists and you will know everything you need to know about AAL/USEB to be a proficient user. You can mimic it or show your cool factor. Dude, no. That's not how this works at all. I still remember sociolinguist Walt Wolfram telling the story many years ago of how he took out his handy list of AAL/USEB features and shared it with a group of Black students, telling them what AAL/USEB was. The students **clapped back**. That's when he says he realized AAL/USEB had variation and the lists weren't cutting it.

Please **don't get it twisted**. I do not have anything personal at all against the researchers who have a features perspective or use a list of features to talk about AAL/USEB. I have done so many times myself in my career. The lists were a start to what has evolved into a more holistic way of approaching the study of AAL/USEB. This is a professional growth area and simply a point of departure. These linguists I have cited—William Labov, Guy Bailey, Walt Wolfram—and many others I have not mentioned have made great contributions to the field and to me personally. We are all forever in their debt for their contributions to and growth of the field. I should also note that in some cases their use of features was pragmatic. That is, describing a feature was low-hanging fruit for earlier AAL/USEB scholars compared to describing a system, especially when you are in a state of discovery and trying to figure out what to do. For your part, let this serve as your personal fix for a pocket AAL/USEB grammar from a features perspective.

I should also be clear that these scholars were often talking about AAVL/VUSEB. I make this point because scholars are sometimes clear about making a distinction between their research on AAVL/VUSEB vs. AAL/USEB. In most research on AAL/USEB, the focus has been on AAVL/VUSEB because some believe AAVL/VUSEB is the "real" AAL/USEB. But many of those scholars also did not believe in variation in AAL/USEB or AAVL/VUSEB, so they really tried to home in on this "real," "authentic," "street" speech that seemed quite "exotic" to them as white, cisgender male (usually), middle- or upper-class researchers. The focus on AAVL/VUSEB has been to the detriment of other varieties of AAL/USEB or even varieties of AAVL/VUSEB. More research has been done on AAVL/VUSEB grammar in the Midwest and Northeast (e.g., Detroit, Philadelphia, New York City, and Washington, DC) than the South/Southeast (e.g., Carolinas, Georgia, Alabama, Mississippi, and Louisiana)—with the exception of Gullah Geechee—even though the Southeast is the cradle of AAL/USEB origins in the U.S. Understandably, those former cities were/are more populous and represent where Black people went during the Great Migration from 1916 to 1970. Nevertheless, the cradle of AAL/USEB still resides in the South/Southeastern U.S. As such, we do not know as much about AAL/USEB speakers today in those areas as we should.

Patterns, Systems, and Structure, Oh My!

Some approaches moved away from listing features of AAL/USEB and, instead, expanded descriptions of it that took into consideration patterns of grammar and systems and principles for explicating grammatical structures. Linguist (syntactician) Lisa Green is one of the biggest proponents of the patterns perspective and one of the scholars who influenced my shift in perspective about AAL/USEB. Her 2002 book *African American English: A Linguistic Introduction* does a lot to live that perspective by not listing a bunch of features as if they make up AAL/USEB. She, instead, provides discussion on a variety of patterns divided into categories of linguistic study (i.e., vocabulary, syntax, phonology, and discourse) but not the usual "features" list. Green (2002) is closer to a traditional grammar book than most books about AAL/USEB. But, still, who wants traditional?

I just need to take another slight break for a testimony. Lisa Green was not the first person to introduce me to this patterns perspective; it was Docta G, Geneva Smitherman, herself. In her writings, she has always approached AAL/USEB as a rich, vibrant, African-centered language. And it is from her writings that I had my first introduction to AAL/USEB as my language of identity (Lanehart 1996) in a way that made me feel seen. *Talkin and Testifyin* (Smitherman 1977) is a classic for a reason. Docta G never did a study on a single AAL/USEB feature as most AAL/USEB researchers did. She always professed the system, the structure, the discourse, the heart of the language: The people and their culture. I do not think AAL/USEB can be separated from the people and their culture. Docta G is partly responsible for my strong sense of language and culture, language and identity, and the language that is AAL/USEB. She is why I resisted studying AAL/USEB through a single feature, vowel, or word because she taught me that AAL/USEB is more than the sum of its parts. She is my Aretha Franklin of AAL/USEB. **Word from the mother** (Smitherman 2006/2022). There's that *DE*-troit soul!

Next you will find an expansion and revision of what is the table of contents (TOC) for Green (2002) that pertains to the grammar of

AAL/USEB. I label the overarching sections as levels of AAL/USEB, as in levels of language—lexical; syntactic and morphosyntactic; phonological; and discourse, nonverbal, and paralinguistic—while still closely following Green's TOC order. This outline provides a departure from the features perspective to the system perspective for the most part. I expand on the TOC to provide some clarity and examples as needed. To get the full details with lots of examples, content, and context, read Green (2002) Chapters 1–5. Remember that this chapter structure for me is about producing a meta-grammar (i.e., thinking about grammar). Also, I attempt to reduce duplication between this part of the chapter and my previous lists by letting the former provide examples and the latter provide context and descriptions.

Lexical Level: Word Classes and Word Formation

- Three types of AAL/USEB lexicon description (Green 2002, 14)
    - A list of lexical items that occur in AAL/USEB (e.g., Major 1994; Smitherman 1994)
    - A list of lexical items and names that are subdivided into thematic topic (e.g., Folb 1980; Lee 2009)
    - A repository of words, distinct from slang, that are part of the African American community (e.g., Dillard 1977)
- Structuring the lexicon
    - Lexical entries for terms in the African American lexicon, e.g., *get over*, *call ___ self*, *come*, *mash*, *-own-*, *some*, *stay*, *steady* (Green 2002, 21–24)
    - Lexical entries for verbal markers, e.g., *be*, *BIN*, *dən* (Green 2002, 25–26)
- Slang as a productive process of adding words to the lexicon

Syntactic Level, Part 1: Verbal Markers

- Auxiliaries (i.e., *have*, *do*, *be*) and modals (i.e., *will/would*, *shall/should*, *can/could*, *may/might*) (Green 2002, 36)

- General description of auxiliaries: Verbal paradigms
- Properties and processes of auxiliaries
  - In auxiliary + main verb sequence paradigms, tense is marked on the auxiliary; in past perfect, the main verb is in the simple past form, but tense is marked on *have* (e.g., had + simple past tense) (Green 2002, 40).
  - Auxiliaries can appear in a contracted, reduced, or zero form, such as 's, 'm, and 'll or 'a, 'd, and Ø (Green 2002, 40).
  - Auxiliaries can host the contracted negator *not* (*n't*); i.e., *n't* can attach to auxiliaries (Green 2002, 41).
  - Auxiliaries can be identified by their property of inverting in yes-no questions, which require a yes or no answer (Green 2002, 41).
  - Auxiliaries do not occur obligatorily in questions (Green 2002, 42).
- Aspectual markers (verbal markers): *Be, BIN, dən*
  - Aspectual *be*
    - Aspectual markers denote meaning in the construction in which they occur. Aspectual *be* denotes habitual or iterative meaning (Green 2002, 47).
    - Summary of properties of aspectual *be*
      - Aspectual *be* is a verbal or aspectual marker that is different from the auxiliary/copula *be* (Green 2002, 51).
      - Aspectual *be* indicates habitual meaning (i.e., an event occurs over and over) (Green 2002, 51).
      - Aspectual *be* occurs before verbs, adjectives, nouns, prepositions, adverbs, *dən*, and at the end of sentences (Green 2002, 52).
  - Unstressed *been/bin* (Spears 2017)
  - Remote past *BIN*
    - Remote past is relative, so it can refer to a time period of 15 minutes ago or 15 years ago (Green 2002, 55).
    - The stress (or pitch accent) distinguishes *BIN* phonetically (i.e., pronunciation) and semantically

(i.e., meaning) from *been* (the unstressed form). . . . One important factor is that stress is associated with meaning, such that stress on *BIN* results in remote past interpretation (Green 2002, 55).
- Three types of *BIN*

  - *BIN$_{STAT}$*
    - In *BIN$_{STAT}$* constructions (where "STAT" refers to state, that which holds constantly), that state started at some point in the remote past and continues to hold up to the moment of utterance or time of speech (Green 2002, 55).

  - *BIN$_{HAB}$*
    - In *BIN$_{HAB}$* constructions (where "HAB" refers to habitual) . . . the activity or state expressed by the verb begins at some point in the remote past and continues habitually, that is, one occasion or from time to time (Green 2002, 57).
    - *BIN$_{HAB}$* differs from *BIN$_{STAT}$* in that none of them can occur in the past form (Green 2002, 57).

  - *BIN$_{COMP}$*
    - In *BIN$_{COMP}$* constructions (where "COMP" refers to complementizer), the activity indicated by the verb ended at some point in the remote past; thus, *BIN$_{COMP}$* constructions are interpreted as meaning finished or ended "a long time ago" (Green 2002, 58).
    - For the most part, the verbs in these constructions are in their past-tense forms, but given variation and phonological processes, the *-ed* may not be pronounced (Green 2002, 58).

- Summary of properties of *BIN* (Green 2002, 60)
  - *BIN* is a verbal or tense/aspect marker.
  - *BIN* is stressed.
  - *BIN* situates something.

- *BIN* occurs before verbs, adjectives, nouns, prepositions, adverbs, and *dən*.
- *Dən*
  - The verbal marker *dən* denotes that an event has ended; it refers to events, such as having changed, having finished, having done all you told me to do, and having pushed it, that have ended (Green 2002, 60).
  - Summary of properties of *dən* (Green 2002, 62)
    - *Dən* is a verbal or tense/aspect marker.
    - *Dən* is unstressed.
    - *Dən* indicates that an event is in the resultant state; that is, it is over. But in some contexts, it occurs with states, which do not have endpoints.
    - *Dən* usually occurs preceding verbs ending in *-ed*; however, it may precede the present form *give*, for example.
  - Aspectual combinations with *dən*: *Be dən* and *BIN dən*
    - *Be dən* (habitual resultant state)
      - Habitual resultant state in which habitual is denoted by *be* and the notion of having ended is denoted by *dən* (Green 2002, 64).
      - The verb is in the past form (Green 2002, 64).
      - This sequence indicates the habitual completion of some event (Green 2002, 64).
    - *Be dən* (future resultant state)
      - Future resultant *be dən* is similar to habitual resultant *be dən* except that it does not indicate habitual meaning (Green 2002, 65).
      - It is used in environments in which some activity will be completed by a future time (Green 2002, 65).
    - *Be dən* (modal resultant state)
      - The *be dən* modal resultant state is used in somewhat threatening situations, situations which ae associated with veiled or mild threats or simply to express imminent actions (Green 2002, 66).

- The constructions in which *be dən* occurs resemble conditionals in that they have an implicit and sometimes explicit *if*-clause and *then*-clause (Green 2002, 66).
- *BIN dən* (remote past resultant state)
  - This *BIN dən* sequence appears to be identical in meaning to the reading of BIN_{COMP} constructions. They both mark remoteness of an event that ended in the past. However, this may be to place emphasis on the resultant state or to redundantly indicate the resultant state (Green 2002, 67).
  - N.B.: "It is slightly misleading to refer to *be dən* and *BIN dən* as separate markers. It is probably more accurate to say that the markers *be* and *BIN* can take sequences of *dən* + verb. Combining them here is for convenience" (Green 2002, 67).
- Preverbal markers: *Finna, steady, come*
  - *Finna*
    - *Finna* (including variants *fixina, fixna,* and *fitna*) indicates that the event is imminent; it will happen in the immediate future (Green 2002, 70).
    - *Finna* precedes nonfinite verbs, which are not marked for tense and agreement (Green 2002, 70).
    - DeBose and Faraclas (1993) refer to *finna* (which they represent as *finta*) as a type of modal marker used to make a weak assertion (Green 2002, 71).
  - *Steady*
    - The marker *steady* (which may also be pronounced as [stʌdi]) precedes a verb form in the progressive (verb+ -*ing*, e.g., *steady talking*, where the verb *talk* takes -*ing*). *Steady* is used to convey the meaning that an activity is carried out in an intense or consistent manner (Green 2002, 71).

- Baugh (1984) defines the marker *steady* as "a predicate adverb" that "indicates that the activity of the corresponding progressive verb is conducted in an intense, consistent, and continuous manner" (3, 5). Because it indicates that an activity is carried out in an intense and consistent manner, it must precede a verb that names an activity. As such, *steady* does not usually precede verbs that name states, such as *have*, *own*, and *know* (Green 2002, 71).
- *Come*
  - A major function of the marker *come* is to mark speaker indignation (Green 2002, 73).
  - Spears (1982, 850) refers to *come* as a semi-auxiliary, unique to AAL/USEB, which (there's only one *come*) expresses speaker indignation (Green 2002, 73).

Syntactic Level, Part 2: From Multiple Negation to Patterns in Question Formation

- Negation
  - Multiple negators such as *don't*, *no*, and *nothing* can be used in a single negative sentence (Green 2002, 77).
  - In negative concord, or multiple negation, constructions, negation can be marked on auxiliaries (e.g., *don't*) and indefinite nouns such as *anybody/nobody* and *anything/nothing* (Green 2002, 77).
  - Pleonastic negation is when the first negative marker does all the work of marking negation because the additional negatives do not contribute additional negative meaning (see Labov 1972; Martin 1992) (Green 2002, 78).
  - Negative inversion is when two sentence- or clause-initial elements, an auxiliary, and indefinite noun phrase are obligatorily marked for negation. Constructions are noted for their superficial resemblance to yes-no questions in that the auxiliary precedes the subject (Green 2002, 78).

- Existential *it* and *dey*
    - *It* and *dey* occur in constructions in AAL/USEB that are used to indicate something exists (Green 2002, 80).
    - Some restrictions are placed on the formation of these existential sentences, and they are important in showing that there is a method in producing them (Green 2002, 81).
    - These existential sentences can only be constructed with an existential element (e.g., *it*) and a following obligatory form of *be* (inflected or aspectual), *have*, or *got* (Green 2002, 81).
- Questions
    - Yes-no questions
    - Questions formed from declarative sentences
    - Questions formed without an auxiliary
    - *Wh*-questions
        - The auxiliary follows the *wh*-word and precedes the subject
        - The auxiliary immediately follows the subject
        - There is no overt auxiliary
    - Indirect questions
    - Embedded questions
- Relative clauses
    - The clauses discussed serve as modifiers or qualifiers of a preceding noun (Green 2002, 89).
    - These clauses may be introduced by an overt relative pronoun, *that* or *who* (Green 2002, 90).
    - Relative clauses that modify nouns in the predicate nominative or object positions are not obligatorily headed by relative pronouns (see Tottie and Harvie 2000; Green 2002, 91).
- Preterite *had*
    - The *had* + verb (verb *-ed*) sequence is not used to indicate action that took place in the past before the past

(i.e., pluperfect); this sequence basically refers to an event in the simple past (Green 2002, 92).

- Other AAL/USEB auxiliaries (Spears 2020)
- Structure of the noun phrase (Mufwene 2022)
- Bare nouns (Spears 2007; Green 2007)

Morphosyntactic Level: Inflections

- Past morphology
    - There is usually no distinction with respect to form between simple past and past participles (Green 2002, 95).
- Verbal -*s*
    - Third-person singular agreement marker
    - Narrative present marker
    - Habitual marker
- Genitive (i.e., possessive) marking
- This is not an obligatory marker (Green 2002, 102).

Phonological Level

This chapter shows that the sound system in AAL/USEB operates according to set rules, so speakers do not delete and add sounds haphazardly. What may sound like ignorant and uneducated speech to those who are unfamiliar with the variety or who have some preconceived notions about the people who use this variety is actually rule-governed language use. This becomes clear once systematic inquiry is made into the sound system of AAL/USEB and descriptions are provided (Green 2002, 119).

- Final consonant sounds
    - One explanation for consonant cluster data in AAL/USEB is that pronunciations in which the final consonant clusters *st*, *sk*, and *nd* are pronounced as *s*, *s*, and *n*, respectively, are a result of a process called consonant cluster reduction (Green 2002, 107).

- A second explanation is that words such as *test*, *desk*, and *hand* are pronounced as [tɛs], [dɛs], and [hæn], respectively, because AAL/USEB, like African languages from which it descended, does not have final consonant clusters (Green 2002, 107).
- Devoicing
  - The process of making a voiced consonant voiceless that applies to some consonants at the ends of words (Green 2002, 116).
- Sound patterns and *th*
  - The occurrence of *t/d* and *f/v* in certain environments is systematic in the sense that each sound is chosen based on phonetic properties and not randomness (Green 2002, 117).
- *r* and *l*: liquid vocalization
  - When *r* and *l* follow vowels within words, they are not necessarily produced as liquids; instead, they may be produced as an unstressed vowel (schwa ə, or *uh* sound) if any sound is produced at all (Green 2002, 120).
- Additional phonological patterns
  - *-in*
    - This pattern is restricted to the suffix *-ing*, that is, to words with more than one syllable, so it never occurs in the *-ing* in words with one syllable (Green 2002, 122).
  - *skr* in *str* clusters
  - *oɪ* and other vowel sounds
    - Older speakers use this pattern (road → [ɹoɪd]) [such as my mom, who is a Louisiana native] (Green 2002, 123).
    - In some regions in which AAL/USEB is spoken, there is lowering of the [ɛr] sound in words such as *prepare*, *care*, and *hair*. Due to lowering, the second syllable in *prepare* is affected, so that syllable almost sounds like *par* [pɑr] (Green 2002, 123).

- Prosodic features: stress and intonation
  - The features discussed here are related to pitch of the voice and rhythm of speech, and they are called prosodic or suprasegmental features. Some specific prosodic features are *stress* (accentuation or emphasis placed on syllables or words) and *intonation* (modulation of the voice or tonal inflection; Green 2002, 124).
  - Green goes on to talk about the importance of research on AAL/USEB prosody, and she tries to contextualize what it means to "sound Black" by focusing on intonational patterns, specifically in questions, then to a focus on stress patterns within words (e.g., PO-lice, "police," and DE-troit, "Detroit"; Green 2002, 124–132).
  - There has been a lot more research on intonation since Green (2002), such as Gooden (2009), Holliday (2016, 2019, 2021), and Holliday and Villarreal (2018).

Speech Events, Discourse, Pragmatics, Nonverbal, and Paralinguistic Levels

- Speech events, verbal genres, discourse genres, and rules of interaction
  - Signifying
  - Indirectness
  - Pointed indirectness
  - Baited indirectness
  - Reading
  - Reading dialect
  - Playing the dozens/snaps
    - A distinction is not always made between signifying and playing the dozens, but according to H. Rap Brown (1972, 205–206), "The dozens is a mean game because what you try to do is totally destroy somebody else with words. . . . Signifying is more humane. Instead of coming down on somebody's mother, you come down on them" (Green 2002, 135).

- Rapping
    - Smitherman (1977, 82) notes that rap is highly stylized and may be used "to convey social and cultural information" or "for conquering foes and women" (Green 2002, 136).
- Marking
- Loud talking
- Woofing
    - A strategy in which boasting is used to intimidate an opponent, thus avoiding violent confrontation (Green 2002, 136).
- Toasts
    - Toasts are tributes, usually poetic, to the grandeur of some character. They are narrated in first person and feature a hero (Green 2002, 137).
- Expressions in nonverbal communication: eye movement and giving dap
    - Eye movement (e.g., cutting eyes, rolling eyes, looking down the nose)
    - Hand on hips, rolling the neck, and moving the head back and forth
    - Handshakes and hand movements, such as giving dap or special hand grips
- Speech events and language use in African American church services
    - Call and response: The interaction between the minister and the congregation is facilitated by call and response, a traditional practice in which the minister makes a statement (a call) and members of the congregation reply (response), indicating that they agree, understand, identify with, or have heard the statement, whether it be an exhortation, instruction, or general information (Green 2002, 147).

- Extensions of call-response
  - *Backchanneling* occurs in the form of short responses to parts of conversations, and it encourages speakers to continue because the listeners are totally engaged in the conversation, in agreement with the speaker's point of view or in awe of it (Green 2002, 154).
- Language use and rap
  - This music type, which combines different technological strategies, such as scratching, sampling, and punch-phrasing, has its roots in a verbal strategy employed in African American communities. *Scratching* refers to the rapid back-and-forth movement of turntables to create a deconstructed sound, and *sampling* involves combining a portion of a record "in the overall mix." *Punch-phrasing* means "to erupt into the sound of turntable #1 with a percussive sample from turntable #2 by def cuing." The use of verbal strategies is a major feature of rap (Green 2002, 156).
- Speech events and communicative competence
  - Researchers, including those in speech pathology and communication disorders, continue to conduct studies that will help to answer questions about the acquisition of AAL/USEB. One important question in that research is, "What kinds of evaluative procedures can be used to determine whether a child is acquiring AAL/USEB normally or whether their speech is impaired (Green 2002, 161)?

Where Does This Leave Us?

And there you have it: A compact overview of approaches to the grammar of AAL/USEB. I was going to supplement the features list and this outline of Green (2002) with additional aspects of AAL/USEB, like grammaticalization, other paralinguistics, and other nonverbal communication, but I decided not to because, again, I don't want this to be a list of features or feed into the ideology that grammar is something you can acquire or learn from a book—at least not my people's grammar 😌.

In all of Green (2002), the most important question was summed up in the last note: "How do we use our knowledge of AAL/USEB grammar to help children?" That has been the basis for much research in AAL/USEB, and that leads to the second question I asked earlier in this chapter: "What is really different about AAL/USEB grammar?" I think I need to add to that question. "Why is difference in AAL/USEB read as deficit?" "Why can't AAL/USEB just be a different variety and not a deficit variety?" "What about African Americans and their language is so grotesque or "exotic" to white people and those using a white gaze and Western European hegemonic ethos that it cannot be more than something that needs to be fixed, eradicated, mocked, scorned, or profited upon at the expense of Black folks?" As Auntie Toni Morrison says,

> The worst of all possible things that could happen would be to lose that language. There are certain things I cannot say without recourse to my language. It's terrible to think that a child with five different present tenses comes to school to be faced with those books that are less than his [sic] own language. And then to be told things about his [sic] language, which is him [sic], that are sometimes permanently damaging. He [sic] may never know the etymology of Africanisms in his [sic] language, not even know that "hip" is a real word or that "the dozens" meant something. This is a really cruel fallout of racism.
>
> (LeClair 1981, 27)

Our children suffer for this. We all suffer for this. How do we use our knowledge of AAL/USEB to help AAL/USEB-speaking children thrive in education, in school, in society, in life in spite of everything against them?

Before tackling these questions, let's talk about who we are and how we do because that's what and where classrooms, education, schooling, and teaching and learning need to be at in order to know how and **where we enter**. And I want to acknowledge that we are not done here yet. As we move through the next chapters, we will emerge at contextualizing AAL/USEB before concluding with responses to the questions I posed. Keep thinking. Next, let's take a little deeper dive into **where we at**.

Questions, Discussion, and Further Inquiry

1. Explore and describe AAL/USEB in social media and other online spaces (e.g., blogs and podcasts).
2. Connect the features list provided in the first part of the chapter and the descriptions and contexts with the second part of the chapter. How might you augment or contextualize the content?
3. Why is AAL/USEB so intriguing to linguists and non-linguists? Why are y'all so interested in AAL/USEB?
4. Which aspects of grammar described here were familiar to you? Which were new?
5. How is AAL/USEB as described here different from your variety?
6. Why is difference in AAL/USEB read as deficit? Why can't AAL/USEB just be a different variety and not a deficit variety?
7. What AAL/USEB words, patterns, and verbal and nonverbal discourse have you experienced that are not discussed in the chapter?
8. What about African Americans and their language is so grotesque or "exotic" to white people with a white gaze and Western European hegemonic ethos that it cannot be more than something that needs to be fixed, eradicated, mocked, scorned, or profited upon at the expense of Black folks?
9. How can/do we use our knowledge of AAL/USEB to help AAL/USEB-speaking children thrive in education, school, society, and life in spite of everything against them?
10. How do people sound like a race (see *raciolinguistics* research)?
11. How can someone be articulate while Black?

References

Alim, H. Samy. 2004. *You Know My Steez: An Ethnographic and Sociolinguistic Study of a Black American Speech Community*. Durham, NC: Duke University Press.

Alim, H. Samy. 2006. *Roc the Mic Right: The Language of Hip Hop Culture*. London: Routledge.

Alim, H. Samy. 2015. Hip Hop Nation Language: Localization and Globalization. In *The Oxford Handbook of African American Language*, edited by Sonja Lanehart, 850–862. Oxford: Oxford University Press.

Bailey, Guy, and Natalie Maynor. 1985. The Present Tense of *Be* in Southern Black Folk Speech. *American Speech* 60.3: 195–213.

Bailey, Guy, and Natalie Maynor. 1987. Decreolization? *Language in Society* 16.4: 449–473.

Bailey, Guy, and Erik Thomas. 2022. Some Aspects of African-American Vernacular English Phonology. In *African-American English: Structure, History, and Use*, Classic Edition, edited by Salikoko S. Mufwene, John R. Rickford, Guy Bailey, and John Baugh, 93–118. London: Routledge.

Baldwin, James. The Blind Men and the Elephant: An Adaptation of an Indian Fable. https://americanliterature.com/author/james-baldwin/short-story/the-blind-men-and-the-elephant

Baugh, John. 1983. *Black Street Speech*. Austin, TX: University of Texas Press.

Baugh, John. 1984. *Steady*: Progressive Aspect in Black Vernacular English. *American Speech* 59.1: 3–12.

Brown, H. Rap. 1972. Street Talk. In *Rappin' and Stylin' Out: Communication in Urban Black America*, edited by Thomas Kochman, 205–207. Urbana, IL: University of Illinois Press.

Crystal, David. 1988. *The English Language*. Harmondsworth, UK: Penguin.

Cukor-Avila, Patricia. 2001. Co-existing Grammars: The Relationship between the Evolution of African American and White Vernacular English in the South. In *Sociocultural and Historical Contexts of African American English*, edited by Sonja L. Lanehart, 93–127. Amsterdam: John Benjamins.

Dayton, Elizabeth. 1996. *Grammatical Categories of the Verb in African-American Vernacular English*. PhD dissertation. University of Pennsylvania.

DeBose, Charles, and Nicholas Faraclas. 1993. An Africanist Approach to the Linguistic Study of Black English: Getting to the Roots of Tense-Aspect-Modality and Copula Systems in Afro-American English. In *Africanisms in Afro-American Language Varieties*, edited by Salikoko S. Mufwene, 364–387. Athens, GA: University of Georgia Press.

Dillard, J.L. 1977. *Lexicon of Black English*. New York: Seabury Press.

Etter-Lewis, Gwendolyn. 1993. *My Soul Is My Own: Oral Narratives of African American Women in the Professions*. London: Routledge.

Folb, Edith A. 1980. *Running' Down Some Lines: The Language and Culture of Black Teenagers*. Cambridge, MA: Harvard University Press.

Foster, Michèle. 1995. "Are You with Me?": Power and Solidarity in the Discourse of African American Women. In *Gender Articulated: Language and the Socially Constructed Self*, edited by Kira Hall and Mary Bucholtz, 329–350. London: Routledge.

Gooden, Shelome. 2009. Authentically Black, Bona Fide Pittsburgher: A First Look at Intonation in African American Women's Language in Pittsburgh. In *African American Women's Language: Discourse, Education, and Identity*, edited by Sonja L. Lanehart, 142–164. Newcastle-upon-Tyne: Cambridge Scholars Publishing.

Green, Lisa. 2002. *African American English: A Linguistic Introduction*. Cambridge: Cambridge University Press.

Green, Lisa. 2007. NPs in Aspectual *Be* Constructions in African American English. In *Noun Phrases in Creole Languages: A Multi-Faceted Approach*, edited by Marlyse Baptista and Jacqueline Guéron, 403–420. Amsterdam: John Benjamins.

Holliday, Nicole R. 2016. Identity Performance among Black/Biracial Men through Intonation: Examining Pitch Accents and Peak Delay. *University of Pennsylvania Working Papers in Linguistics* 22.2.9: 71–80. DOI: 10.1177/00754242211024722

Holliday, Nicole R. 2019. Variation in Question Intonation in the Corpus of Regional African American Language. *American Speech* 94.1: 110–130.

Holliday, Nicole R. 2021. Intonation and Referee Design Phenomena in the Narrative Speech of Black/Biracial Men. *Journal of English Linguistics* 49.3: 283–304. DOI: 10.1177/00754242211024722

Holliday, Nicolle R., and Daniel Villarreal. 2018. How Black Does Obama Sound Now?: Testing Listener Judgments of Intonation in Incrementally Manipulated Speech. *University of Pennsylvania Working Papers in Linguistics* 24.2.8: 57–66. https://repository.upenn.edu/pwpl/vol24/iss2/8

Ice-T, and Heidi Siegmund. 1994. *The Ice Opinion*. New York: St. Martin's Press.

Labov, William. 1969. The Logic of Nonstandard English. *Georgetown Monographs in Languages and Linguistics* 22. Washington, DC: Georgetown University Press.

Labov, William. 1972. *Language in the Inner City: Studies in the Black English Vernacular*. Philadelphia: University of Pennsylvania Press.

Lanehart, Sonja L. 1996. The Language of Identity. *Journal of English Linguistics* 24.4: 322–331.

Lanehart, Sonja L. 2002. *Sista, Speak! Black Women Kinfolk Talk about Language and Literacy*. Austin, TX: University of Texas Press.

Lanehart, Sonja L. 2012/2018. Re-viewing the Origins and History of African American Language. In *English Historical Linguistics: An International Handbook*, vol. 2 *(HSK 34.2)*, edited by Alexander Bergs and Laurel J. Brinton, 1826–1839. Berlin: Mouton de Gruyter.

LeClair, Thomas. 1981. The Language Must Not Sweat: A Conversation with Toni Morrison. *The New Republic*, March 21. https://newrepublic.com/article/95923/the-language-must-not-sweat

Lee, Margaret G. 2009. Selling Decency and Innocence: Names of Singing Groups in the *Malt Shop Memories* Collection. *Names* 57.3: 162–174.

Major, Clarence. 1994. *Juba to Jive: A Dictionary of African-American Slang*. New York: Penguin Books.

Martin, Stefan E. 1992. *Topics in the Syntax of Nonstandard English*. PhD dissertation. University of Maryland.

Martin, Stefan E., and Walt Wolfram. 2022. The Sentence in African-American Vernacular English. In *African-American English: Structure, History, and Use*, Classic Edition, edited by Salikoko S. Mufwene, John R. Rickford, Guy Bailey, and John Baugh, 11–40. London: Routledge.

Mitchell-Kernan, Claudia. 1972. Signifying, Loud-talking, and Marking. In *Rappin' and Stylin' Out: Communication in Urban Black America*, edited by Thomas Kochman, 315–335. Urbana, IL: University of Illinois Press.

Morgan, Marcyliena. 1996. Conversational Signifying: Grammar and Indirectness among African American Women. In *Interaction and Grammar*, edited by Elinor Ochs, Emmanuel Schegloff, and Sandra Thompson, 405–434. Cambridge: Cambridge University Press.

Morgan, Marcyliena. 2001. "Nuthin' But a G Thang": Grammar and Language Ideology in Hip Hop Identity. In *Sociocultural and Historical Contexts of African American English*, edited by Sonja L. Lanehart, 187–210. Amsterdam: John Benjamins.

Morgan, Marcyliena. 2022. More than a Mood or an Attitude: Discourse and Verbal Genres in African-American Culture. In *African-American English: Structure, History, and Use, Classic Edition*, edited by Salikoko S. Mufwene, John R. Rickford, Guy Bailey, and John Baugh, 277–312. London: Routledge.

Mufwene, Salikoko. 2022. The Structure of the Noun Phrase in African-American Vernacular English. In *African-American English: Structure, History, and Use*, Classic Edition, edited by Salikoko S. Mufwene, John R. Rickford, Guy Bailey, and John Baugh, 75–89. London: Routledge.

Rambsy II, Howard, and Briana Whiteside. 2015. African American Language and Black Poetry. In *The Oxford Handbook of African American Language*, edited by Sonja Lanehart, 706–722. Oxford: Oxford University Press.

Reed, Ishmael. 1976/1989. *Flight to Canada*. New York: Antheneum.

Rickford, John R. 1999. *African American Vernacular English: Features, Evolution, and Educational Implications*. Malden, MA: Wiley Blackwell.

Rodgers, Carolyn. 1969. Black Poetry: Where It's At. *Negro Digest* 18.11: 7–16.

Smitherman, Geneva. 1977. *Talkin and Testifyin: The Language of Black America*. Boston: Houghton Mifflin.

Smitherman, Geneva. 1994. *Black Talk: Words and Phrases from the Hood to the Amen Corner*. New York: Houghton Mifflin.

Smitherman, Geneva. 1998. Ebonics, *King*, and Oakland: Some Folk Don't Believe Fat Meat Is Greasy. *Journal of English Linguistics* 26.2: 97–107. DOI: 10.1177/007542429802600202

Smitherman, Geneva. 2006/2022. *Word from the Mother: Language and African Americans*. London: Routledge.

Smitherman, Geneva, and Denise Troutman-Robinson. 1988. Black Women's Language. In *The Reader's Companion to the U.S. Women's History*, edited by Wilma Mankiller, Gwendolyn Mink, Marysa Navarro, Barbara Smith, and Gloria Steinem, 65–66. Boston: Houghton Mifflin.

Spears, Arthur K. 1982. The Black English Semi-auxiliary "Come." *Language* 58.4: 850–872. DOI: 10.2307/413960

Spears, Arthur K. 2000. Stressed *Stay*: A New African-American English Aspect Marker. Paper presented at the Annual Meeting of the American Dialect Society, Chicago.

Spears, Arthur K. 2001. Directness in the Use of African American English. In *Sociocultural and Historical Contexts of African American English*, edited by Sonja L. Lanehart, 239–259. Amsterdam: John Benjamins.

Spears, Arthur K. 2007. Bare Nouns in African American English (AAE). In *Noun Phrases in Creole Languages: A Multi-Faceted Approach*, edited by Marlyse Baptista and Jacqueline Guéron, 421–434. Amsterdam: John Benjamins.

Spears, Arthur K. 2017. Unstressed *been*: Past and Present in African American English. *American Speech* 92.2: 151–175.

Spears, Arthur K. 2020. Rickford's List of African American English Grammatical Features: An Update. In *The Routledge Companion to the Work of John R. Rickford*, edited by Renée Blake and Isabelle Buchstaller, 79–89. London: Routledge.

Tatum, Beverly Daniel. 1992. *"Why Are All the Black Kids Sitting Together in the Cafeteria?" And Other Conversations about Race*. New York: Basic Books.

Tottie, Gunnel, and Dawn Harvie. 2000. It's All Relative: Relativization Strategies in Early African American English. In *The English History of African American English*, edited by Shana Poplack, 198–232. Malden, MA: Blackwell.

Troutman, Denise. 2001. African American Women: Talking that Talk. In *Sociocultural and Historical Contexts of African American English*, edited by Sonja L. Lanehart, 211–238. Amsterdam: John Benjamins.

Digital Media

Harvey, Steve. 1997. *One Man*. HBO Home Video. 90 minutes.

Chapter 6

Where Your People At?
Regional and Geographic Variation

Introduction: A New Day Is Dawning

Before continuing with the big questions asked in previous chapters, let's think about AAL/USEB regional/geographic and social communities over these next two chapters. Much of the early research on AAL/USEB focused on "authentic" speakers who researchers believed to be only African American, "urban," low-income, male teenagers. Women need not apply. Much of my contribution to AAL/USEB research has critiqued the lack of inclusion in AAL/USEB research, namely African American women, but also LGBTQIA+ folks (Lanehart 2001, 2015, 2021)—but still not enough. There was also the lack of inclusion of signed language in African American communities. These omissions were the case because most research in the mid-20th century did not go beyond AAVL/VUSEB in low-income urban areas. The definition back then for AAVL/VUSEB, which was equivalent to most for AAL/USEB, was believed to be "that relatively uniform grammar found in its most consistent form in the speech of [B]lack youth from 8 to 19 years old who participate fully in the street culture of the inner cities" (Labov 1972, xiii). To all those who persisted with such a narrow view of AAL/USEB—treating AAL/USEB and AAVL/VUSEB interchangeably: Why did y'all ever think AAL/USEB was simply the language of a **mannish boy who was smellin himself**?

According to Mary Bucholtz (2003), this limited view of AAL/USEB was because of "strategic essentialism" (see McElhinny 1996; Spivak 1988), or low-hanging fruit as I've noted earlier in the book:

Where Your People At? 123

As an ideology, essentialism rests on two assumptions; (1) that groups can be clearly delimited; and (2) that group members are more or less alike. The idea of authenticity gains its force from essentialism. . . . Yet despite these serious problems, essentialism is also an import intellectual and social tool. . . . I briefly illustrate the uses of strategic essentialism in two different areas of sociolinguistics that took shape in the 1970s: language and gender studies, and research on African American Vernacular English. In both of these sociolinguistic undertakings, researchers focused on highly "marked," socially marginalized groups (women and African Americans) in part to recognize and legitimate their widely devalued linguistic practices. . . . A strategic use of essentialized and hence authentic identity is . . . evident in sociolinguists' validation of African American Vernacular English (AAVE) as a legitimate linguistic variety, a revolutionary viewpoint that challenged generations of racism, linguistic and otherwise. Indeed, what made this challenge so powerful was precisely the sociolinguistic commitment to describing the speech of inner-city youth, who had been—and continue to be—maligned and misrepresented in public discourse. In such a context, a demonstration of, say, the linguistic flexibility of bidialectal middle-class African Americans would have failed to persuade skeptical teachers, policy-makers, and researchers in other disciplines of the value of AAVE. Thus, the most useful conceptualization of the AAVE speech community at the time, both politically and theoretically, was one in which those speakers whose speech was mislabeled as substandard or even as not really language at all were placed at the very center, as the most competent and systematic speakers of a complete and systematic variety.

(Bucholtz 2003, 400–402)

This is a very good answer to my question. However, some researchers lost the plot because, as Bucholtz also states,

What makes some essentializing efforts strategic is that they are undertaken to achieve a short-term goal with awareness of their limitations in the long term. Although not all participants who commit themselves to an essentialist position necessarily recognize it as a temporary tactic.

(2003, 402)

In other words, some researchers are still looking to do sociolinguistic interviews with **June Bug, Ray Ray, and Pookie**. That might be fine for places that there hasn't been AAL/USEB research, but really? C'mon, man.

But today is a new day because emerging Scholars of Color in linguistics are **in the house**, and they are not their (white) academic parents. Like me, they asking, "Why we keep having to fight the same battles from the 1960s?" "Why haven't people gotten it yet?" This was supposed to be short term. Orlando Taylor (1975, 1983) tried to tell us, but some folks **hard headed**. I cannot solve these issues in a couple of chapters, but I can at least include varieties of groups in AAL/USEB communities for you to get acquainted with. Here's my attempt to provide a glimpse of some of the communities and varieties that make up AAL/USEB:

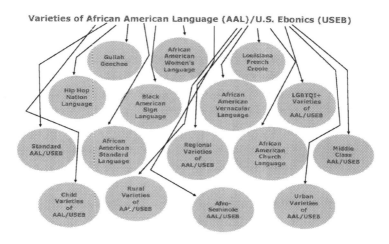

Figure 6.1 Varieties of AAL/USEB Tree Diagram. Tree diagram of varieties of African American Language.

For too long, AAL/USEB was viewed as homogeneous. Linguists believed that all AAL/USEB speakers sounded alike. That's right. Black people in Michigan sounded the same as Black people in California, and they sounded the same as Black people in New York and Georgia. This belief is contrary to the sociolinguistic mantra, Rule #2 in Chapter 2, that says all languages vary because all languages change or they die. I think the mistake was that researchers didn't think of AAL/USEB in the same way as most languages are thought of. That is, if you study Spanish, do you believe all Spanish language users sound the same? Do they all have the exact same language identity? Are their vowel spaces the same? Are their vocabularies all the same? Of course not. We know there is variation within Spain as well as all its former colonies because we know that a primary reason for language variation is distance, such as rivers, oceans, and mountains, or separation, such as social or psychological, like racism, anti-Blackness, and *misogynoir* (Bailey 2013, 2021).[1] Those separations form different varieties of the same language but also different languages. James Baldwin's famous 1979 *New York Times* article, "If Black English Isn't a Language, Then Tell Me, What Is?" explains it even better:

> People evolve a language in order to describe and thus control their circumstances, or in order not to be submerged by a reality that they cannot articulate. . . . [L]anguage is also a political instrument, means, and proof of power. It is the most vivid and crucial key to identity.
>
> (1979, E19)[2]

---

1 Moya Bailey coined the term in 2010 while a graduate student at Emory University (2013, 2021) and while writing on the Crunk Feminist Collective blog (see Cooper, Morris, and Boylorn 2017). The *Crunk Feminist Collective* is a group of Hip Hop Feminists of Color. They define *crunk feminism* as "the animating principle of our collective work together and derives from our commitment to feminist principles and politics, and also from our unapologetic embrace of those new cultural resources, which provide or offer the potential for resistance. *Crunk(ness)* is our mode of resistance that finds its particular expression in the rhetorical, cultural, and intellectual practices of a contemporary generation."
2 Baldwin also discusses how French in various parts of France and in French colonies varies and why, but I was unable to include that because of the strict *New York Times* 50-word copyright policy. Please read the full article online.

Give it up for the inimitable James Baldwin, y'all, or Uncle Jimmy as we know him. I'm so glad this third wave of Black sociolinguistics researchers **got next/now**.

Gullah Geechee

We have discussed Gullah Geechee in Chapters 3 and 4, but I would be remiss to not include it here as a regional variety of AAL/USEB. As you should recall, Gullah Geechee is an AAL/USEB variety spoken primarily along the coast and Sea Islands of South Carolina and Georgia. There is much debate about the origins of Gullah Geechee as noted by Mufwene (1997), but the consensus is that it is a creole and it is now in need of revitalization due to more contact with mainland varieties of English and a great decline in the number of speakers. Turner (1949) and Weldon and Moody (2015) provide historical overviews of Gullah Geechee. Cunningham (1970) provides a description of syntactic characteristics of Gullah Geechee. Because it originated from Africans in America and is the language of African Americans, it is considered a variety of AAL/USEB since AAL/USEB is language of, relating to, or characteristic of African Americans; language used by and among African Americans. Moody (2011) and Weldon (1998) provide studies that further demonstrate the connection between AAL/USEB development and Gullah Geechee.

Gullah Geechee has a rich history and shows the remnants of a language borne out of necessity. Gullah Geechee is described as an African English-lexifier creole (see Chapter 2 for a discussion on creoles). There is no particular African language ascribed to Gullah Geechee because, as Uncle Jimmy noted, African slaves who survived the Middle Passage intentionally comprised a variety of different African languages so the colonizers could successfully establish chattel slavery for as long as possible to their benefit and our subjugation by language isolation. In other words, we couldn't converse with each other. Gullah Geechee was a necessity just like Haitian Creole, Jamaican Creole, and the other Caribbean languages that bear witness to settler colonialism and chattel slavery. The physical barriers and high concentration of enslaved Africans in comparison to the number of white colonizers and enslavers that the Sea Islands contained helped sustain Gullah Geechee all these years and the differences we see between Gullah Geechee and all the other varieties of AAL/USEB.

Ironically, the isolation from mainland economies in conjunction with white flight due to lack of a plantation economy, the influx of white tourists, and the increased ability to converse with mainland English speakers has led to the endangerment of Gullah Geechee. Native speakers leave the islands for better opportunities. South Carolina has created tourist attractions like Hilton Head and a better infrastructure than Georgia. Without the settler-colonial, plantation economy on the islands, there is little left to sustain the island economies of the Gullah Geechee who remain. In order for families to continue to live and grow and thrive on the islands, the remaining Gullah Geechee have had to resort to a tourist industry economy that requires showing off their language, culture, and community for (white) tourists who want a glimpse of a bygone era (cf. Hawaii and other indigenous communities). Still, taking charge of their future in this way is better than letting someone else determine it. Current examples of Gullah Geechee can be found in Bible translations, Julie Dash's (1991) award-winning film *Daughters of the Dust*, Hilton Head resort workers, and Sapelo Island.

Urban and Rural

Most early research on AAL/USEB was done in urban areas like Detroit, Philadelphia, New York City, and Washington, DC. What's odd about that is AAL/USEB developed in the Southeastern U.S. There are scattered studies of AAL/USEB in Southern states by some early AAL/USEB researchers, but the focus was not on where AAL/USEB began but, instead, where it ended up, so to speak, for white researchers to get access. That is, the focus was on those African Americans who left the South fleeing from daily segregation and brutality for the hope—a fairy tale—of a better life up North. That's not how it worked out, as we know. There is just as much segregation and brutality up North as there is down South—they just have their own flair for it. As such, scholars such as Malcolm X and Docta G refer to the different regions as Down South (i.e., Southern states) and Up South (i.e., Northern states).

In addition to a Northern/Up South focus was a particular predilection for the speech of adolescent and teenage African American males in these areas, as noted earlier in this chapter. Researchers were known to get Black men to collect data on street corners and among gangs or in housing projects. It boggles my mind that it was not until the 2010s that someone—a white male researcher—thought to conduct a linguistic study of the language of the Reverend Doctor Martin Luther King Jr. (MLK) as an AAL/USEB speaker (see Wolfram et al. 2016). Maybe it was because people were in denial about MLK as an AAL/USEB speaker despite the work of Arthur Spears on Standard AAL/USEB, African American/USEB Standard Language, and grammatical camouflage (e.g., Spears 2015) or the work done on intonation and stress (e.g., Holliday 2019; Thomas 2015) or the work done by Docta G on AAL/USEB history and education (e.g., Smitherman 1999). These may be the same people who sing Old Negro Spirituals at HBCU (Historically Black Colleges and Universities) commencements while denouncing the actual AAL/USEB used in the Old Negro Spirituals (see Rickford and Rickford 2000, 74–75). This isn't new. **Not all skin folk yo kinfolk** and **respectability politics** are fierce. White people did a number on some Black folks who believe **white is right**. Think Samuel L. Jackson's character, Stephen, in *Django Unchained* (Tarantino 2012) and remember, "**Massa, we sick?**" And though they may say they loathe white people for all the atrocities against Black people and, well, because slavery, they also worship the ground they walk on because they want to be just like them with all the privilege whiteness affords—some all the way down to the skin (think a reverse Rachel Dolezal). It is not always or simply because they love white and hate Black, but sometimes just the despair of knowing that in the Good Ole U.S. of A., regardless, they are always viewed as being nothing but a [nɪgə]. W.E.B. DuBois (that's [duˈbɔɪz], not [duˈbwɑ]) talked about it as *double consciousness*, others talked about it as a *push-pull syndrome*—"*pushing* toward white American culture while simultaneously *pulling* away from it" (Smitherman 1977, 10–11). I don't want to neglect the other issue: Racism does push some Black folk toward assimilation, but more like the Borg from *Star Trek: The Next Generation* (Roddenberry 1987–1994). It's not pretty. There is no assimilation; only annihilation.

In addition, the Rev. Dr. King wasn't just African American, he was a Southern Black HBCU-educated Baptist preacher. It doesn't get much Blacker than that. He was a "I shall not be moved" Black man. He was a preacher, after all. He could moan like Aretha. He had charisma. He had **swagger**. But he wasn't from Up South, so maybe that's why it took so long. Wait! Malcolm X's speech hasn't been linguistically analyzed either, though Mary Hoover, an African American linguist who was former dean at Howard University, does refer to his speech as "an excellent example of a [S]tandard Black English speaker" (Hoover 1978, 72). Maybe he was the **uppity** kind and that wasn't okay (**sipping tea**). Despite the focus on urban and Up South, there are clearly some gaps. I have to wonder why. Why African American adolescent and teenage males in urban areas, often gang-affiliated, Up South, poor, miseducated, hanging on the corner, etc.? Is that really how researchers saw/see us; reduced to the worst image they could approach for study? I guess that's not too hard to comprehend when you think of how "research" on AAL/USEB started with those who thought it was akin to "baby talk." That means that's the level of intelligence ascribed to Black folk. From there, I guess Nonstandard Negro English as a moniker was an upgrade.

In 1988, Guy Bailey and Patricia Cukor-Avila decided that there was enough research on urban Up South AAVL/VUSEB and it was time for a look at rural Down South AAVL/VUSEB. That's right, Bailey and Cukor-Avila have been researching rural Down South AAVL/VUSEB in Texas for more than 30 years. That is the kind of dedication it takes to get a sense of a community. They are some of the first researchers to take notice of *had* + past in AAL/USEB (e.g., "She had told me about that"). And this is why this type of longitudinal research is important: We don't know what we don't know. *Had* + past has been part of my language for as long as I can remember, but I never thought anything about it. It was just language to me. I thought everybody used *had* + past and that it was just WAmE. That's only one of what I am sure are many aspects of AAL/USEB that are waiting to be "discovered."

Walt Wolfram is another researcher who has been embedded in a variety of linguistic communities in North Carolina for 30 years in his role as the William C. Friday Distinguished University Professor at North Carolina State University (NCSU). Walt and his team have documented and studied several varieties in North Carolina with his establishment of the *Language and Life Project* at NCSU. In addition to his work on AAL/USEB in North Carolina is his research on Ocracoke and Lumbee English. Because of his community research, which focused on sociocultural and historical contexts, he's even produced work comparing all of these varieties given their proximity to one another. His work on multiple generations of AAL/USEB speakers and comparisons between urban and rural AAL/USEB of Black families in the area is important sociolinguistic research. In addition, Wolfram (2004) provides research on urban AAL/USEB. Walt is one of the early white AAL/USEB researchers who has evolved in his research and perspective more than any other researcher. He's one of the first white researchers, along with Bailey and Cukor-Avila, to recognize the importance of sociocultural and historical contexts in sociolinguistic research. He is also one of the few white researchers to acknowledge past limitations in early AAL/USEB research and accept his part in it.

What we have learned from Bailey and Cukor-Avila's and Wolfram's research in rural areas is that there are differences between rural and urban AAL/USEB—as one would expect. Proximity and integration or segregation play roles in the varieties in addition to the sociocultural and historical contexts of the speakers and geographic areas. In some cases, rural AAL/USEB in North Carolina seems closer to rural Southern White American Vernacular English a few generations ago, whereas younger rural North Carolina AAL/USEB speakers are converging more toward urban North Carolina AAL/USEB speakers because of interaction but also because of the prestige of urban AAL/USEB for these speakers. It's like back in my day when you'd spend summers with your grandparents, though, in my case, I was going from big city Houston to small city Baton Rouge, which are both Southern cities. In the traditional cases, it was going from small towns Down South to "sophisticated" big cities Up South for the summers, or vice versa. When you visited your Up South relatives, you were told you sounded country. When you went back home Down South, you were told you sounded citified or proper after spending time Up South identifying with your people's language there. In either case, your variety was different from family in different parts of the country, though you certainly shared some things. For example, Bridget Anderson's (2002) research on the language of African Americans who migrated to Detroit shows that they have similarities to those Down South because of their language of identity (Lanehart 1996). Down South folks keep saying Up South folk citified, Up South folk keep saying Down South folk countrified, and Anderson (2002) saying both the Up South and Down South folks share some things so maybe they both country. Maybe it's a [təmeto]/[təmɑto] kind of thing, but we should not get caught up on thinking similarities in AAL/USEB across the U.S. means the same. There are similarities across regional and social varieties of AAL/USEB, just like there are similarities of dialects of any language. If there weren't similarities, then they'd be different languages because they wouldn't be mutually intelligible. But just as we do not say Mexican Spanish is the same as Cuban Spanish or Venezuelan Spanish, we should not be lulled into thinking that AAL/USEB is homogenous and, therefore, all African Americans talk the same. That's like saying all Black people look alike 😒. That sounds like some Walking Eagle shite, right there (see www.urbandictionary.com/define.php?term=Walking%20Eagle).

CORAAL, et al.

We are not going to talk about all the regional varieties of AAL/USEB because that would be a whole other book. But what I can do is point you to an excellent resource: *CORAAL*, or the *Corpus of Regional African American Language*, that is housed at the University of Oregon and can be found at https://oraal.uoregon.edu/coraal. *CORAAL* is the only large-scale public corpus of AAL/USEB that exists currently and was made possible by funding from the National Science Foundation (Grant No. BCS-1358724)—your public dollars at work—and the University of Oregon. The project team was headed by Tyler Kendal and Jason McLarty with much of the website work done by Charlie Farrington and Kaylynn Gunter.

CORAAL houses recorded speech from regional varieties of AAL/USEB that were sourced from several researchers who were gracious enough and able to provide their data. *CORAAL* includes audio recordings along with time-aligned, orthographic transcriptions so that those who want to use the resources can do so. Kendall et al. (2018a) and Kendall et al. (2018b) describe how the initial contributions were mostly from Washington, DC, over a period of several decades that included data from Ralph Fasold's 1970s Washington, DC, research (e.g., Fasold 1972), Minnie Quartey's 2015–2017 dissertation data in Washington, DC, and Walt Wolfram's 1960s Detroit research (Wolfram 1969). The corpus includes supplements with data from Rochester, New York, by King (2018) and King et al. (2020); Atlanta, Georgia, by Farrington et al. (2020); and Princeville, North Carolina, by Rowe et al. (2018).

While *CORAAL* is an important research outlet, it is difficult to produce such scholarship. Unfortunately, Institutional Review Boards (IRB) and permissions for data sharing and use did not conceive of this type of opportunity decades ago, so it is more difficult in some instances to acquire such work for online data sources. [N.B.: Unfortunately, because of some IRB agreements, researchers were required to destroy their audio recordings.] It is also important to note that some researchers just do not support Open Access Scholarship and, therefore, we do not have access to as much data as is available and necessary to provide a full compendium of AAL/USEB recorded data.

The website has recently been reorganized and renamed to *ORAAL*, or *Online Resources for African American Language*, with its new home at https://oraal.uoregon.edu/. ORAAL is devoted to providing information about language and African American communities. In addition to finding out more about the project and *CORAAL*, it includes research resources, educational resources, a glossary of terms, and lots of information about AAL/USEB.

A more recent collection and analysis of regional phonetic AAL/USEB data is provided by Taylor Jones in his dissertation, *Variation in African American English: The Great Migration and Regional Differentiation* (2020). His dissertation abstract is as follows:

> While African American English is among the best studied language varieties, it was historically taken to be relatively uniform, and it is only recently that regional variation in AAE has become an object of sustained study among sociolinguists. There has been as of yet no comprehensive, large-scale

description of regional variation in AAE comparable to existing descriptions of white varieties of English, like that in the Atlas of North American English (ANAE) [Labov et al. 2008]). In this dissertation, I provide the first ever analysis of regional variation in the AAE vocalic system, across the United States, arguing that there is considerable regional variation in AAE, that it patterns with movement of people during the Great Migration, and that it cannot be characterized solely by the presence or absence of the proposed African American Vowel Shift. To do so, I introduced a novel reading passage specifically designed to elicit naturalistic AAE speech, read by hundreds of participants across the US, and apply traditional sociophonetic methods, spatial statistics, and clustering analyses.
(https://repository.upenn.edu/dissertations/AAI27955096/)

As you can see from the dissertation abstract, Jones (2020) is in line with the perspective of AAL/USEB provided in this book, despite not using my term 😊: AAL/USEB includes regional variation across the U.S. that can be examined in its vocalic system (as well as all of its systems). This dissertation provides the evidence.

From Regional to Social Variation

Although there is so much more that could be said about regional or geographic variation in AAL/USEB, that would be another book in itself. And though that book has not been written yet, I am not the one who is going to do it right now. *The Oxford Handbook of African American Language* (Lanehart 2015) has a ten-chapter section devoted to AAL/USEB lects and variation. In addition to Gullah Geechee (Weldon and Moody 2015) are chapters that discuss regional varieties in Texas (Cukor-Avila and Bailey 2015), the Mississippi Delta (Wilkerson 2015), Atlanta (Kretzschmar 2015), Pittsburgh and the Lower Susquehanna Valley (Bloomquist and Gooden 2015), Philadelphia (Labov and Fisher 2015), New York City (Blake, Shousterman, and Newlin-Łukowicz 2015), and California (Rickford 2015). I point you there and to the stacks for more information. In the meantime, let's move on to social variation.

Questions, Discussion, and Further Inquiry

1. Which regional varieties of AAL/USEB are you familiar with?
2. Why don't language users sound the same, have the same language identity, have the same vowel spaces, or have the same vocabularies?
3. Do you believe that there is such a thing as an "authentic" speaker? Please elaborate.
4. Do you believe there is such a thing as a speech community? Please elaborate.
5. Why we keep having to fight the same battles from the 1960s? Why haven't people gotten it yet?
6. How is it possible that African American adolescent and teenage males in low-income urban areas, often gang-affiliated, Up South, miseducated, hanging on the corner, etc. could best represent authentic AA(V)L users to researchers?
7. How is *CORAAL* important to research on AAL/USEB?
8. How had you considered regional differences in AAL/USEB before reading this chapter/book?
9. If you haven't checked out a language corpus, check out *CORAAL* and report what you discover about language and variation in AAL/USEB.
10. What are some things missing in regional/geographic variation in AAL research that wasn't discussed in this chapter? What are you interested in AAL research that's missing in this chapter?

References

Anderson, Bridget. 2002. Dialect Leveling and /ai/ Monophthongization among African American Detroiters. *Journal of Sociolinguistics* 6.1: 86–98.

Bailey, Moya. 2013. New Terms of Resistance: A Response to Zenzele Isoke. *Souls: A Critical Journal of Black Politics, Culture, and Society* 15.14: 341–343. DOI: 10.1080/10999949.2014.884451

Bailey, Moya. 2021. *Misogynoir Transformed: Black Women's Digital Resistance*. New York: New York University Press.

Baldwin, James. 1979. If Black English Isn't a Language, Then Tell Me, What Is? *The New York Times* July 29: E19. https://archive.nytimes.com/www.nytimes.com/books/98/03/29/specials/baldwin-english.html?_r=1&oref=slogin

Blake, Renée, Cara Shousterman, and Luiza Newlin-Łukowicz. 2015. African American Language in New York City. In *The Oxford Handbook of African American Language*, edited by Sonja Lanehart, 280–298. Oxford: Oxford University Press.

Bloomquist, Jennifer, and Shelome Gooden. 2015. African American Language in Pittsburgh and the Lower Susquehanna Valley. In *The Oxford Handbook of African American Language*, edited by Sonja Lanehart, 236–255. Oxford: Oxford University Press.

Bucholtz, Mary. 2003. Sociolinguistic Nostalgia and the Authentication of Identity. *Journal of Sociolinguistics* 7.3: 398–416. https://escholarship.org/uc/item/0sz2z8fc

Cooper, Brittney C., Susana M. Morris, and Robin M. Boylorn, eds. 2017. *The Crunk Feminist Collection*. New York: Feminist Press at the City University of New York.

Cukor-Avila, Patricia, and Guy Bailey. 2015. Rural Texas African American Vernacular English. In *The Oxford Handbook of African American Language*, edited by Sonja Lanehart, 181–200. Oxford: Oxford University Press.

Cunningham, Irma Aloyce Ewing. 1970. *A Syntactic Analysis of Sea Island Creole ("Gullah")*. PhD dissertation. University of Michigan.

Farrington, Charlie, Tyler Kendall, Patrick Brooks, Emma Mullen, and Chloe Tacata. 2020. *The Corpus of Regional African American Language: ATL (Atlanta, GA 2017)*. Version 2020.05. Eugene, OR: The Online Resources for African American Language Project.

Fasold, Ralph W. 1972. *Tense Marking in Black English: A Linguistic and Social Analysis*. Arlington, VA: Center for Applied Linguistics.

Holliday, Nicole. 2019. Variation in Question Intonation in the Corpus of Regional African American Language. *American Speech* 94.1: 110–130.

Hoover, Mary Rhodes. 1978. Community Attitudes toward Black English. *Language in Society* 7.1: 65–87. DOI: 10.1017/S0047404500005339

Jones, Taylor. 2020. *Variation in African American English: The Great Migration and Regional Differentiation*. PhD dissertation. University of Pennsylvania.

Kendall, Tyler, Ralph Fasold, Charlie Farrington, Jason McLarty, Shelby Arnson, and Brooke Josler. 2018a. *The Corpus of Regional African American Language: DCA* (Washington DC 1968). Version 2018.10.06. Eugene, OR: The Online Resources for African American Language Project.

Kendall, Tyler, Minnie Quartey, Charlie Farrington, Jason McLarty, Shelby Arnson, and Brooke Josler. 2018b. *The Corpus of Regional African American Language: DCB (Washington DC 2016)*. Version 2018.10.06. Eugene, OR: The Online Resources for African American Language Project.

King, Sharese. 2018. *Exploring Social and Linguistic Diversity across African Americans from Rochester, New York*. Ph.D. dissertation. Stanford University.

King, Sharese, Charlie Farrington, Tyler Kendall, Emma Mullen, Shelby Arnson, and Lucas Jenson. 2020. *The Corpus of Regional African American Language: ROC (Rochester, NY 2018)*. Version 2020.05. Eugene, OR: The Online Resources for African American Language Project.

Kretzschmar, Jr., William A. 2015. African American Voices in Atlanta. In *The Oxford Handbook of African American Language*, edited by Sonja Lanehart, 219–235. Oxford: Oxford University Press.

Labov, William. 1972. *Language in the Inner City: Studies in the Black English Vernacular*. Philadelphia: University of Pennsylvania Press.

Labov, William, Sharon Ash, Charles Boberg. 2008. *The Atlas of North American English: Phonetics, Phonology, and Sound Change*. Berlin: De Gruyter Mouton. DOI: 10.1515/9783110167467

Labov, William, and Sabriya Fisher. 2015. African American Phonology in a Philadelphia Community. In *The Oxford Handbook of African American Language*, edited by Sonja Lanehart, 256–279. Oxford: Oxford University Press.

Lanehart, Sonja L. 1996. The Language of Identity. *Journal of English Linguistics* 24.4: 322–331.

Lanehart, Sonja L., ed. 2001. *Sociocultural and Historical Contexts of African American English*. Amsterdam: John Benjamins.

Lanehart, Sonja L., ed. 2015. *The Oxford Handbook of African American Language*. Oxford: Oxford University Press.

Lanehart, Sonja L. 2021. Say My Name: African American Women's Language. *Gender & Language* 15.4: 559–568.

Lanehart, Sonja. 2023. *Language in African American Communities*. London: Routledge.

McElhinny, Bonnie. 1996. Strategic Essentialism in Sociolinguistic Studies of Gender. In *Gender and Belief Systems: Proceedings of the Fourth Berkeley Women and Language Conference*, edited by Natasha Warner, Jocelyn Ahlers, Leela Bilmes, Monica Oliver, Suzanne Wertheim, and Melinda Chen, 469–489. Berkeley, CA: Berkeley Women and Language Group.

Moody, Simanique. 2011. *Language Contact and Regional Variation in African American English: A Study of Southeast Georgia*. Ph.D. dissertation. New York University.

Mufwene, Salikoko. 1997. Gullah's Development: Myths and Sociohistorical Evidence. In *Language Variety in the South Revisited*, edited by Cynthia Bernstein, Thomas Nunnally, and Robin Sabino, 113–123. Tuscaloosa, AL: University of Alabama Press.

Rickford, John R. 2015. African American Vernacular English in California: Over Four Decades of Vibrant Variationist Research. In *The Oxford Handbook of African American Language*, edited by Sonja Lanehart, 299–315. Oxford: Oxford University Press.

Rickford, John Russell, and Russell John Rickford. 2000. *Spoken Soul: The Story of Black English*. New York: John Wiley and Sons.

Rowe, Ryan, Walt Wolfram, Tyler Kendall, Charlie Farrington, and Brooke Josler. 2018. *The Corpus of Regional African American Language: PRV (Princeville, NC 2004)*. Version 2018.10.06. Eugene, OR: The Online Resources for African American Language Project.

Smitherman, Geneva. 1977. *Talkin and Testifyin: The Language of Black America*. Boston, MA: Houghton Mifflin.

Smitherman, Geneva. 1999. *Talkin that Talk: Language, Culture, and Education in African America*. London: Routledge.

Spears, Arthur. 2015. African American Standard English. *The Oxford Handbook of African American Language*, edited by Sonja Lanehart, 786–799. Oxford: Oxford University Press.

Spivak, Gayatri Chakravorty. 1988. Subaltern Studies: Deconstructing Historiography. In *Selected Subaltern Studies*, edited by Ranajit Guha and Gayatri Chakravorty Spivak, 3–32. Oxford: Oxford University Press.

Taylor, Orlando. 1975. Black Language and What to Do about It: Some Black Community Perspectives. In *Ebonics: The True Language of Black Folks*, edited by Robert L. Williams, 28–39. St. Louis: The Institute of Black Studies.

Taylor, Orlando. 1983. Black English: An Agenda for the 1980's. In *Black English: Educational Equity and the Law*, edited by John Chambers, Jr., 133–143. Ann Arbor, MI: Karoma.

Thomas, Erik. 2015. Prosodic Features of African American English. In *The Oxford Handbook of African American Language*, edited by Sonja Lanehart, 420–435. Oxford: Oxford University Press.

Turner, Lorenzo Dow. 1949. *Africanisms in the Gullah Dialect*. Chicago: University of Chicago Press.

Weldon, Tracey. 1998. Exploring the AAVE-Gullah Connection: A Comparative Study of Copula Variability. Ph.D. dissertation. The Ohio State University.

Weldon, Tracey L., and Simanique Moody. 2015. The Place of Gullah in the African American Linguistic Continuum. In *The Oxford Handbook of African American Language*, edited by Sonja Lanehart, 163–180. Oxford: Oxford University Press.

Wilkerson, Rose. 2015. African American English in the Mississippi Delta: A Case Study of Copula Absence and r-Lessness in the Speech of African American Women in Coahoma County. In *The Oxford Handbook of African American Language*, edited by Sonja Lanehart, 201–218. Oxford: Oxford University Press.

Wolfram, Walt. 1969. *A Sociolinguistic Description of Detroit Negro Speech*. Washington, DC: Center for Applied Linguistics.

Wolfram, Walt. 2004. The Grammar of Urban African American Vernacular English. In *Handbook of Varieties of English*, vol. 2., edited by Bernd Kortmann and Edgar Schneider, 111–132. Berlin: Mouton de Gruyter.

Wolfram, Walt, Caroline Myrick, Jon Forrest, and Michael J. Fox. 2016. The Significance of Linguistic Variation in the Speeches of Rev. Dr. Martin Luther King Jr. *American Speech* 91.3: 269–300.

Filmography

Dash, Julie, director and writer. 1991. *Daughters of the Dust*. Kino International. 112 minutes.

Roddenberry, Gene, creator. 1987–1994. *Star Trek: The Next Generation*. Paramount Domestic Television. 178 episodes.

Tarantino, Quentin, director and writer. 2012. *Django Unchained*. Columbia Pictures. 165 minutes.

Digital Media

Corpus of Regional African American Language. https://oraal.uoregon.edu/coraal

Online Resources for African American Language (ORAAL). https://oraal.uoregon.edu/

Walking Eagle. www.urbandictionary.com/define.php?term=Walking%20Eagle

Chapter 7

Where My *Shawtys* At?
Social and Gendered Variation

Introduction: *It's About to Be Lit Up in Here*

In addition to the many regional varieties of AAL/USEB (i.e., those associated with anywhere you think of as a region or has some sort of geographical barrier like mountains and rivers), there are also numerous social or demographic varieties. Distinct varieties of AAL/USEB emerge based on myriad sociocultural, historical, ideological, identity-based, and social-psychological contexts. Variation can be seen in spaces such as with DeBose's (2015) study of African American Church Language; Champion and McCabe's (2015) and Green's (2011) studies of age/generation; Rickford's (1999) study of AAVL/VUSEB; Britt and Weldon's (2015) and Weldon's (2021) studies of Middle-Class AAL/USEB; Spears's (2015) study of African American/USEB Standard Language; Rahman's (2015) study of spaces of laughter; and AAL/USEB studies in culture, literature, the arts, and more. There is AAL/USEB social variation wherever and however African Americans reflect their identities, their ideologies, and the interstices of space and place.

We will explore some of these spaces here, specifically, Black American Sign Language (Black ASL); Middle-Class AAL/USEB; Standard African American Language/USEB and African American Standard Language; African American Women's Language; Hip Hop Nation Language; and sexuality, gender, and gender identity in AAL/USEB. There are many more social varieties of AAL/USEB than this, such as African American child language (see Lisa Green

DOI: 10.4324/9781003204756-7

2011; and Part IV of Lanehart 2015), but this is a good introduction that should help you discover and explore other varieties.

Black American Sign Language, or Black ASL

Let's talk about a traditionally overlooked variety of AAL/USEB: Black American Sign Language, or Black ASL. According to Hill et al. (2015), African Americans in deaf communities developed their own signing practices while being denied access to American Sign Language (ASL) used by white Americans and taught in schools for the deaf due to segregation. Black ASL studies include McCaskill et al.'s (2011) comparisons between Black ASL and white ASL, Hill's (2012) study of variation in Black ASL communities, Lucas et al.'s (2015) study of the relationship between AAL/USEB and Black ASL, and Bayley and Lucas's (2015) and Hill et al.'s (2015) study of the grammar of Black ASL. Clark (2007, 2010) explores navigating and negotiating deafness for African Americans and the cultural identities expressed in Black ASL. McCaskill et al. (2011) provide a good history of Black ASL. Hill et al. (2015) discuss a website hosted by Gallaudet University, the premier university for the deaf and deaf studies in the U.S., that provides online information and resources through *The Black ASL Project*. There is also a film, *Signing Black in America*, produced by Hutcheson, Cullinan, and Wolfram (2020), that explores Black ASL and provides stories of those in Black deaf communities who suffered from segregation and racism in communities and schooling. It is part of Walt Wolfram's *Language and Life Project* at NCSU, which includes his multi-documentary, award-winning series *Talking Black in America*. I am one of several scholars on the advisory board for this documentary series.

I want to give props to Carolyn McCaskill, a deaf African American woman and Professor of Deaf Studies and ASL at Gallaudet University. She is also in the 2022 class of the Alabama School for the Deaf Hall of Fame. She received all of her degrees from Gallaudet University—BA, MA, and PhD. I also want to give props to Joseph Hill, a deaf African American man who is an Associate Professor of ASL and Interpreting Education as well as Assistant

Dean for Faculty Recruitment and Retention at Rochester Institute of Technology. Hill is also a PhD graduate of Gallaudet University. More notably, he is the first deaf African American to receive a PhD in Linguistics in the U.S.[1] The dedication with which Hill and McCaskill have worked to put Black ASL on the map, particularly in their collaboration with Ceil Lucas and Robert Bayley, is nothing short of phenomenal and worthy of a shout out. Thank you.

What shocks me but doesn't is that this amazing work is all in the 21st century—as if Black deaf people in America weren't here before then and that they didn't have a language worth studying. I watched *CODA* (Heder 2021, i.e., Child of Deaf Adults) on Apple TV+ and was reminded of a high school friend who was a CODA. I spent time hanging out at her home, but I was not fully aware of how hard being a CODA must have been for her. But now, thinking about that same situation for a Black ASL CODA or just Black ASL user in general makes my head spin because, as we know, the situation is infinitely more difficult for African Americans in situations similar to white people. It's like when people say, "When the U.S. sneezes, the rest of the world catches a cold"; but for Black America, it's more like we catch the flu—or die. I am just so grateful to these researchers for doing this work and showing us that Black ASL is a variety distinct from ASL and is truly a variety of the varied AAL/USEB communities that **keep on keepin on**.

Standards in Language Use in African American Communities

Folks have been talking about a Standard African American Language, or SAAL/SUSEB, for a while now. In 1970, Orlando Taylor noted that there was a variety of AAL/USEB he referred to as *Black Standard English* (BSE). Next is an excerpt from Orlando Taylor's section of a report that was submitted by Roger Shuy to the Office of Education in the U.S. Department of Health, Education, and Welfare in 1970. Part I of the report contained sections from five fields of

---

[1] Carolyn McCaskill earned her PhD in Special Education Administration and Supervision.

language study represented by Speech/Communication, Education (Early Childhood Education), Sociolinguistics, Psychology (Communicative Competence), and Linguistics/Linguistic Anthropology. Frederick Williams was the lead writer for Speech/Communication, and Orlando Taylor wrote the response to Williams's comments. His discussion on this issue in connection to SAmE is fascinating:

> In all of the discussions about Black English–Standard English, little is ever mentioned about Black Standard English. Black Standard English is characterized primarily by a standard syntax, plus a few [B]lack syntactic elements. The remainder of Black Standard English may include varying degrees of [B]lack vowel patterns, ethnically marked suprasegmental features, and [B]lack, lexical items. This rubric would be especially useful for categorizing Black educated speech. The speaker is able to move to a more standard speech or a [B]lacker speech depending on the situation.
>
> Why can't Black Standard English be included in the rubric of Standard English, described, and left alone? To me, Standard English is a concept in search of a definition. It appears to represent the language of the socially, economically, politically, and educationally prestigious groups of Americans. By definition, the term is almost synonymous with white prestige speech. It is wide enough to include the language of all prestigious white groups in the country (despite a wide range of phonological and suprasegmental differences) while excluding all [B]lack speakers except those who can "switch" into one of the acceptable patterns. Since Standard English is a relatively flexible concept, I am suggesting that it be expanded to include Black Standard English. Of course, many people will reject this suggestion. I submit that Black Standard English is spoken by a substantial portion of the [B]lack population, but is rejected by white America. This rejection is related to rejection of all [B]lack people except those who assume white-like behavior, including language.
>
> (Taylor 1970, 16–17)

Taylor (1975) again references the need for more research on BSE, and Hoover (1978) goes on to reference Taylor's call for research on

BSE. Hoover (1978) points to Mitchell-Kernan (1971) and her use of the term "good English" in reference to what Taylor and Hoover call BSE. So, if we go to the use of "good English" as synonymous with SAAL/SUSEB, then we are headed down a rabbit hole. But what is fascinating about equating SAAL/SUSEB with "good English" is that "good English" is also SAmE. And if "good English" is SAAL/SUSEB and SAmE, then SAAL/SUSEB is—**shut yo mouth!** Now you see why Taylor's argument is so fascinating. It also aligns with Spears (2015).

Hoover et al. (1976) and Hoover (1978, 72) provide a table that compares Vernacular Black English (VBE), Standard Black English (SBE), and SAmE. In it is an overview that includes phonology, grammar, vocabulary, and tone/intonation, which is described as language levels. In this language levels grid table, VBE is shown to contain vernacular features in all four areas (i.e., phonology, grammar, vocabulary, and tone/intonation). SBE contains vernacular features in varying degrees according to the situation in everything except grammar, where it contains very few vernacular features. SAmE contains very few vernacular features in any of the areas. The table represents her view of SAAL/SUSEB, which aligns more with Taylor (1983) than Taylor (1970). Taylor (1983) sees SBE as spoken by "Black speakers who use Standard English phonology and grammar when speaking informally, while simultaneously using Black rhetorical style, prosodic features, and idioms" (Taylor 1983, 135). Hoover gives a shoutout to Taylor's work in fitting fashion:

> In most previous surveys of attitudes toward Black English, parents were given a choice only between "network" English (general Standard English spoken by newscasters on national television stations) and nonstandard (vernacular) Black English, if given a choice at all. Such a choice and terminology implies [sic] that Black English is by definition "nonstandard." Orlando Taylor has attempted to deepen understanding of Black English and to move away from the conception that it has no internal differentiation into levels according to social situation **(unlike any other lect in the world)** [emphasis added], and that that one undifferentiated form is at the bottom of the scale, being inherently "nonstandard" in the eyes of its own users

> (as well as perhaps in the eyes of others). Taylor has called attention to the existence of a form of English among Black people that can be considered a "[S]tandard Black English."
>
> (Hoover 1978, 69)

Thank you! And all of this talk was going on 50 years ago!

I noted earlier that I do not tend to use "Standard American English," or SAmE, as a term. As you have seen in this book, I have used the term White American English, or WAmE, to reference what are seen as mainstream, educated, respectable, etc. varieties of American English because the underlying assumption is that these are by, about, and for white people. When we say "Standard American English," we are referencing how we perceive white people to speak because, **let's just be real for a moment**, white people named what we value from their Western European perspectives and they dominate lexicography or, more specifically, dictionary making. Anyway, in this line of thought, Spears, Hoover, and others **feel some kind of way about** that. To Hoover (1978) and Spears (2015), if you're going to require a comparison of AAVL to SAmE, then it is only fitting that you actually compare SAAL to SAmE and not AAVL.

Arthur Spears has been talking about definitions and varieties of AAL/USEB for a while now too. Spears (1988) is what **hipped** me to the importance of definitions when describing and researching language uses in African American communities. His work is what I most rely on for this discussion because he has written most extensively since the 1980s. Spears (2015) notes that

> varieties fitting Taylor's (1983) characterization of (what [he] call[s]) SAA[L] are, in [his] experience, those of younger (roughly under 60) Blacks from solidly middle-class backgrounds. This group controls an SAA[L] variety with no vernacular features, though on certain occasions they may use a variety with vernacular features.
>
> (Taylor 1983, 791)

However, Spears (2015) also defines AASL (he actually uses the term "African American Standard English" and explains why he uses "English") as a standard variety (composed of many subvarieties) of American English that has distinctively Black (i.e., African American) grammatical features, hereinafter DBGFs. DBGFs are found uniquely, or nearly so, in AAE varieties. An example of a DBGF is what linguists term *stressed BIN* . . . . AASE is a type of AAE: it has DBGFs, but none that are stigmatized or considered nonstandard (e.g., the use of *ain't*). For the most part, no one but an AAE specialist could detect the DBGFs in AASE because they are grammatically camouflaged.

(Spears 2015, 786)

Spears (1982) introduces camouflaged AAL/USEB forms in his discussion of the semi-auxiliary *come*, which expresses indignation, as you may recall from Chapter 5 (e.g., "He *come* walkin in here like he owned the damn place," 852).[2] As you might imagine, *camouflaged* forms are those that appear to be similar to something you think you already know or you are familiar with, but you're not, so stop **fronting**. It's like what we think of as "false friends" (i.e., false cognates) in HEL[3] for words in a different language that we think we know because they sound nearly the same or are spelled nearly the same, so we assume they are the same, such as English *embarrassed* and Spanish *embarazada*, meaning "pregnant." Same principle here. WAmE thinks AAL/USEB semi-auxiliary *come* means one thing when it doesn't. It has a different meaning in AAL/USEB; hence, it is a camouflaged form. This is how you can have *distinctively Black grammatical features* (*DBGFs*) that can be AAL/USEB and not stigmatized: white folks just don't know what you talkin bout.

Speaking of "talkin bout," there is a grammaticalized form of this expression in AAL/USEB that is rendered as *talmbout*.[4] *Grammaticalization* happens when grammar (i.e., grammatical function)

---

2 Remember, another example of camouflaged AAL is counterfactual *call*, "She call herself singing."
3 Remember, "HEL" is the abbreviation for History of the English Language.
4 Jones (2016) also discussed this as a camouflaged form, though not one that would be part of AASL.

is created from a lexical form or construction. Put in another way, a lexical cluster, such as *talking about*, gets reduced to *talmbout* and, in this case, serves as a quotative—a grammatical function. This is the same thing that happened with *let's*, which is a reduction of the lexical cluster "let us" meaning "allow us" and is now an auxiliary, as in "let's you and me play ball." Of course, *talmbout*[5] is a part of Black Twitter, like *wypipo* "white people" or *yt* "white," but it is cemented with the Janelle Monáe song "Hell You Talmbout" (2013). But I digress—just a little.

Just to be clear about the distinction between SAAL and AASL because Spears's (2015) use of the latter makes explicit claims that Hoover (1978) and Taylor (1983) did not make:

> [T]he term *AASE* explicitly references a variety including DBGFs, which Hoover (1978) and Taylor (1983) did not label. Keep in mind that some grammatical features associated with AAE (particularly AAVE) occur also in non-AAE varieties, e.g., *ain't* and multiple negation. AASE is also a variety with no vernacular features, as noted above. The use of the term *AASE* is important since it makes explicit claims that Hoover (1978) and Taylor (1983) did not make.
>
> In sum, SAAE is the cover term for the varieties characterized by Hoover (1978) and Taylor (1983). SAAE varieties, stated differently, are those that have no vernacular features (Taylor 1983) or have only a few—if any (Hoover 1978). Hoover (1978) and Taylor (1983) did not explicitly characterize the notion DBGF, so the varieties that they describe cannot be fully distinguished from AASE, which is claimed to have DBGFs. AASE is a different conceptualization of a Black standard in that it explicitly includes a number of DBGFs in the Black standard. This view of AASE is in most details in accord with my earlier statements on the Black standard (Spears 1982, 1988, 2007; Spears and Hinton 2010, inter alia), though I have used terms other than AASE.
>
> (Spears 2015, 791)

---

5 *Talmbout* also carries a regional index pointing to the American South.

For Spears, SAAL/SUSEB is what African Americans under the age of 60 use and AASL is what African Americans generally over 60 acquired when they were "raised in all-Black, multiclass communities, under segregation and roughly the twenty years thereafter; and members of the contemporary Black elite . . . which . . . included the most educated, highest income, and wealthiest members of Black communities" (Spears 2015, 792). Spears has talked about the Black elite in several of his writings. He is one of them and speaks from the experience of growing up in these communities. The way in which the temporal-spatial dimension separating the types of AAL/USEB Black folks acquire intersect with class distinctions, as Spears points out, has also been portrayed in literature. In Lorraine Hansberry's (1959) play *A Raisin in the Sun*, the character Beneatha is introduced with the following stage direction:

> Her speech is a mixture of many things; it is different from the rest of the family's insofar as education has permeated her sense of English—and perhaps the Midwest rather than the South has finally—at last—won out in her inflection; but not altogether, because over all of it is a soft slurring and transformed use of vowels which is the decided influence of the Southside.

Coming from the working-class Younger family depicted in the play, Beneatha's use of language represents intergenerational class mobility at the time that Spears pinpoints. Her speech demonstrates a high level of formal education—she is a college student with plans to attend medical school—which is a clear marker of upper-class status or, at least, a trajectory toward it. **Yet and still**, her English is spatially marked as Black in association with the then, and largely still, segregated Southside of Chicago.

Being from Houston with my family from Louisiana, I am familiar with the Black elite, the Black Bourgeoisie, the Jack and Jill, and Black cotillion folk (see Frazier 1957). My family was not part of any of that, but we knew who they were. Growing up in Houston, there were a couple of communities of them. When I was 12, we moved to the up-and-coming Black middle-class part of town, but it was nothing compared to the well-known, well-established Black areas. But Spears (2015) speaks to the period when, because of segregation, Black folks of all varieties lived, worked, played, and worshiped together. That's when doctors, lawyers, preachers, and teachers were at the top of our communities and neighborhoods. Multiple classes of people were together and acquired language varieties of AAL/USEB on a continuum that included the oft sought after by researchers AAVL/VUSEB as well as AASL, African American Church Language, and Middle-Class AAL/USEB. Spears's work also reminds me of my mother, who, as noted in *Sista, Speak!* (Lanehart 2002), says that Black folks' call for school desegregation didn't mean they wanted to be in schools sitting next to white children. Black folks simply wanted equity and equality. Nearly 70 years later and we still have neither.

Middle-Class Language Use in African American Communities

In the research on SAAL/SUSEB and AASL, there's a lot of talk about African American middle-class people, but SAAL/SUSEB and AASL are not labeled or discussed as Middle-Class AAL/USEB, or MCAAL/MCUSEB. Sociolinguist Tracey Weldon has been talking specifically about MCAAL/MCUSEB for nearly two decades, and she now has a book to show for all of her efforts, titled (what else?) *Middle-Class African American English* (Weldon 2021). She didn't even need a subtitle because the title says it all and she's the first person to write a book-length manuscript devoted to the subject. Simply defined, MCAAL/MCUSEB is language spoken by and among middle-class African Americans in the same way that AAL/USEB is language spoken by and among African Americans.

I'm not going to do a book review right here, but I do want to highlight a couple of things it includes that I think are important: She digs deep into the role of a term like "middle class" in its historical application to African Americans. She is very particular about definitions, as she should be. I had to say this to reinforce its significance to me and how I've approached writing this book—just in case you forgot.

One of the things I find fascinating about her discussion of the emergence of MCAAL/MCUSEB is that it started with colorism "color discrimination." Colorism arose in communities around the world along with race and racism. *Colorism* is the belief that "**bright/light and (damn near) white**" folk are better than darker-skinned folks. This is a view both inside and outside Black communities (think **brown paper bag test**, in which Blacks could only be accepted into bourgeoisie African American social clubs, fraternities, and sororities if they were lighter than a brown paper bag). And when I say Black communities here, I mean the African Diaspora because a lot of folk who Black ain't claiming it. I did not realize the extent of colorism beyond African American communities until I moved to San Antonio and saw it alive and well among Hispanics/Latinx. When I saw it there—Chicanx vs. Latinx vs. Hispanic or East Coast vs. West Coast vs. South Texas vs. Latin America, etc.—I was shocked, but I began to see it throughout the African Diaspora. I saw it among different Asian groups, Middle Eastern groups, and any group that had a range of skin color that separated white from Black.

What's shocking but not surprising is how this self-hatred manifested as even more hatred toward African Americans. There is really nowhere to hide if you are Black. Remember the days of 9/11 and the Persian Gulf War when "[sændnɪgɚ]" came to prominence as a slur? If you're not white, you're just different shades/varieties of [nɪgɚz] in the view of the dominant group (i.e., dominant in status, wealth, and prestige since it is not by numbers). And, unfortunately, this view is found both with ingroup and outgroup communities. It is ingrained in the fabric of our (i.e., Black) communities and in our language varieties. Think of all the different words we use in Black communities to talk about skin color to remind us every day of its salience and capital (e.g., high yellow, redbone, red, bright skinned, light skinned, trigueño, mulato, moreno, prieto, zambo, negrita/o, etc.). It literally translates to capital because we know that darker-skinned workers are often paid less or not as readily employed to front-of-the-house work, so to speak, as their lighter-skinned brothas and sistas. We see it in our own families with our siblings, aunts, uncles, and cousins. And don't start railing off a list of exceptions. I know there are nuances, but I am talking about people's everyday lives here.

The white-adjacency of mulattos often meant they chose to emulate whiteness. Here's where you can see the bubbling up of the idea of respectability. Over the decades of near-white Blacks feeling close to the status and power of whites meant distancing themselves from "unmixed Negroes" (Landry 1987, 25; as quoted in Weldon 2021, 5). They had different jobs, different styles of dress, different worldviews, and, of course, different ways of speaking. But there was still a problem. Near-white or white-adjacent is not the same thing as being white (see Nella Larsen's 1929 novel *Passing*, which was made into a Netflix movie in 2021). Class or status differences do not turn Black people into white people. As I noted in Chapter 3, "compassionate, liberal educators . . . will change the color of a student's vowels because they cannot change the color of their students' skins" (Sledd 1969, 1312). Blacks buy into letting society try to force this unnatural and failed metamorphosis which has simply led to what W.E.B. DuBois (1903, 159) talked about as double consciousness, the idea of this two-ness by trying to have their feet in two different worlds. Isn't there something about how you can't serve two masters because you will hate the one and love the other; you will be devoted to one and despise the other? Yeah, I get that.

Weldon discusses three key phases of the emergence of the African American middle class: (1) Mulattos who lived during post-Civil War to 1915, which included Black Reconstruction; (2) 1915–1960 during Jim Crow, World Wars I and II, and the Great Migration, which segregated Blacks from whites and forced Black people to live amongst themselves in multiclass communities as discussed in the previous section but more often poor, underserved communities; and (3) after 1960 during the civil rights movement, integration, and where we are today. For Weldon (2021), defining or delimiting MCAAL/MCUSEB includes, of course, SES (socioeconomic status), but SES is tricky in the best of circumstances and is highly variable and contested in definition and in practice. For African Americans, Weldon (2021) determines that middle class includes having a college education or some form of higher education whether completed or not; white-collar employment or employment that requires the use of WAmE; and, roughly, a family income that is twice the poverty level—adjusted for Blackness, of course. As you can see, middle class in African American communities comes with some caveats such that Weldon (2021, 15) acknowledges that in the spirit of Bourdieu's concept of symbolic capital and Weber's emphasis on the social psychological component of class identity, some aspects of this project will allow for consideration of speakers who fall above or below the limits of middle-class status as defined by traditional socioeconomic indicators, but whose experiences, practices, and perspectives are otherwise consistent with those who meet these criteria.

We are indebted to Weldon's continued interest and research in MCAAL/MCUSEB. As a variationist sociolinguist, her book contains data and analysis of several studies that take a features perspective of AAL/USEB, as well as a more quantitative approach. She's got the goods on investigating a continuum of AAL/USEB speech and speaker attitudes and perceptions. This is all a far cry from strategic essentialism in the 1960s and 1970s that set the standard for a focus on AAVL:

> Middle-class African American speakers, falling outside the limits of this "street" or 'vernacular' culture [i.e., "the speech of Black youth from 8–19-year-old who participate fully in the street culture of the inner cities" (Labov 1972, xiii), were dismissed as linguistic "lames" and systematically excluded from consideration in AAE research. In fact, with the exception of Wolfram's 1969 social stratification study in Detroit, Michigan, almost none of the seminal studies on AAE gave any serious consideration of middle-class speakers.
> (Britt and Weldon 2015, 800–801)

The consequences of this exclusion of most African Americans reverberated for decades. Linguistic anthropologist Marcyliena Morgan's comment about this strikes the right chord:

> Because vernacular AAE has been defined as hip, male, adolescent, street, or gang-related speech, nonvernacular speech is described as weak, lame, or white (Labov 1972). Those who do not fit the model of the vernacular-idealized speaker . . . are therefore, according to this sociolinguistic paradigm, not African American or, to put it in modern terms, not the "authentic Other."
> (Morgan 1994, 135; as quoted in
> Britt and Weldon 2015, 801)

None of this should come as a surprise based on what we have discussed throughout this book and especially this chapter.

Later in this book, we will provide a broader context for the issues raised by those studying AASL, SAAL/SUSEB, and MCAAL/MCUSEB that involve ideas of language and identity, but next let's look at another overlooked area in AAL/USEB research: African American women.

African American Women's Language, or AAWL

African American Women's Language (AAWL) is an important variety of AAL/USEB, but it has been understudied because Black male "urban" teenagers' speech was the stuff of gold. So, as usual, Black women had to wait their turn. Cultural and linguistic anthropologist Claudia Mitchell-Kernan was one of the first African Americans to include African American women as a central part of linguistic research (see Mitchell-Kernan 1972). She interviewed three generations of women in her family for her dissertation (Mitchell 1969). Marcyliena Morgan followed suit in her dissertation (Morgan 1989). I continued that legacy with my dissertation (Lanehart 1995). This was much-needed research given the rift between white women feminism and their disregard for African American women and their struggles as well as contributions. It was necessary because prior (and continuing) research on women's language meant white women's language. Seminal research on women's language was always white women. As a result, research associated with white women's language was mistakenly applied to AAWL[6] in the same way that traditional medical research tries to apply studies done on

---

6 I was summarily dismissed from an Honors thesis committee at UTSA because I insisted a student include research on AAWL to analyze the language of the Black women in her project. Her advisor, a white woman historical linguist, only had her read research on white women's speech and the student's analysis consisted of applying white women's speech norms to African American women. When the African American women's language differed from the white women's language and the literature the student had read, the student's analysis framed the African American women's speech as, essentially, grotesque.

white men to all populations. Black women are not white women, just like Black women are not Black men (Stanback 1985). It's in the name! But as Hull et al. (1982) said, "All the women are white, all the Blacks are men, but some of us are brave." Amen!

In *Sista, Speak!* (Lanehart 2002), I present research on language, education, and literacy for three generations of my maternal family because I know that the language of African American women, and certainly African American women in the South, matter. *Sista, Speak!* is based on my dissertation research. Doing *that* dissertation set me on the road to doing work that I love to do because it's personal—not business—as I discussed in Chapter 1. Those three generations of women—Granny (b. 1920), Mom (b. 1946), my mom's baby sister/my aunt (b. 1960), Sis (b. 1964), and me—are still very much part of the story of AAWL, even though Granny **went to be with the Lord** in December 2017 after a long bout with Alzheimer's. Each of these women had poignant stories and experiences related to their ideologies, attitudes, and beliefs about language and identity, education, and schooling. A significant finding, ironically, was that the more education they had, the less they believed in what I termed the *Ideology of Opportunity* (i.e., the belief that SAmE/WAmE would provide them with better educational, financial, and career opportunities), the *Ideology of Progress* (i.e., the belief that SAmE/WAmE would allow them to overcome the adversities and shortcomings of their "deficient" and "deprived" culture), and the *Ideology of Emancipation* (i.e., the belief that SAmE/WAmE would provide them autonomy and empower and emancipate them from the lack of power that Black language and life had inscribed). Isn't it like the letdown you have after passing your dissertation defense and submitting it to the graduate school or winning the Hunger Games that is tenure and promotion? Asking for a friend. *Sista, Speak!* has reinforced over and over again to me how so many African Americans have bought into the lie that is white supremacy that shows up every single day as anti-Black racism.

African American Women's Language: Discourse, Education, and Identity (Lanehart 2009) arose from a conference on AAWL. What I loved about the conference was the space that was created for Black creativity and community. This was a space to acknowledge and celebrate African American women and girls. The book provides a collection of research from a variety of contexts, perspectives, and interdisciplinary studies that address AAWL. As such, I focused on having Black women talk about Black language. It was important and necessary to center African American women and girls in a way linguistics had often overlooked. Research ranges from traditional features to discourse analysis to auto-ethnography and more. AAWL was investigated and celebrated. And the question of "What is Linguistics?" is answered as, "It's what we choose to make of it in our exploration and study of the language of Black women." **Yassss, queens!** *Linguistics* is defined by the Linguistic Society of America as the "scientific study of language and its applications," but Black scholars and Black women decidedly **clapped back** at the colonial view of positivist and behavioralist notions of science and its white gaze. As Morgan (2021) says, **we don't play**.

Jacobs-Huey (2006) focuses on AAWL and Black women's hair. Black women's hair is **a whole thing**, so I will not deal with that here (see Banks 2000). Suffice it to say, Jacobs-Huey (2006) is a must-read because, for Black women, hair is just not simply hair (see the Will Smith slap of Chris Rock heard round the world at the 2022 Academy Awards over Jada Pinkett Smith's baldness due to alopecia). **Okurrr**? That's why we can have a whole book and more about the complexities of hair talk. AAL/USEB lexicon around hair includes "nappy," "good hair," "kitchen," "natural," "straightened," "creamy crack," "relaxer," "locs," "corn rows," "press 'n curl," "hot comb," "baby hair," "edges," "(hair is) laid," and a lot more that negotiate between anti-Blackness and **respectability politics** to "**Say it loud, I'm Black and I'm proud**." We see the policing of Black women's hair in the military, PreK–12, jobs, sports, etc. How come you think so many Black women talk about relaxing or straightening their hair for job interviews for fear of being seen as "unprofessional" if they wear their hair natural? This is the language that Black women speak with a nod of the head and a proverbial **h/t** that says, "**I see you**."

Hudson (2001) provides an overview of research and characteristics of AAWL at the time and indicates the importance of AAWL in broader AAL/USEB communities. Michèle Foster's research focuses on the language of Black women teachers (see Foster 1997) and

Where My *Shawtys* At? 155

their uses of AA(W)L in classrooms to help students learn. Gwendolyn Etter-Lewis provides linguistic and Black Feminist research on AAWL in one of my favorite books of all time, *My Soul Is My Own: Oral Narratives of African American Women in the Professions* (1993) as well as a co-edited book with Michèle Foster, *Unrelated Kin: Race and Gender in Women's Personal Narratives* (1996). Her work uses discourse and narrative analyses. Etter-Lewis gets at the **nitty gritty** of AAWL in Black women's narratives and discourse.

Marcyliena Morgan's research focuses on *discourse genres*, "language and communication styles which commonly occur in socially, culturally, and politically defined contexts" (Morgan 2022, 277), and *verbal genres*, "speaker's use of culturally significant varieties and styles which mediate, constitute, and construct contexts" (Morgan 2022, 277). She's helped to expand our understanding of indirectness, directness, directed discourse, reading, and signifying (see Chapter 5 for definitions and examples), which combine to mark AAL/USEB as distinct across generation, gender, and class (see Morgan 2004). While Morgan (2015) provides a thorough overview of the theories and research on AAWL over the decades, Morgan (2004) is **my jam**! It is a **dope** study of the acquisition of AAWL in intragenerational and intergenerational women's communities of an intriguing discourse genre: Laughter. It is one of my **Top Five** articles about AA(W)L. **Periodt**! She talks about how signifying laughter is acquired and passed down from generation to generation of Black women. The chapter

> addresses the complexity of African American women's stories by exploring how language and interactions frame and reveal the buried truth, depth, and richness of African American women's lives. I focus on the body of linguistic and symbolic resources they employ to express their ideas, identities, roles, and relations to each other.
>
> (Morgan 2004, 52)

But the laugh; oh, the laughter:

> [W]hat I call "the Black woman's laugh" (Morgan 2002) can seem out of context if one does not possess the interpretive

framework to recognize and respond to that which is implicit and indexed and that which is explicit. This is because the Black woman's laugh often occurs within narratives and discussions of bigotry, patriarchy, paternalism, social class privilege, sexism, and other situations that may also be responded to with outrage and indignation. Consequently, in conversations and narratives, African American women's laughter often signals an indirect critique on situations in which injustice and the exercise of power highlight the event under discussion. [Men also use this laugh but within the culture it seems to occur more frequently among women without additional comment.] This laugh is easily misinterpreted because it occurs as a reflex within discourse that is tragic or may have dire consequences for the speaker, who never provides an explanation for why she's laughing.

(Morgan 2004, 61–62)

I highly recommend you read her chapter because I cannot include here her transcriptions and analysis. I do love, however, the different ways laughter is used by older Black women, younger Black women, and the misinterpretations and missteps by Black girls and young Black women as they acquire and practice their signifying laughter and loud talk.

Denise Troutman's research on AAWL is greatly influenced by earlier Black women researchers and primarily uses discourse analysis to explore AAWL. Her research **takes it home** for Black women and girls and their community discourse. Troutman (2001, 213) breaks down characteristics of AAWL as including:

- reported speech (Etter-Lewis 1991, 1993);
- cooperative or collaborative speech (Etter-Lewis 1991, 1993);
- "little" usage (Etter-Lewis 1991, 1993);
- reading dialect, which is one form of signifying (Morgan 1996);
- culturally-toned diminutives (Troutman 1996);
- performance (Foster 1995);
- assertiveness (Stanback 1985; Troutman 1996); and
- "smart talk," one form of assertiveness (Stanback 1985).

Reported speech in Black women's narratives is when they attribute something as coming from authority figures in their lives, especially fathers (e.g., "My father said . . ." or "My mother would say . . .") (Etter-Lewis 1991, 1993). Etter-Lewis (1991, 1993) notes that in her Black women's oral narratives, Black women willingly engaged in cooperative and collaborative speech interchanges in order to work together, such as a participant asking permission to share a story and then with Etter-Lewis evaluating the story with the participant. Then there's "little" usage, where accomplished Black women use the word "little" to refer to something that is actually very important and highly significant (e.g., "I wrote a little book, *Beloved*, that garnered some attention"). *Culturally toned diminutives* are a major conversational feature of AAWL. They express solidarity and familiarity. Examples are *girl, sista, sista friend, honey, honey child, child, baby, baby girl* (this is one my mom's oldest sister always used with her), *precious, muh'dear* (Troutman 2001, 217), *girlfriend*, and *queen*.[7] Foster (1995, 333) defines *performance* as "a special kind of communicative event in which there is a particular relationship among stylized material, performer, and audience." Teachers use this sometimes in order to make concepts concrete. They perform (or enact) the meaning of a concept instead of just providing a rote definition (Troutman 2001, 218; see Foster 2001).

Stanback (1982, 1985), as quoted in Troutman (2001, 219), claims that African American women communicate in an assertive, outspoken way, just as African American men, due to African American women's work in public spheres. African American women, however, must curtail their outspokenness as a result of community standards, which only allow assertiveness to a certain point for women. This shows up in stereotypes of Black women. Rachel Weissler has extended research on AAWL to address stereotypes of Black women, such as the "Angry Black Woman" (Weissler 2021; Weissler and Boland 2019).

While *sweet talk* is used with children, female friends, and relatives to affirm and support, *smart talk* is a form of assertiveness that is reserved for put-downs (2001, 222). *Signifying*, an indirect

---

7 Some might argue that [bɪtʃ] should be included as a term of endearment.

form of ritualized insult, is one form of smart talk. Just watch some episodes of *Good Times* (Monte and Evans 1974–1979) where JJ and Thelma interact or JJ and Willona or Willona and Bookman for examples of signifying and smart talk. Troutman's more recent work focuses on the intersectionality of (im)politeness (Troutman 2010, 2022).

All I will say for Docta G here is *Word from the Mother* (Smitherman 2006/2022) is *Talkin that Talk* (Smitherman 2000) while *Talkin and Testifyin* (Smitherman 1977) and being *Articulate* [**AF**] *While Black* (Alim and Smitherman 2012). **Ain't she *the* woman?! Word**!

Hip Hop Nation Language, or HHNL

Speaking of overlooking Black women, let's talk about Hip Hop.

> Hip Hop began in the early 1970s by marginalized youth of the South Bronx in New York City. The culture gave these youth a platform to be seen and heard, which placed them at the center—for better or for worse. The four original elements of Hip Hop are writing (aerosol art), DJing, breaking and MCing; knowledge of self and community was added later. MCing (rapping) is the most notable and perhaps lucrative of the elements. Rap music unapologetically articulates the social, political, cultural, and economic issues in Black communities by employing the Black Language. Moreover, there is no Hip Hop without Black Language—no matter the element. The whole culture revolves around the elaborate Black storytelling that catches audiences' ears, imaginations, and hearts. . . .
>
> While these adolescents were trying to out-rhyme each other to be the best MC, they created their own words, phrases, and definitions that then became part of a deep and broad Black Language lexicon, style, and linguistic philosophy that spread even further during events, mixtapes, radio, and the military. *This created a symbiotic relationship: what you heard on the streets, you heard on the track and if you heard it on a track, then you heard it on the streets. There is no separating Black*

Language from Hip Hop. There is no separating Hip Hop from Black Language. This is how we do.
(www.blacklanguagesyllabus.com/black-language-and-hip-hop.html).

Hip Hop is reflected across subcultures and communities of African Americans and, as such, is part of AAL/USEB. Hip Hop as a variety of AAL/USEB is part of the African American communities that have a strong identity in Hip Hop and is an intersection of culture, music, and language. To paraphrase KRS-One in the song *Hip Hop Lives* (2007), Hip means to know, Hop is a form of movement. Therefore, Hip Hop is more than music, knowledge, and/or movement: It's intelligent movement.

Hip Hop Nation Language (HHNL) refers to language and language use within the *Hip Hop Nation* (HHN), as conceptualized by H. Samy Alim (see Alim 2015), as a global network of individuals and communities that engage in Hip Hop culture (Alim 2006, 2; Alim et al. 2010). The HHN has been called the "locus of Hip Hop cultural activity" (Alim 2006, 4). Though Alim coined the terms HHN and HHNL, several Black women scholars investigated and invoked Hip Hop culture as a linguistic manifestation in and of AAL/USEB before him, such as J. Morgan (2000), M. Morgan (2001), and Pough (2004); contemporaneously, such as Richardson (2006) and Smitherman (2006), which is now a 2022 Routledge Classic[8]; and after him, such as Blake and Shousterman (2010). In fact, Black women have viewed HHN and HHNL from a Black Feminist perspective despite being overlooked, underappreciated, and under-represented (e.g., Brown 2009; Brown and Kwakye 2012; J. Morgan 2018; Perry 2004). But this is nothing new. Remember, Zora (Neale Hurston) told us long ago: *Mules and Men* (1935). But also remember the Black women who have trailblazed, such as Erykah Badu, Missy Elliott, MC Lyte, Lauryn Hill, Queen Mary J. Blige, Queen Latifah, Lil' Kim, Salt-N-Pepa, Sister Souljah, Eve, Trina, Brandy, and Da Brat, to those who walk in the trails they blazed, such as Noname, Lizzo, Nicki Minaj, Cardi B, Megan Thee Stallion, Doja Cat, and

---

8 Smitherman (2006/2022) is Hip Hop in action, or HHNL.

OSHUN. And let's not forget that Hip Hop is not just rap, as these women artists demonstrate so well.

In addition to the citations I have provided, I also recommend you explore the rich resources provided by *Rap Genius* and its *Rap Stats* tool, the Rap Research Lab's *Rap Almanac* database, *Mappers Delight XR*, *Maximum Distance Minimum Displacement* exhibit, MIT's *Hip Hop Word Count* database, *Urban Dictionary*, and the *Black Language Syllabus* created by April Baker-Bell and Carmen Kynard to get a fuller sense of the intersection of Hip Hop and AAL/USEB that yields HHNL.

As you do that, I'd like to note a particular research project that has not been published but is excellent work on how global and how deep HHNL is. Ayesha Malik—my former student at UTSA and former research assistant-turned-writing-partner who is now a lawyer—is a Pakistani American, Muslim, Hip Hop head who calls Islam Hip Hop's (un)official religion (Malik 2015, 2016, 2018, 2019). [9] As she discusses, the Islamic association to Hip Hop culture originated via the Nation of Gods and Earths (NGE, or the "Five Percent Nation"), which made way for the Nation of Islam (NOI) and Sunni Islam (Mohaiemen 2008).

Malik notes that Islamic imagery, symbolism, beliefs, and phrases are so pervasive in Hip Hop that they are frequently used by even non-Muslim Hip Hop artists—both intentionally (to make a statement about identity to those in the know) and unintentionally (as many features have been bleached of their origins). This same Islamic iconography, philosophy, and language is used in the streets by members of the HHN. She conducted research on the invisibility of Black Muslims in America; the religious and sociopolitical history of the civil rights movement and how this bled into Hip Hop (i.e., Martin Luther King Jr., the Church, and integration versus Malcolm X, Farrakhan, the Nation of Islam, and Black separatist nationalism); the importance of the oral transmission of knowledge

---

9 Please note that this discussion of Ayesha Malik's research was reviewed and revised by her in December 2021. She adds, "I'm not just a Muslim girl who got excited by hearing *shaytan* in a Lauryn Hill song once upon a time. It [Islam and Hip Hop connections] came up a lot and it [Islam] was foundational."

to Five Percenters; the locus (or should I say, "Mecca") of early Hip Hop in the Bronx in New York City; and the distinctively Islamic elements in HHNL, including an examination of the frequency of use of these patterns of Islamic influence by Hip Hop artists who demonstrate their varying affiliation to Islam[10] through their lyrics over time; and what use of these features mean for artists in conveying identity (Malik 2019). She demonstrates the influence of Islam in these artists' lyricism, in addition to comments or references they have made outside of their music.

In interrogating the intersection of religion, Hip Hop culture, and HHNL, Malik discusses four ways Islamic influence is in HHNL:

1 word formation often used in artist, group, song, and album naming through the use of backronyms, such as *CREAM* ("cash rules everything around me"); acronyms, such as *NWA* ("Niggaz Wit Attitudes"), and *A$AP* ("Always $trive and Prosper");[11] and abbreviations, such as *KRS-One* ("Knowledge Reigns Supreme Over Nearly Everyone") and *RZA*, pronounced /rɪzə/ ("Ruler, Zig-Zag-Zag, Allah");
2 slang, such as *G* (meaning "God," not "gangsta"), *drop knowledge*, *word is bond*, *peace*, and *cipha* or *cipher*;[12]
3 the use of spoken Islamic Arabic, such as *shaytan* ("devil") and *deen* ("faith"), *Sirat al-mustaqeem* ("the straight path"); Islamic

---

10 In Malik (2019), the use of the Islamic features identified was examined in the lyrics of Lauryn Hill and Jay-Z, who both exhibit a fluid association to the Five Percent Nation; Erykah Badu, who has a strong Five Percent affiliation; and Yasiin Bey, formerly Mos Def, who converted to Sunni Islam from Five Percent ideology. "Tobe Nwigwe (from Alief, TX, really blew up this past year) is a devout Christian [and Islam is] very present in his music. He's [often] dropping Islam references (Malik, personal communication December 2021). See, for example, his video "Shine" at https://youtu.be/Pmr9jXy3zQQ.
11 According to Ayesha Malik (personal communication, December 2021): "While more popular in the 1990s, early 2000s, acronyms/backronyms are part of the culture (literally artists are still doing this). Hip Hop heads still use the slang. Jay-Z is dropping 'alhamdulillah' in *4:44*."
12 According to Ayesha Malik (personal communication, December 2021): "Cipher is literally Arabic for 'zero,' they [Hip Hop artists with ties to Islam] are all about the numerology and symbology and Supreme Alphabet/Mathematics."

discursive tradition, or *dhikr*, such as *Bismillah* ("in the name of God"), *Alhamdullillah* ("praise be to God"), *Allahu akbar* ("God is great"), and *Inshallah* ("God willing"); and inclusion of Quranic verses; and

4 speech acts that reflect Islamic teachings in songs as a moral practice to prevent other Muslims from engaging in *haram*, or forbidden, acts, as commanded in Surat al-Imran (Quran 3, 104), like Lupe Fiasco's "Muhammad Walks."

I did not know the extent of the connection prior to Malik's research, but it is clear that the influence and integration of Islam and Hip Hop is there because the legends of Hip Hop tell us. As she discusses, the Islamic association to Hip Hop culture originated via the Nation of Gods and Earths, or Five Percenter sect of Islam (such as Wu Tang Clan), which made way for the inclusion of Nation of Islam and Sunni Islam beliefs in Hip Hop (Mohaiemen 2008).[13]

This discussion is not to ignore the influence of Christianity and West African religious traditions. However, we cannot and should not ignore non-Western religious origins in Hip Hop and HHNL. As Malik says in defense of the significance and pervasiveness of Islam in Hip Hop and HHNL (personal communication, December 2021):

I know HH builds on its foundations. If Islam was just a trend, why is someone who wasn't NY HH in the 90s, and by stark contrast is Houston 2020 rap, building off Mos Def's "Umi Says" and talking about "shaytan" (see https://youtu.be/Pmr9jXy3zQQ)? How do you look at Wu Tang, Mos Def, and those "90s" artists and think no one carried those torches or paid homage? Why would Kendrick Lamar, Frank Ocean, who are most definitely not Muslim, be using Allah? It's not just cause

---

13 See Talib Kweli's Facebook video interview with Raekwon where he says "Mathematics was definitely the way of life for us. It wasn't actually lessons it was a way of life" (https://fb.watch/aiVSGs33Ac/).

it sounds better in lyrics. I mean, I'm just saying, of course HH wouldn't exist without West African drum circles. That's where the roots are from. But Black American Islam has something to do with it, too, and it's persisted. Raekwon is literally talking about the backronym/song CREAM and Five Percenters in this clip: https://fb.watch/afdehCY5pp/.

Changes that occurred in Hip Hop were about expansion to other regions beyond the East Coast origins and the strong Black Muslim influence. According to H. Samy Alim in a personal communication, "What happened commercially was the industry began looking to the South for 'fresh' talent. There was less Muslim influence in the music of Southern artists, well, because there are less Muslims in the South!" (January 2022).

Last, but not least, let's not forget the poetics of Hip Hop and HHNL. Hip Hop consists of linguistic acrobats and poets who innovated and spread HHNL in the streets. According to Adam Carpenter (personal communication, December 2021),

> HHNL has influenced AAL through the proliferation of poetic conventions. For instance, the use of simile, not just when doin the **dozens/cappin**, but also in regular speech, is powered by Hip Hop—even if Hip Hop is merely fostering mechanisms that originated in West Africa, before being incubated in Negro spirituals then the blues. Similes pop up all the time in AAL. Extended metaphor and allusion also play a more dominant role in AAL than they do in White speech, and it seems Hip Hop may deserve the credit for that as well. . . . Adam Bradley's *Book of Rhymes: The Poetics of Hip Hop* **goes IN**—and from the perspective of the use of literary devices in AAL, that book's **crazy** relevant.

According to Bradley (2009/2017), Hip Hop is the source of some of the most exciting developments in verse today. That's why Kendrick Lamar can win a Pulitzer Prize for *DAMN*, and Jay-Z wrote *Decoded*.

Sexuality and Gendered Identity in Language Use in African American Communities

As is the case with much research on variation in AAL/USEB beyond AAVL/VUSEB, there is not enough research in *gender* (i.e., as a social construction and not the biological, binary, sex-based construction), *gender identity* (i.e., a person's sense of their gender and their expression of it, which may not correspond to their assigned sex), and *sexuality* (i.e., one's sexual orientation). These areas are understudied or overlooked in their linguistic relationship to AAL/USEB. Though AAWL is still in need of much research, it is the most studied area of this grouping of least studied areas in AAL/USEB research around gender (i.e., not cis-male), sexuality (i.e., usually heterosexual), and gender identity (i.e., almost always based on assigned sex at birth). This is exacerbated by what seems to be a rule of some sort in sociolinguistics: two degrees of separation beyond white, heterosexual, and (cis-gender) male, or *WHAM* as I call it, is too much (Lanehart 2019). So, you can study white women's speech or white gay men's speech, but Black gay men's speech or Black lesbians' speech is a little much. Pushing the envelope to three degrees of separation or more is a unicorn. I think this is where sociolinguistics and Intersectionality Theory need to collide, and sociolinguistics has not been a very willing partner until recently. However, if sociolinguistics is the study of language in society, social and cultural contexts, and social factors, which include the Big Five (i.e., age, gender/sex, SES, region, and race/ethnicity), then sociolinguistics needs to catch up to and grow into its definition.

Tackling intersectionality means knowing what it means and using it appropriately. *Intersectionality* was coined by Kimberlé Crenshaw in 1989, even though the concept of intersectionality was developing and developed before she coined the term in all the Black Feminist/Womanist thinkers before her (see King 1988). Crenshaw (1991, 1244) originally

> used the concept of intersectionality to denote the various ways in which race and gender interact to shape the multiple dimensions of Black women's employment experiences. My

objective there was to illustrate that many of the experiences Black women face are subsumed within the traditional boundaries of race or gender discrimination as these boundaries are currently understood, and that the intersection of racism and sexism factors into Black women's lives in ways that cannot be captured wholly by looking at the race or gender dimensions of those experiences separately.

In February 2020, Crenshaw did an interview with *TIME* where she explained what intersectionality means today:

A lens, a prism, for seeing the way in which various forms of inequality often operate together and exacerbate each other. We tend to talk about race inequality as separate from inequality based on gender, class, sexuality, or immigrant status [and] how some people are subject to all of these.

The experience of intersecting oppressions is more than the sum of its parts. I hope that provides the clarity you need for intersectionality versus intersecting oppressions and how they can be used in sociolinguistics research to move it into the 21st century responsibly.

Gender has been understudied in Black communities in particular, but that has been the case for the fullest meanings of gender and gender identity. The International Gender and Language Association (IGALA) was founded in 1999 and emerged out of the University of California Berkeley, a bastion of white feminist language research, and launched its journal, *Gender and Language* (*G&L*), in 2007, providing a space to include research on not just AAWL but more inclusive views of gender and gender identity. Unfortunately, IGALA did not realize the hope of a more inclusive space and neither did *G&L* for much of its history. It was easier to find an article on white women around the world than Black or other Women of Color here in the Americas. In a way, gender in sociolinguistics was like AAL/USEB: Scholars took the low-hanging fruit first. Well, the tree is **grown** now, so it's time to see the **white meat** (I hope you understand the irony here of this mixed metaphor).

Fortunately, with this third wave of AAL/USEB research and researchers, these barriers and shackles of white supremacy, heteronormativity, and gender normativity are being broken because they represent more of those identities for Black folx (e.g., queer, nonbinary, trans, and all that is LGBTQIA+) in a forward-and-out way and have a **white meat** line of research interests in language use in Black communities than previous waves did or could represent. While Barrett (1998) provides some early work in the area of African American drag queens, Campbell-Kibler and miles-hercules (2021) (race and gendering beyond hegemonic binaries), Cornelius (2020) and Cornelius and Barrett (2020) (African American gay males), Lane (2019) (Black queer women), Lopez and Bucholtz (2017) (media representations of race, gender, and sexuality), and miles-hercules (2020, forthcoming) (intersectionality of gender and gender identity in AAL/USEB) dig deeper into sexuality, gender, and gender identity in AAL/USEB than any previous research. miles-hercules in particular has become the face of gender identity in African American communities' research, and I look forward to seeing more of what they have to say.

We are seeing more representations of African Americans beyond gendered binaries and heteronormativity and their representations of femininity and masculinity and the impact on AAL/USEB (e.g., *WAP* by Cardi B featuring Megan Thee Stallion 2020 or *MONTERO* by Lil Nas X 2021). Now let's get a corresponding increase of public performances, personal discourses, and AAL/USEB research beyond two degrees of separation. Where my **shawtys** at?

Questions, Discussion, and Further Inquiry

1 Have you noticed variation in signed languages before reading this book?
2 How can you identify Standard African American Language?
3 What are the noticeable differences in SAAL/AASL and AAVL?
4 In your own words, from a historical standpoint, why do you think the study of Middle-Class African American Language is an important field of study?
5 What solutions can you think of for Black women's speech to be researched just to the same or better extent than other varieties of AAL/USEB?

6 Why is hair more than just hair for Black women?
7 What needs to be troubled about tone, im/politeness, and emotion in relation to Black women?
8 What does Hurston mean when she says "women are the mules of the earth," and how does that manifest in research on AAL/USEB and how AAWL is viewed?
9 What is *intersectionality* as theorized by Kimberlé Crenshaw, and how has it been co-opted?
10 Make a Venn diagram of likenesses and differences between AAL/USEB, HHNL, Hip Hop, and Rap.
11 What do you think is the current state of HHNL with respect to religious influence and its impact on AAL/USEB more broadly?
12 Why do you think it's been difficult to find or conduct research beyond two degrees of separation from WHAM?
13 How do you understand the distinctions between *sex*, *gender*, *gender identity*, and *sexuality* and their significance in AAL research and AAL speech communities?
14 What are some things missing in social variation in AAL research that weren't discussed in this chapter? What are you interested in about AAL research that's missing?

References

Alim, H. Samy. 2006. *Roc the mic right: The Language of Hip Hop Culture*. London: Routledge.

Alim, H. Samy. 2015. Hip Hop Nation Language: Localization and Globalization. In *The Oxford Handbook of African American Language*, edited by Sonja Lanehart, 850–862. Oxford: Oxford University Press.

Alim, H. Samy, Awad Ibrahim, and Alastair Pennycook, eds. 2010. *Global Linguistic Flows: Hip Hop Cultures, Youth Identities, and the Politics of Language*. London: Routledge.

Alim, H. Samy, and Geneva Smitherman. 2012. *Articulate while Black: Barack Obama, Language, and Race in the U.S.* Oxford: Oxford University Press.

Banks, Ingrid. 2000. *Hair Matters: Beauty, Power, and Black Women's Consciousness*. New York: New York University Press.

Barrett, Rusty. 1998. Markedness and Styleswitching in Performances by African American Drag Queens. In *Codes and Consequences: Choosing*

Linguistic Varieties, edited by Carol Myers-Scotton, 139–161. Oxford: Oxford University Press.

Bayley, Robert, and Ceil Lucas. 2015. Phonological Variation in Louisiana ASL: An Exploratory Study. In *New Perspectives on Language Variety in the South: Historical and Contemporary Approaches*, edited by Michael D. Picone and Catherine Evans Davies, 565–580. Tuscaloosa, AL: University of Alabama Press.

Blake, Renée, and Cara Shousterman. 2010. Diachrony and AAE: St. Louis, Hip-Hop, and Sound Change Outside of the Mainstream. *Journal of English Linguistics* 38.3: 230–247. DOI: 10.1177/0075424210374955

Bradley, Adam. 2009/2017. *Book of Rhymes: The Poetics of Hip Hop*. New York: Civitas Books.

Britt, Erica, and Tracey Weldon. 2015. African American English in the Middle Class. In *The Oxford Handbook of African American Language*, edited by Sonja Lanehart, 800–816. Oxford: Oxford University Press.

Brown, Ruth Nicole. 2009. *Black Girlhood Celebration: Toward a Hip-Hop Feminist Pedagogy*. New York: Peter Lang.

Brown, Ruth Nicole, and Chamara Jewel Kwakye, eds. 2012. *Wish to Live: The Hip-Hop Feminism Pedagogy Reader*. New York: Peter Lang.

Campbell-Kibler, Kathryn, and deandre miles-hercules. 2021. Perception of Gender and Sexuality. In *The Routledge Handbook of Language, Gender, and Sexuality*, edited by Jo Angouri and Judith Baxter, 52–68. London: Routledge.

Champion, Tempii B., and Allyssa McCabe. 2015. Narrative Structures of African American Children: Commonalities and Differences. In *The Oxford Handbook of African American Language*, edited by Sonja Lanehart, 492–511. Oxford: Oxford University Press.

Clark, Heather D. 2007. Signing and Signifyin': Negotiating Deaf and African American Identities. *Ethnic Studies Review* 30.1: 115–124.

Clark, Heather D. 2010. *We Are the Same But Different: Navigating African American and Deaf Cultural Identities*. PhD dissertation. University of Washington.

Cornelius, Brianna R. 2020. Talkin' Black and Sounding Gay: An Examination of the Construction of a Multiplex Identity via Intraspeaker Variation. Ph.D. dissertation. University of South Carolina.

Cornelius, Brianna R., and Rusty Barrett. 2020. You Met My Ambassador: Language and Self-monitoring at the Intersection of Race and Sexuality. In *The Oxford Handbook of Language and Race*, edited by H. Samy Alim, Angela Reyes, and Paul V. Kroskrity, 315–341. Oxford: Oxford University Press. DOI: 10.1093/oxfordhb/9780190845995.013.17

Crenshaw, Kimberlé. 1989. Demarginalizing the Intersection of Race and Sex: A Black Feminist Critique of Antidiscrimination Doctrine, Feminist Theory

and Antiracist Politics. *University of Chicago Legal Forum* 1989.1.8: 139–167. http://chicagounbound.uchicago.edu/uclf/vol1989/iss1/8
- Crenshaw, Kimberlé. 1991. Mapping the Margins: Intersectionality, Identity Politics, and Violence against Women of Color. *Stanford Law Review* 43.6: 1241–1299.
- DeBose, Charles. 2015. African American Church Language. In *The Oxford Handbook of African American Language*, edited by Sonja Lanehart, 677–690. Oxford: Oxford University Press.
- DuBois, W.E. Burghardt. 1903. *The Souls of Black Folk: Essays and Sketches*. Chicago: A.C. McClurg & Co.
- Etter-Lewis, Gwendolyn. 1991. Black Women's Life Stories: Reclaiming Self in Narrative Texts. In *Women's Words: The Feminist Practice of Oral History*, edited by Sherna Berger Gluck and Daphne Patai, 43–62. London: Routledge.
- Etter-Lewis, Gwendolyn. 1993. *My Soul Is My Own: Oral Narratives of African American Women in the Professions*. London: Routledge.
- Etter-Lewis, Gwendolyn, and Michèle Foster, eds. 1996. *Unrelated Kin: Race and Gender in Women's Personal Narratives*. London: Routledge.
- Foster, Michèle. 1995. "Are You with Me?": Power and Solidarity in the Discourse of African American Women. In *Gender Articulated: Language and the Socially Constructed Self*, edited by Kira Hall and Mary Bucholtz, 329–350. London: Routledge.
- Foster, Michèle. 1997. *Black Teachers on Teaching*. New York: The New Press.
- Foster, Michèle. 2001. Pay Leon, Pay Leon, Pay Leon, Paleontologist: Using Call-and-Response to Facilitate Language Mastery and Literacy Acquisition among African American Students. In *Sociocultural and Historical Contexts of African American English*, edited by Sonja L. Lanehart, 281–298. Amsterdam: John Benjamins.
- Frazier, E. Franklin. 1957. *Black Bourgeoisie*. New York: Free Press/Simon & Schuster.
- Green, Lisa J. 2011. *Language and the African American Child*. Cambridge: Cambridge University Press.
- Hansberry, Lorraine. 1959. *A Raisin in the Sun*. New York: Random House.
- Hill, Joseph. 2012. *Language Attitudes in the American Deaf Community*. PhD dissertation. Gallaudet University Press.
- Hill, Joseph, Carolyn McCaskill, Robert Bayley, and Ceil Lucas. 2015. The Black ASL (American Sign Language) Project. In *The Oxford Handbook of African American Language*, edited by Sonja Lanehart, 316–337. Oxford: Oxford University Press.
- Hoover, Mary Rhodes. 1978. Community Attitudes toward Black English. *Language in Society* 7.1: 65–87. DOI: 10.1017/S0047404500005339

Hoover, Mary Rhodes, Dwight Brown, Shirley Lewis, Shirley Hicks, and Robert Politzer. 1976. SCRDT Black English Tests for Students (with Teacher's Manual). Stanford, CA: Stanford Center for Research and Development of Teaching.

Hudson, Barbara Hill. 2001. *African American Female Speech Communities: Varieties of Talk.* Westport, CT: Bergin & Garvey.

Hull, Gloria T., Patricia Bell Scott, and Barbara Smith, eds. 1982. *All the Women Are White, All the Blacks Are men, but Some of Us Are Brave: Black Women's Studies.* New York: The Feminist Press.

Hurston, Zora Neale. 1935. *Mules and Men.* New York: Lippincott.

Jacobs-Huey, Lanita. 2006. *From the Kitchen to the Parlor: Language and African American Women's Hair Care.* Oxford: Oxford University Press.

Jay-Z. 2010. *Decoded.* New York: Spiegel & Grau.

Jones, Taylor. 2016. AAE Talmbout: An Overlooked Verb of Quotation. *University of Pennsylvania Working Papers in Linguistics* 22.2: 11. https://repository.upenn.edu/pwpl/vol22/iss2/11

King, Deborah. 1988. Multiple Jeopardy, Multiple Consciousness: The Context of a Black Feminist Ideology. *Signs: Journal of Women in Culture* 14.1: 42–72.

Labov, William. 1969/1972. *Language in the Inner City: Studies in the Black English Vernacular.* Philadelphia: University of Pennsylvania Press.

Landry, Bart. 1987. *The New Black Middle Class.* Los Angeles: University of California Press.

Lane, Nikki. 2019. *The Black Queer Work of Ratchet: Race, Gender, Sexuality, and the (Anti)Politics of Respectability.* Cham, Switzerland: Palgrave Macmillan.

Lanehart, Sonja L. 1995. *Peculiar to Your Mind: Language, Literacy, and Uses of Identity.* PhD dissertation. University of Michigan at Ann Arbor.

Lanehart, Sonja L. 2002. *Sista, Speak! Black Women Kinfolk Talk about Language and Literacy.* Austin, TX: University of Texas Press.

Lanehart, Sonja, ed. 2009. *African American Women's Language: Discourse, Education, and Identity.* Newcastle-upon-Tyne: Cambridge Scholars Publishing.

Lanehart, Sonja, ed. 2015. *The Oxford Handbook of African American Language.* Oxford: Oxford University Press.

Lanehart, Sonja. 2019. Can You Hear (and See) Me Now?: Race-ing American Language Variationist/Change and Sociolinguistic Research Methodologies. In *Understanding Critical Race Research Methods and Methodologies: Lessons from the Field*, edited by Jessica DeCuir-Gunby, Thandeka Chapman, and Paul A. Schutz, 34–47. London: Routledge.

Larsen, Nella. 1929. *Passing.* New York: Knopf.

Lopez, Qiuana, and Mary Bucholtz. 2017. "How My Hair Look?" Linguistic Authenticity and Racialized Gender and Sexuality on *The Wire*. *Journal of Language and Sexuality* 6.1: 1–29. DOI: 10.1075/jls.6.1.01lop

Lucas, Ceil, Robert Bayley, Carolyn McCaskill, and Joseph Hill. 2015. The Intersection of African American English and Black American Sign Language. *International Journal of Bilingualism* 19.2: 156–168. DOI: 10.1177/1367006913489204

Malik, Ayesha M. 2015. Islam, Hip Hop's (Un)Official Religion: Examining Distinctively Islamic Features in Hip Hop Nation Language. Paper presented at the 6th Biennial International Conference on the Linguistics of Contemporary English, University of Wisconsin Madison, Madison, WI, August 19–23.

Malik, Ayesha M. 2016. Islam, Hip Hop's (Un)Official Religion: Examining Distinctively Islamic Features in Hip Hop Nation Language. Paper presented at the 83rd Southeastern Conference on Linguistics, New Orleans, March 28–31.

Malik, Ayesha M. 2018. Islam, Hip Hop's (Un)Official Religion: Examining Distinctively Islamic Features in Hip Hop Nation Language. Paper presented at the Annual Meeting of the American Dialect Society, Salt Lake City, UT, January 4–7.

Malik, Ayesha M. 2019. Islam, Hip Hop's (Un)Official Religion: Examining the Use of Islamic Features by Lauryn Hill, Erykah Badu, Jay Z, and Yasiin Bey (Mos Def). Paper presented at the Annual Meeting of the American Dialect Society, New York, January 3–6.

McCaskill, Carolyn, Ceil Lucas, Robert Bayley, and Joseph Hill. 2011. *The Hidden Treasure of Black ASL: Its History and Structure*. Washington, DC: Gallaudet University Press.

miles-hercules, deandre. 2020. *"A Way to Lift Each Other Up": Black-femme—ininities and Materiality of Discourse*. MA thesis. University of California Santa Barbara.

miles-hercules, deandre. Forthcoming. The Real Tea: Language at the Intersections. In *The Oxford Handbook of Language and Sexuality*, edited by Kira Hall and Rusty Barrett. Oxford Handbooks Online. DOI: 10.1093/oxfordhb/9780190212926.001.0001

Mitchell, Claudia. 1969. *Language Behavior in a Black Urban Community*. PhD dissertation. University of California Berkeley.

Mitchell-Kernan, Claudia. 1971. *Language Behavior in a Black Urban Community*. Monograph No. 2, Language Behavior Research Laboratory, Berkeley, CA.

Mitchell-Kernan, Claudia. 1972. Signifying, Loud-talking, and Marking. In *Rappin' and Stylin' Out: Communication in Urban Black America*,

edited by Thomas Kochman, 315–335. Urbana, IL: University of Illinois Press.
Mohaiemen, Naeem. 2008. Fear of a Muslim Planet: Hip Hop's Hidden History. In *Sound Unbound: Sampling Digital Music and Culture*, edited by Paul D. Miller, 313–336. Cambridge, MA: MIT Press.
Morgan, Joan. 2000. *When Chickenheads Come Home to Roost: A Hip Hop Feminist Breaks It Down*. New York: Touchstone.
Morgan, Joan. 2018. *She Begat This: 20 Years of the Miseducation of Lauryn Hill*. New York: 37 Ink.
Morgan, Marcyliena Hazel. 1989. *From Down South to Up South: The Language Behavior of Three Generations of Black Women Residing in Chicago*. PhD dissertation. University of Pennsylvania.
Morgan, Marcyliena Hazel. 1994. The African American Speech Community: Reality and Sociolinguistics. In *Language and Social Construction of Identity in Creole Situations*, edited by Marcyliena Morgan, 121–148. Los Angeles: UCLA Center for African American Studies.
Morgan, Marcyliena Hazel. 1996. Conversational Signifying: Grammar and Indirectness among African American Women. In *Interaction and Grammar*, edited by Elinor Ochs, Emmanuel Schegloff, and Sandra Thompson, 405–434. Cambridge: Cambridge University Press.
Morgan, Marcyliena Hazel. 2001. "Nuthin but a G thang": Grammar and Language Ideology in Hiphop Identity. In *Sociocultural and Historical Contexts of African American English*, edited by Sonja Lanehart, 187–210. Amsterdam: John Benjamins.
Morgan, Marcyliena Hazel. 2002. *Language, Discourse, and Power in African American Culture*. Cambridge: Cambridge University Press.
Morgan, Marcyliena Hazel. 2004. Signifying, Laughter, and the Subtleties of Loud Talking: Memory and Meaning in African American Women's Discourse. In *Ethnolinguistic Chicago: Language and Literacy in Chicago's Neighborhoods*, edited by Marcia Farr, 51–78. Mahwah, NJ: Lawrence Erlbaum.
Morgan, Marcyliena Hazel. 2015. African American Women's Language: Mother Tongues Untied. In *The Oxford Handbook of African American Language*, edited by Sonja Lanehart, 817–833. Oxford: Oxford University Press.
Morgan, Marcyliena Hazel. 2021. Counterlanguage Powermoves in African American Women's Language Practices. *Gender and Language* 15.2: 289–299. https://doi.org/10.1558/genl.20317
Morgan, Marcyliena Hazel. 2022. More than a Mood or an Attitude: Discourse and Verbal Genres in African American Speech. In *African-American English: Structure, History, and Use, Classic Edition*, edited

by Salikoko S. Mufwene, John R. Rickford, Guy Bailey, and John Baugh, 277–312. London: Routledge.
Perry, Imani. 2004. *Prophets of the Hood: Politics and Poetics in Hip Hop*. Durham, NC: Duke University Press.
Pough, Gwendolyn. 2004. *Check It while I Wreck It: Black Womanhood, Hip-Hop Culture and the Public Sphere*. Boston: Northeastern University Press.
Rahman, Jacquelyn. 2015. African American Divas of Comedy: Staking a Claim in Public Space. In *The Oxford Handbook of African American Language*, edited by Sonja Lanehart, 723–739. Oxford: Oxford University Press.
Richardson, Elaine. 2006. *Hiphop Literacies*. London: Routledge.
Rickford, John R. 1999. *African American Vernacular English: Features, Evolution, Educational Implications*. Malden, MA: Blackwell.
Sledd, James. 1969. Bi-dialectalism: The Linguistics of White Supremacy. *English Journal* 58.9: 1307–1329.
Smitherman, Geneva. 1977. *Talkin and Testifyin: The Language of Black America*. Boston: Houghton Mifflin.
Smitherman, Geneva. 2000. *Talkin that Talk: Language, Culture, and Education in African America*. London: Routledge.
Smitherman, Geneva. 2006/2022. *Word from the Mother: Language and African Americans*, Classic Edition. London: Routledge.
Spears, Arthur K. 1982. The Black English Semi-Auxiliary "Come." *Language* 58.4: 850–872. DOI: 10.2307/413960
Spears, Arthur K. 1988. Black American English. In *Anthropology for the Nineties*, edited by Johnnetta B. Cole, 96–113. New York: Free Press.
Spears, Arthur K. 2007. Bare Nouns in African American English (AAE). In *Noun Phrases in Creole Languages*, edited by Marlyse Baptista and Jacqueline Guéron, 421–434. Philadelphia: John Benjamins.
Spears, Arthur K. 2015. African American Standard English. In *The Oxford Handbook of African American Language*, edited by Sonja Lanehart, 786–799. Oxford: Oxford University Press.
Spears, Arthur K., and Leanne Hinton. 2010. Languages and Speakers: An Introduction to African American English and Native American Languages. *Transforming Anthropology* 18.1: 3–14.
Stanback, Marsha Houston. 1982. Language and Black Woman's Place: Toward a Description of Black Women's Communication. Paper presented at the Speech Communication Association.
Stanback, Marsha Houston. 1985. Language and Black Woman's Place: Evidence from the Black Middle Class. In *For Alma Mater: Theory and Practice in Feminist Scholarship*, edited by Paula A. Treichler, Cheris

Kramarae, and Beth Stafford, 177–193. Chicago: University of Chicago Press.

Taylor, Orlando. 1970. Response to "Social Dialects and the Field of Speech." In *Sociolinguistic Theory, Materials and Training Programs: Three Related Studies. Final Report*, edited by Roger Shuy, 14–22. Washington, DC: Center for Applied Linguistics.

Taylor, Orlando. 1975. Black Language and What to Do about It: Some Black Community Perspectives. In *Ebonics: The True Language of Black Folks*, edited by Robert L. Williams, 28–39. St. Louis: The Institute of Black Studies.

Taylor, Orlando. 1983. Black English: An Agenda for the 1980's. In *Black English: Educational Equity and the Law*, edited by John Chambers, Jr., 133–143. Ann Arbor, MI: Karoma.

Troutman, Denise. 1996. Culturally-toned Diminutives within the Speech Community of African American Women. *Journal of Commonwealth and Postcolonial Studies* 4.1: 55–64.

Troutman, Denise. 2001. African American Women: Talking that Talk. In *Sociocultural and Historical Contexts of African American English*, edited by Sonja L. Lanehart, 211–238. Amsterdam: John Benjamins.

Troutman, Denise. 2010. Attitude and Its Situatedness in Linguistic Politeness. *Poznań Studies in Contemporary Linguistics* 46.1: 85–109.

Troutman, Denise. 2022. Sassy Sasha?: The Intersectionality of (Im)politeness and Sociolinguistics. *Journal of Politeness Research* 18.1: 1–29. DOI: 10.1515/pr-2019-0005

Weissler, Rachel Elizabeth. 2021. *Leveraging African American English Knowledge: Cognition and Multidialectal Processing*. PhD dissertation. University of Michigan at Ann Arbor.

Weissler, Rachel Elizabeth, and Julie Boland. 2019. Sounding Like a Stereotype: The Influence of Emotional Prosody on Race Perception. In *Proceedings of the 19th International Congress of Phonetic Sciences*, edited by Sasha Calhoun, Paola Escudero, Marija Tabain, and Paul Warren, 2169–2173. Melbourne, Australia: Australasian Speech Science and Technology Association Inc.

Weldon, Tracey L. 2021. *Middle-Class African American English*. Cambridge: Cambridge University Press.

Filmography

Hall, Rebecca, director and screenplay writer. 2021. *Passing*. Netflix. 99 minutes.

Heder, Sian, director. 2021. *CODA*. Apple TV+. 111 minutes.

Hutcheson, Neal, Danica Cullinan, and Walt Wolfram, producers. 2017. *Talking Black in America*. Language & Life Project at North Carolina State University. 60 minutes. https://languageandlife.org/documentaries/talking-black-in-america/

Hutcheson, Neal, Danica Cullinan, and Walt Wolfram, producers. 2020. *Signing Black in America*. Language & Life Project at North Carolina State University. 27 minutes. www.TalkingBlackinAmerica.org

Monte, Eric, and Mike Evans, creators. 1974–1979. *Good Times*. CBS. 133 episodes.

Discography

Cardi B featuring Megan Thee Stallion. 2020. WAP. Single. Atlantic.

Jay-Z. 2017. *4:44*. Studio album. Roc Nation.

KRS–One. 2007. Hip Hop Lives (I Come Back). Track 2 on *Hip Hop Lives* (with Marly Marl). KOCH-RECORDS.

Lamar, Kendrick. 2017. *DAMN*. Studio album. TDE, Aftermath, and Interscope.

Lil Nas X. 2021. MONTERO (Call Me by Your Name). Track 1 on *MONTERO*. Columbia.

Monáe, Janelle. 2013. Hell You Talmbout. Track 22 on *The Electric Lady*. Atlantic.

Nwigwe, Tobe. 2019. Shine. Track 9 on *Three Originals*. Tobe Nwigwe.

Digital Media

The Black ASL Project. http://blackaslproject.gallaudet.edu/BlackASLProject/Welcome.html

Black Language Syllabus. April Baker-Bell and Carmen Kynard. www.blacklanguagesyllabus.com/black-language-and-hip-hop.html

International Gender and Language Association (IGALA). https://igalaweb.wixsite.com/igala

Kweli, Talib. Raekwon on Being Muslim & How NGE Ties into Wu Tang. 2021. *Facebook* September 21. https://fb.watch/aiVG9067nN

MIT's *Hip Hop Word Count*. https://docubase.mit.edu/project/hip-hop-word-count/.

North Carolina Language and Life Project. https://languageandlife.org/

Rap Genius. https://genius.com/rap-genius

Rap Genius' *Rap Stats*. https://genius.com/rapstats.

Rap Research Lab's *Mapper's Delight XR*. www.rapresearchlab.com/mappers-delight.

Rap Research Lab's *Maximum Distance. Minimum Displacement*. www.rapresearchlab.com/max-min.

Rap Research Lab's *Rap Almanac Database*. www.rapresearchlab.com/rapalmanac.

Steinmetz, Katy. 2020. She Coined the Term "Intersectionality" over 30 Years Ago. Here's What It Means to Her Today. *TIME*. https://time.com/5786710/kimberle-crenshaw-intersectionality/

Urban Dictionary. www.urbandictionary.com/define.php?term=The%20Urban%20Dictionary

Chapter 8

This Is Why We Can't Have Nice Things

Pop Culture, Social Media, and Digital Media

Introduction: *Whatcha Know Good*?[1]

AAL/USEB is ubiquitous. Not because Black folk are physically everywhere but because the appropriation of Blackness and Black culture is. Think TikTok and Instagram viral videos that continuously perpetuate the new dance craze or the new non-Black reality star or influencer. TikTok and Instagram[2] are hot spots for cultural theft from Black folks, or "appropriation" to be polite—so much so that Black folks have had to boycott these social media/digital platforms to highlight the theft and show the audacity of non-Black people who stole content from them without any credit or **h/t**. Instead,

---

1 This was a standard greeting from my maternal grandfather, the gentlest man I've ever known. RIP, Grandpa. Funny that I had no idea that this is what he was saying when I was younger because it never occurred to me that he was saying "know" and not "no." Also, his name was "Isaac," but I didn't realize that until I was an adult because, to this day, he is called [ˈaɪyi]. Same thing with my paternal grandfather's name. His name was "Isaiah." However, I didn't know that till only a few years before he died when I'd written him and he responded with the correct spelling of his name. To this day, he is called [aɪˈzɛɣ]. My cousin was named after him and his name was spelled "Izell."
2 Both TikTok and Instagram are digital social media platforms, but they differ. While both TikTok and Instagram allow for the posting of short and extended videos, TikTok focuses on videos that are set to music and that often depict dances or miming that make use of trending songs. Instagram is a platform where photos can be shared but where TikToks are cross-posted (Jamie Thomas, personal communication, December 2021).

DOI: 10.4324/9781003204756-8

they think it's a white Gen Z[3] thing when, in reality, **it's a Black thang**. From dance moves to dialogues, Black folks gettin ripped off, repackaged, and repurposed for white audiences and white wealth portfolios.[4] AAL/USEB is where language resides, so we are going where the language is and how it gets used by Black folks.

Afrofuturism and Ebonics

I was enthralled with HBO's *Watchmen* in the fall of 2019 and then HBO's *Lovecraft Country* in the summer of 2020 during the COVID-19 pandemic, a very ugly and hotly contested presidential race, and **Freedom Summer** 2020 after the murders of Ahmaud Arbery,[5] Breonna Taylor,[6] and George Floyd.[7] I/we needed these

---

3 Gen Z refers to those born between 1997 and 2012 and follow millennials. They are digital natives (i.e., raised on the internet and social media). Millennials, aka Gen Y, refers to those born between 1981 and 1996 and follow Gen X. Gen X refers to those born between the mid-1960s to 1980. Gen X follows baby boomers.
4 Theft from Blacks by whites is nothing new. There's a PBS *American Masters* documentary of Buddy Guy where Brits talk about how they honored Black talent and couldn't understand how white Americans didn't do that. The white Americans simply stole Black people's music without attribution or **respeck**—the era of race music in the early 20th century and its influence and appropriation by white musicians, blue-eyed soul, boy bands, and even rap artists. You know who they are, so I don't have to name them.
5 Ahmaud Arbery, a 25-year-old Black man, was jogging in a neighborhood when three white men chased him down and killed him near Brunswick, Georgia, on February 23, 2020. The three men were convicted of the murder on November 24, 2021.
6 Breonna Taylor, a 26-year-old Black woman medical worker, was murdered during a police raid with a no-knock search warrant at her apartment in Louisville, Kentucky, on March 13, 2020. Taylor's partner shot at the police officers because he thought they were burglars. In the gunfire exchange, Taylor was shot several times and killed. The police officers were never tried for the murder.
7 George Floyd, a 46-year-old Black man, was murdered by Derek Chauvin, a white police officer, in Minneapolis, Minnesota, on May 25, 2020, while being arrested on suspicion of using a counterfeit $20 bill. Officer Chauvin held his knee on Floyd's neck until he died as other police officers stood by with guns pointed and bystanders videorecorded the murder. Chauvin was convicted of murder on April 20, 2021.

This Is Why We Can't Have Nice Things   179

Afrofuturistic television shows. Regina King was the Black woman superhero **we didn't know we needed**. The fullness of her Blackness and the Black love between her and Cal in the limited series was everything. And what about her superhero name: Sister/a Night? It doesn't get Blacker than that by referencing both the Traditional Black Church (sacred)—where people are called Sistas and Brothas in their righteousness—and the secular, her righteous killing and [kɪkæsɪŋ] dressed in a nun's habit while wielding a balaclava in a [**bædæs**] full-length black leather hooded coat. The fact that HBO's *Watchmen* is reenvisioned as an Afrofuturistic remix of the original very white graphic novel and is a retelling of the Tulsa Race Massacre in 1921 is life giving.

Okay, definition break. *Afrofuturism*, in my very simplistic telling of it, is a future in which the Black people win and thrive. Okay, that's too simplistic—but, basically, it's a future with Black liberation and joy. It's a retelling of history, the present, and the future with Black people as the storytellers and in control of their destinies, hopes, and dreams. It's a (re)telling in which Black people inhabit all past, present, and future; you know, because Black people didn't just appear during slavery in the U.S. and neither does their history. What might be your (white people's) **fear of a Black planet** is our (Black people's) vision of joy. In Afrofuturism, we are the captains of our ships now. The future is **Black and it's beautiful**. There's a lot more theoretical detail to Afrofuturism, but this is what we will work with here.

So, given that, in HBO's *Watchmen*, that means you can have a Black woman be the hero and the god despite the title, Watch*men*, obscuring that.[8] We get a retelling of history, present, and future. White people thought they won the war but realized it was just a battle, and now they are trying to change the future. What they don't know is, **they ain't slick**. Black folks **got this on lockdown**. Cal,

---

8 Once upon a time, all writing used a so-called generic masculine form that was supposed to include all genders. Then people realized the problem with that and the need to be more inclusive, so they stopped doing that ☺. Because this is a revision of an existing older graphic novel, then, the creators rightfully maintained the so-called generic gender name even though the god in the revision is a woman—and Black at that.

the Black man superhero/god, realizes the power lies in the hands of Sista Night, a Black woman superhero who, as **Big Freedia** says in "Formation" (Beyoncé 2016a), "I **did not come to play** with you **hoes**; I came to *slay*, [bɪtʃ]." The End. **Nuff said**. HBO's *Watchmen* doesn't need a season two of the Sista Night storyline because she **did that thang**.

In HBO's *Lovecraft Country*, developed by Misha Green, a Black woman, we see yet a different Afrofuturistic take on the Tulsa Race Massacre. In this version, the white folks dominated because they had the magic. However, the pain they inflicted during the enslavement of Black people, the slave patrols, and Jim Crow was with Black folks waiting until they could turn the tables. Black women **showed up, showed out**, and **turned this mutha out**. We saw the pain of Black men, written on their bodies and souls, but Black women saved them. Hippolyta Freeman was the Black Doctor Who we need(ed). Like Afrofuturism itself, where time is not linear, Hippolyta took us backwards, forwards, sideways, and leftways. And when she was **good and ready**, she **took care of business, TCB**, y'all. And while Christina Braithwaite is concerned about her lack of power as a white woman, Ruby is able to see that white feminism is not the answer for Black women. Ruby walks in Black Feminisms while stomping on white feminism's blind spots and shortcomings. **Girrrrl**, Black folks took the magic, stomped on it, blew it and white folks up, and **kept it moving**. Know that HBO's *Lovecraft Country* is defined as horror because racism is horror,[9] enslavement of Black folks is horror, **sundown towns** are horror, and let us not forget, **Jig-a-Bobo** and the **Topsy and Bopsy** twins in this series are horror. Misha Green takes horror and provides an Afrofuturistic lens and gives us Black triumph and joy with three generations of Black women: Hippolyta Freeman, sisters Ruby and Letti Baptiste, and Diana Freeman. The future is Black, y'all.

I've included HBO's *Watchmen* and *Lovecraft Country* because they represent *embodied sociolinguistics* (Bucholtz and Hall 2016),

---

9 Some even believe that racism is like a virus (see Anderson 2021; Anderson et al. 2021).

which asserts that "language lives on the body."[10] Depictions and enactments of Afrofuturism live in and on the body. The language of Black people in Afrofuturism is Ebonics in the fullest senses of its definition. The leading Afrofuturist writers are Black women: Octavia Butler, N.K. Jemisin, Nalo Hopkinson, Nnedi Okorafor, and Tananarive Due. Afrofuturism, like Hip Hop, incorporates more than one artistic element. There's the graphic work of Black Kirby (aka John Jennings and Stacey Robinson) and Tim Fielder; the science of Alondra Nelson; the music of Sun Ra, Grace Jones, George Clinton, Parliament Funkadelic, and Janelle Monáe; the visual art of Renee Cox, Kerry James Marshall, and Wangechi Mutu; and, of course, the 2018 Marvel Universe movie *Black Panther*, directed by Ryan Coogler. And there's so much more. Afrofuturism is speaking Black Language all over the place and in so many ways. We come to **slay**, y'all, with "hot sauce in [our] bag, swag" (Beyoncé 2016a).

Ya Man, Steve Harvey: *Blacktainment* Extraordinaire

Steve Harvey, Tiffany Haddish, and Kevin Hart are making money off of their shrewdness of giving the people what they want: Black culture, Black Language, and Blacktainment (Black + entertainment). AAL/USEB has become quite performative. It's all over the place. And while these performers are "authentic" in their language use, they are also, well, performers. It's like the ESPN folks' obsession with Stuart Scott: **cain't get enough**. These performers are **making bank**. They aren't the only ones. There are many Black performers who are making bank because they are giving the people what they want: **Blackity Black Black** content. Some see the Black male performers in particular as modern-day minstrels of sorts in that they are performing Blackness in a stereotypical

---

10 I'm using the title from a wonderful NWAV49 (2021) symposium, "Language Lives on the Body: Rethinking Epistemologies of Linguistic Variation," chaired by Aris Clemons with paper presentations by deandre miles-hercules, Alexus Brown, and Jazmine Exford to explain embodied sociolinguistics. https://virtual.oxfordabstracts.com/#/event/2091/symposium/9

way. Think 1970s **Blaxploitation** (Black + exploitation) films: *Sweet Sweetback's Baadasssss Song* (1971), *Shaft* (1971), *Super Fly* (1972), *Blacula* (1972), *Cleopatra Jones* (1973), *Foxy Brown* (1974), *Uptown Saturday Night* (1974), *Dolemite* (1975), *Mandingo* (1975), *Let's Do It Again* (1975), and *Sparkle* (1976). Read and watch up, **Youngbloods**.

Blacktainment is big, though. It's not just comedy, game shows, and movies. It's also music, dance, and other creative arts. TikTok and Instagram are spaces for showcasing creativity of Black folks, but, as I noted earlier, they also expose Black creatives to appropriation, aka theft, without attribution and, therefore, without **bank**. In other words, Black folks ain't gettin paid for their creativity like the non-Black people (it ain't just white folks) who stealin they stuff is gettin paid. But in the comedy world, Harvey, Haddish, and Hart, as well as Eddie Murphy, Tracey Morgan, Tyler Perry, and Chris Rock, are getting paid like nobody's business. They laughin all the way to the bank. Their use of AAL/USEB is distinctive. How they parlay their Blackness varies a little bit, but they all capitalize on their Black Language and Black cultural signposts in particular. They are famous famous Black performers who use all the vernacular aspects of AAL/USEB with wit, charm, and cool.

Steve Harvey in his crossover to white likability is known for his mustache, "authenticity," and style. His original style was, as some might say, **ratchet**. He dressed in pimp suits. One of my favorite comedy special performances of his was in the yellow suit (Harvey 1997) or the skit about **[gʌmənt] cheese** (Harvey 1995; I'll let you Google them). Steve was lookin sharp. But that was back when he hadn't crossed over. He was **Blackfamous**, but not famous famous. *The Root* former senior writer Michael Harriot explains *Blackfamous* on Twitter in a December 13, 2019, post as

> The gap between [B]lack stardom and white anonymity. For instance: The highest possible rating on the "[B]lackfamous" scale would be someone EVERY [B]lack person knew but was unknown by EVERY white person. So, I ask: "Who is the most '[B]lackfamous' person of all time?"
>
> (https://twitter.com/michaelharriot/status/1205695846391721986)

Essence online published the top 13 (www.essence.com/celebrity/blackfamous-celebrities/), which included Frankie Beverly (and Maze), Gerald Levert, Teena Marie, Leon, and Millie Jackson. Check it out. Do you know all or some of these Blackfamous performers who are all invited to **the cookout?** I'm not going to tell you who these Blackfamous stars are. Time for you to do a little work again, like YouTube sensation "TwinsthenewTrend." **If you [dõ] know, you [bɛrə] [æks] somebody**. And AAL/USEB and Blackness are **all up in here** with these folks and more who you likely don't know. At least the article provides pictures so you'll know if you're on the right track when you do your internet searches. Then think about why they are Blackfamous and not famous famous (i.e., white famous). That's just the top 13 from an informal poll. There are so many more. For comedians, I'd add Rickey Smiley, Katt Williams, and Sommore for sure. Check em out. They all play with Black Language and culture in ways that make them important to Black audiences but not as interesting to white ones. They are too **real** instead of being just "authentic."[11] Think Denzel Washington giving his acceptance speech for winning the Academy Award for *Training Day* (2001) instead of *Malcolm X* (1992).

There's a long history of ridiculing Blackness and Black Language by white folks. That's minstrelsy. We think of it mostly these days as white people wearing blackface, but it extends to language as well. During the Ebonics Controversy, there were plenty of places that were willing to translate WAmE into mock Ebonics. Mock Ebonics, Ebonics "humor," and the like are examples of *linguistic racism* (Ronkin and Karn 1999; Scott 1998), or *linguisticism*. Rickford and Rickford (2000) note that "Ebonics jokes fall into four main categories: *-onics* jokes; jokes involving the verb *be*; translation humor; and racial caricatures" (2000, 204). Poking fun at the very word Ebonics was the first step. It involved adding *-onics* to make further "fun" and show their racism: For example, Irish American Speak = Leprechaunics, Native American Speak = Kimosabics, Spanish American Speak = Burritonics, and Oakland School Board Speak

---

11 For more on Black entertainment, see Rickford and Rickford (2000), Chapter 4, "Comedians and Actors," in *Spoken Soul*.

= Moronics (Rickford and Rickford 2000, 204). Invariant *be* (see Chapter 5) jokes were to be expected because it is quite visible in AAL/USEB and had been "recognized" by white folks for decades as a stereotyped feature of AAL/USEB, as seen in the movie *Airplane!* The scene is with Barbara Billingsley (aka the mom on *Leave It to Beaver*), a white woman passenger who served as the jive translator of two Black male passengers played by Norman Alexander Gibbs ("First Jive Dude") and Al White ("Second Jive Dude"). I don't know which is worse: The script in "**jive talk**" or the translations of it. This is typical of AAL/USEB representation in media and typical of how media expects and wants AAL/USEB to be represented by anyone who is willing: As **jive talk**. **Ooh, chile**, don't get me started on all the **Blackfishing** on social media.

The Queen of Soul to Spoken Soul

Aretha Franklin. I feel like I should just be able to stop writing now because . . . Aretha Franklin. **Nuff said**. But I know you need more. But when you say it, **put some respeck on it**. Just listen to the music. Listen to the soul. Her performance at the 2015 Kennedy Center Honors paying tribute to Carole King and the song King wrote but Aretha **owned**, "(You Make Me Feel Like) A Natural Woman" (https://youtu.be/8cF0tf35Mbo), was certainly not written in AAL/USEB, but everything about that performance by Aretha was all Black, all AAL/USEB, all the time. Just watch the reaction from the audience, especially Viola Davis and President Barack Obama. That's how I felt every Sunday morning when my mom played the all-time best-selling Aretha Franklin album *Amazing Grace* (1972): "Amazing Grace." "Mary, Don't You Weep." **Lord, [hæmɜ˞si]**. Al Green was played other days of the week. No one can outdo Al Green on a song about love other than Aretha since she is next to nobody, Baby!. "Love and Happiness" (Green 1972). "Let's Stay Together" (Green 1973). Classics. But "Respect," "I Never Loved a Man (The Way I Love You)," "Dr. Feelgood," "Do Right Woman, Do Right Man," and "Ain't No Way"—all on Franklin's 1967 album). This is being African American. This is being in community. This is Black excellence. Oh, to be **young, gifted, and Black**. I'm not saying that all African Americans think or act or feel the same way I do about Aretha and Al or even James Brown, the Godfather of Soul, and Prince, His Royal Badness/[**bædæs**] and The Purple One, but they do represent Blackness and Black excellence. They are our classical musicians among many others.

When we talk about Ebonics, we have to think about music because it's not just about the words. Language is so much more than just the words. The paralinguistic aspects of language give you **all the feels**. Aretha is the Queen of Soul because no one—and I mean no one—can sing pain, love, and pure joy like she can with a moan and groan (though some may make an argument for Mahalia Jackson). We get it in the tone, the rhythm, the head position, the facial expression, the eyes, the whole package. Of course, this reflects my biases, generation, and sociocultural context because not all Black folks are the same. "Singers, Toasters, and Rappers" in Rickford and Rickford (2000) provides a good overview as well as a case for Mahalia Jackson.

Although music is diverse and dependent on one's taste, Black music artists and performers reflect their language and sociocultural contexts in their music. Think of Beyoncé's performance at the Super Bowl L (50) Halftime show in 2016 with her new release, "Formation," and marking the 50th anniversary of the Black Panther Party. She did **slay**. That performance was epic. And I love that the ancestors refused to let Beyoncé fall (see www.youtube.com/watch?v=3hZFz3bHUAg). Speaking of "Formation," let's talk about the release of *Lemonade* (Beyoncé 2016b) and the revelation to many a white folk that Beyoncé is Black. There's a great *Saturday Night Live* skit on this that is a must see (https://youtu.be/ociMBfkDG1w) because we, **fam**, all knew it just like we all knew Whitney Houston was Black even before she married Bobby Brown and despite the whitewashing attempts by her handlers and studio. *Lemonade* is a masterpiece and statement of Afrofuturism that cannot be denied. Beyoncé proudly and defiantly proclaims her Blackness. I don't mean just African Americanness; I mean, like, Black Diaspora, Ebonics, all that. In other words, Beyoncé's *Lemonade* is, in particular, Black Feminist **AF** and one of the most profound visual albums ever. Being a visual album makes it worthy of linguistics research as a statement in Ebonics. Follow that up with her BeyChella, I mean Coachella, performance in 2018 (www.youtube.

com/watch?v=lC9JUCHzC3s). I hope you take up that challenge along with all the other Black music and performances that drip with Ebonics, like Nina Simone and Mary J. Blige but also Missy Elliott, Janelle Monáe, Kendrick Lamar, Silk Sonic, Noname, Lizzo, Megan Thee Stallion, and all the Blackfamous musicians. Again, it's not just the lyrics. It's **all the things** (see www.blacklanguagesyllabus.com/).

Black Twitter and Language Use in African American Communities

"What is Black Twitter?" I remember asking that of my friends at one point. "What is it?" "Where can I go to find it?" "Who is it?" Stop. Just stop embarrassing yourself. Black Twitter is not a place or person per se. *Black Twitter* is when Black people on Twitter tweet, retweet, like, respond, and comment collectively about a thing. When white folks mess up, Black people on Twitter—Black Twitter—will be sure to point it out (well, **er'ybody** and Fox "News"). When Black folks mess up, Black people on Twitter—Black Twitter—will be sure to point it out (think Dave Chappelle, Kevin Hart, Bill Cosby, Candace Owens, and Nicki Minaj). There are some notable Black Twitter participants such as Brittney Cooper (@ProfessorCrunk), Nikole Hannah-Jones aka Ida Bae Wells (@nhannahjones), Tressie McMillan Cottom (@tressiemcphd), Michael Harriot (@michaelharriot), Tananarive Due (@TananariveDue), Sherrilyn Ifill (@SIfill), Joy Reid aka Joy-Ann (Pro-Democracy) Reid 👀 (@JoyAnnReid and @thereidout), Imani Perry (@imaniperry), Jemele Hill (@jemelehill), and Charles Blow (@CharlesMBlow). But Black Twitter has regular Black folk too. And those regular Black folk use Black Language. They have manipulated the keyboard to represent AAL/USEB in a way that regular print media or even TV just can't or won't.

Linguistically, Black Twitter has provided a lot of respellings and just plain ol Black Language for the masses. Michael Harriot is a self-described "world-renowned **wypipologist**." On Black Twitter, it's *wypipo*. You may say and write "white people," but that doesn't cover it all. Harriot defines *wypipologist* as "a professional who has specialized knowledge in the field of Caucasian culture, including the political, economic, and social habit of white people and their history" (www.michaelharriot.com/). You see, it's not just about a respelling; it's about the heart and truth of the matter. It's the **white meat**. That's what I'm **talmbout** (i.e., another Black Twitter respelling). "Toward a Description of African American Vernacular English Dialect Regions Using 'Black Twitter'" (Jones 2015) goes into the linguistics of it all. He says there are more than 30 common respellings, such as *bofum* "both of them," *bednot* "better not," and *ioneem* "I don't even" (Jones 2015, 414). He provides samples of entire sentences that reflect AAVL; you know, like it's a system with rules and . . . Let me **stop messin**:

(1) *ioneem kno chu talmbout*
    I don't even know what you are talking about

(2) *yeen kno nun bout dat*
    you ain't know nothing about that

(3) *iont mess w those mufuggas nomo*
    I don't mess with those motherfuckers no more

He also provides a table with a sample of AAVL forms queried on Twitter (Jones 2015, 415) that includes additional respellings such as *nuffin/nutn/nuttin* "nothing," *sumfin* "something," *sholl* "sure," and *doe* "though." These are Black people using Black Twitter to express themselves and say what they want to say and how they want to say it in a space they took over for themselves and **for all the world to see**. Now, go back to Chapter 5 and do your thang with figuring all this linguistics out.

Digital Media and the Performance of Language Use in African American Communities

Podcasts, online magazines, blogs, vlogs, video games, memes, gifs, emojis, emoticons, memojis, etc. are all part of digital media. We interact with them digitally. Black people have made a home with digital media. However, like with social media, there are both pros and cons. Black folk have found places and spaces to express themselves, but that also means others have done the same to express their anti-Blackness and to steal (and I said steal, not appropriate, borrow, or imitate) our stuff, including **Blackfishing** and **digital blackface**. I told you not to let me get started on this. I'm not going to re-inflict trauma by sharing anti-Black visual images. There's enough of that. I will not share the vitriol that is so easy to find that makes fun of the deaths of Black people. I'll let you go out and find the mock AAL/USEB, nonverbal gifs and memes, digital blackface, Ebonics "humor," and all the **things that make you wanna go hmmmm** or **make you wanna holler, throw up both your hands**, à la Marvin Gaye (1971). So, instead, let's talk about how Black people **do** on digital media.

Let's start with online magazines since I love *The Root: The Blacker the Content the Sweeter the Truth*. *The Root* includes the podcasts *Very Smart Brothas*, which covers Black news, opinions, politics, and culture, and *The Glow Up*, which covers beauty and style. Of course, it all crosses platforms so you'll find it all online, Twitter, Instagram, and podcasts along with videos, photos, stories, and more. This is where the **Blackfamous** and **Black famous famous** folks be. There's so much more: *Essence* (a magazine that was created more than 50 years ago for Black women), *Blavity* (a website created by and for Black millennials), *The Grio*, and *Atlanta Black Star* (focuses on Black news, politics, entertainment, culture, and more). You can do a search for Black digital media to find many more online magazines and websites.

Podcasts for Black folks include *Therapy for Black Girls* (yes, I started with this one because I support Black therapy, especially for Black women),[12] *The Stoop*, *GirlTrek* (I discovered this during **Freedom Summer 2020**, and it was lifegiving as the world's largest Black women's and girls' health movement), *Red Table Talk*, *The Black Guy Who Tips*, *Where's My 40 Acres?*, *Black Me Up*, *This Week in Blackness* (aka *TWiB!*), *The Read* by Kid Fury and Crissle West, *The Black Language Podcast*, *Intersectionality Matters* and *Under the Blacklight* by the African American Policy Forum, *Here*

---

12 *Therapy for Black Girls* does include resources for Black people of all genders and gender identities.

to Slay by Roxane Gay and Tressie McMillan Cottom, and dozens more. Again, a search for Black podcasts will yield scores available on a variety of platforms.

I Refuse to *Eat the Cake*

I know AAL/USEB in digital spaces is important. I know AAL/USEB in pop culture and social media is important. I also know I have my limits. I hope you've received enough guidance, instruction, and learning to access all the places and spaces around you and beyond you that AAL/USEB and Black people occupy. Listen to the language and representation in your music, video games, TV programs and films, and podcasts. Critique the visual images of the memes, gifs, and other visual imagery in their language and representation of Black Language and Black folks. It's all there for you to see in Black and white. I won't show you the images and break them down in this book no matter how many times I'm told to "**Eat the cake, Anna Mae**!"

Questions, Discussion, and Further Inquiry

1. Provide examples of AAL/USEB, including its geographic and social varieties, from:

    a   Social media
    b   Digital media and podcasts
    c   Music and Hip Hop
    d   Films and TV
    e   Visual images (e.g., gifs, memes, emojis, emoticons)
    f   Dance

2. What first comes to mind when you think of AAL in digital media/social media?
3. How do you disentangle, in your own words, the differences between so-called Gen Z language and pop culture creation and AAL/USEB and Black culture creation?
4. Why is the subsection titled "Afrofuturism and Ebonics" and not "Afrofuturism and AAL/USEB"?
5. What is Black Twitter? How do you find it? Have you ever engaged with it or observed it? Provide current examples.

6 What are some Black Twitter word creations or respellings?
7 What is Afrofuturism? What examples do you know besides the ones discussed in this chapter?
8 What would your conceptualization of an Afrofuturism film entail?
9 What are some examples of *embodied sociolinguistics*?
10 How do you feel about the language used in Spotify Wrapped, and how does that usage relate to this bigger picture?
11 What are some examples of digital blackface and Blackfishing?
12 What are some solutions you could imagine to these issues in the media relating to appropriation of Black Language?
13 Who is the most Blackfamous person of all time that *you* know of?
14 How is Beyoncé's visual album *Lemonade* Afrofuturism and Blackity Black Black?
15 Who's a present-day example of Aretha Franklin, Al Green, James Brown, and/or Marvin Gaye in their music, performance, and messaging in Black Language and culture?
16 What does "eat the cake, Anna Mae" reference, and what does it mean for this chapter?
17 What do you think mock Ebonics says about the people and spaces that employed or employ it? What are some current people or spaces that engage in mock Ebonics?

References

13 Celebrities Who Are "Blackfamous," According to Black Twitter. November 4, 2020. www.essence.com/celebrity/blackfamous-celebrities/

Anderson, Riana Elyse, Nia Heard-Garris, and Ryan C. T. DeLapp. 2021. Future Directions for Vaccinating Children against the American Endemic: Treating Racism as a Virus. *Journal of Clinical Child & Adolescent Psychology*, 1–16. DOI: 10.1080/15374416.2021.1969940

Bucholtz, Mary, and Kira Hall. 2016. Embodied Sociolinguistics. In *Sociolinguistics: Theoretical Debates*, edited by Nikolas Coupland, 173–197. Cambridge: Cambridge University Press.

Jones, Taylor. 2015. Toward a Description of African American Vernacular English Dialect Regions Using "Black Twitter." *American Speech* 90.4: 403–440. DOI: 10.1215/00031283-3442117

Rickford, John Russell, and Russell John Rickford. 2000. *Spoken Soul: The Story of Black English*. New York: John Wiley and Sons.

Ronkin, Maggie, and Helen E. Karn. 1999. Mock Ebonics: Linguistic Racism in Parodies of Ebonics on the Internet. *Journal of Sociolinguistics* 3.3: 360–380.

Scott, Jerrie C. 1998. The Serious Side of Ebonics Humor. *Journal of English Linguistics* 26.2: 137–155.

Filmography

Chanda, Devin, Matt Mitchener, and Charles Todd, directors. *Buddy Guy: The Blues Chase the Blues Away*. 2021. American Masters Film. PBS. 83 minutes. www.pbs.org/wnet/americanmasters/stream-buddy-guy-blues-chase-blues-away-documentary/17954/

Coogler, Ryan, director. 2018. *Black Panther*. Marvel Studios.

Craine, William, director. 1972. *Blacula*. Power Productions/American International Productions.

Doctor Who. 1963–present. Created by Sydney Newman, C.E. Webber, and Donald Wilson. BBC. 866 episodes.

Fleischer, Richard, director. 1975. *Mandingo*. Paramount Pictures.

Fuqua, Antoine, director. 2001. *Training Day*. Warner Bros.

Harvey, Steve. 1995. *That's Deep*. HBO Comedy Half-Hour. HBO. 30 minutes.

Harvey, Steve. 1997. *One Man*. HBO Home Video. 90 minutes.

Hill, Jack, director. 1974. *Foxy Brown*. American International Pictures.

Leave It to Beaver. 1957–1963. Created by John Connelly and Bob Mosher. MCA TV. 134 episodes.

Lee, Spike, director. 1992. *Malcolm X*. Warner Bros.

Lovecraft Country. 2020. Developed by Misha Green. HBO. 10 episodes.

Martin, D'Urville, director. 1975. *Dolemite*. Dimension Pictures.

O'Steen, Sam, director. 1976. *Sparkle*. RSO/Warner Bros.

Parks, Gordon, director. 1971. *Shaft*. Shaft Productions/Metro-Goldwyn-Mayer.

Parks, Gordon, director. 1972. *Super Fly*. Superfly Ltd/Warner Bros.

Poitier, Sidney, director. 1974. *Uptown Saturday Night*. Warner Bros.

Poitier, Sidney, director. 1975. *Let's Do It Again*. Warner Bros.

Starrett, Jack, director. 1973. *Cleopatra Jones*. Warner Bros.

Van Peebles, Melvin, director. 1971. *Sweet Sweetback's Baadasssss Song*. Yeah, Inc.

Watchmen. 2019. Created by Damon Lindelof. HBO. 9 episodes.

Zucker, David, Jim Abrahams, and Jerry Zucker, directors. 1980. *Airplane!* Paramount Pictures.

Discography

Beyoncé. 2016a. Formation. Track 12 on *Lemonade*. Parkwood/Columbia.
Beyoncé. 2016b. *Lemonade*. Parkwood/Columbia, visual album.
Franklin, Aretha. 1967. Do Right Woman, Do Right Man. Track 9 on *I Never Loved a Man the Way I Love You*. Atlantic.
Franklin, Aretha. 1967. Dr. Feelgood. Track 7 on *I Never Loved a Man the Way I Love You*. Atlantic.
Franklin, Aretha. 1967. I Never Loved a Man (The Way I Love You). Track 3 on *I Never Loved a Man the Way I Love You*. Atlantic.
Franklin, Aretha. 1967. Respect. Track 1 on *I Never Loved a Man the Way I Love You*. Atlantic.
Franklin, Aretha. 1968. Ain't No Way. Side B Track 5 on *Lady Soul*. Atlantic.
Franklin, Aretha. 1972. *Amazing Grace*. Atlantic.
Franklin, Aretha. 1972. Amazing Grace. Side 2 Track 3 on *Amazing Grace*. Atlantic.
Franklin, Aretha. 1972. Mary, Don't You Weep. Side 1 Track 1 on *Amazing Grace*. Atlantic.
Gaye, Marvin. 1971. Inner City Blues (Make We Wanna Holler). Track 9 on *What's Going On*. Tamla.
Green, Al. 1972. Love and Happiness. Track 3 on *I'm Still in Love with You*. Hi.
Green, Al. 1973. Let's Stay Together. Track 1 on *Let's Stay Together*. Hi.

Digital Media

Aretha Franklin Brings President Obama to Tears Performing at Kennedy Center Honors. *YouTube*, uploaded by FNA Music Group, December 30, 2015. www.youtube.com/watch?v=8cF0tf35Mbo
Atlanta Black Star. https://atlantablackstar.com/
Beyoncé Live at Super Bowl 2016. Formation + Final—Full Performance. *YouTube*, uploaded by BEYONCÉ Paris, August 11, 2019. www.youtube.com/watch?v=3hZFz3bHUAg
Beyoncé—The BeyChella Show 2 2018—Full Show—Second Show—Week Two. *YouTube*, uploaded by BEYONCÉ Paris, August 5, 2018. www.youtube.com/watch?v=lC9JUCHzC3s
The Black Guy Who Tips. www.theblackguywhotips.com/
The Black Language Podcast. Hosted by Anansa Benbow. https://blacklangpod.buzzsprout.com/
Black Me Up. Hosted by Lily L and Dae Yunique. https://pod.link/BlackMeUpPodcast

Blavity. https://blavity.com/

Dr. Riana Elyse Anderson—TEDxDetroit 2021. Hosted by TEDxDetroit. https://youtu.be/pLLlOJH0EQo

Essence. www.essence.com/

GirlTrek. www.girltrek.org/

The Glow Up. Hosted by Casey Carter and Naomi Raven. https://theglowupcast.com/

The Grio. https://thegrio.com/

Harriot, Michael [@MichaelHarriot]. "Blackfamous." *Twitter*, December 13, 2019. https://twitter.com/michaelharriot/status/1205695846391721986

Harriot, Michael. "Wypipologist." www.michaelharriot.com/

Here to Slay. Hosted by Roxane Gay and Tressie McMillan Cottom. A Luminary original podcast. www.heartoslay.com/

Intersectionality Matters. Hosted by Kimberlé Crenshaw. African American Policy Forum. www.aapf.org/intersectionality-matters

The Read. Hosted by Kid Fury and Crissle West. http://thisistheread.com/

Red Table Talk. Hosted by Jada Pinkett Smith, Willow Smith, and Adrienne Banfield-Norris. https://redtabletalk.com/

The Root. www.theroot.com/

The Stoop. www.thestoop.org/

Therapy for Black Girls. https://therapyforblackgirls.com/

This Week in Blackness. Hosted by Elon James White. https://thisweekinblack.livejournal.com/

TwinsthenewTrend YouTube Channel. Hosted by Tim Williams and Fred Williams. www.youtube.com/channel/UCopm4iCRGWS6PkLB8uDe-Wg

Under the Blacklight. Hosted by Kimberlé Crenshaw. African American Policy Forum. www.aapf.org/blacklight

Very Smart Brothas. www.theroot.com/very-smart-brothas

Where's My 40 Acres? https://open.spotify.com/show/3IurP0FS6QHvdeUnOfCB6P

Chapter 9

It's Not the Shoes, Bruh! You Black!

African American Language Use in AmeriKKKa's Educational ApparatU.S.

Introduction: *That's the Way of the World*

The serious study of AAL/USEB was spurred by a concern after court-mandated school desegregation that AAL/USEB, particularly AAVL/VUSEB, was hindering African American children's educational achievement. As such, language and linguistics scholars have been studying the connection between AAL/USEB and education for more than 60 years. There has been much research on AAL/USEB and reading, writing, learning, communication or speech disorders, codeswitching/styleshifting, and other applied linguistics and educational linguistics concerns. Historically, these studies presumed something was wrong with Black children: "Why are Black children struggling readers?" (i.e., "Why can't Malik read?") "Why are Black children struggling writers?" (i.e., "Why can't Malik write?") "Why don't Black children speak like white children? (i.e., "Why can't Malik use correct/good English?") "Why aren't Black children the same as white children?" (i.e., "Why we gotta educate other people's children?"; see Delpit 2006). Those deficit and racist perspectives were challenged and soundly throttled, but they still remain in scholarship that seeks to "discover" why Black children just cain't be like white children or why Black children just won't go away. Those perspectives are ever with us—like cockroaches. Given the American educational system and their (i.e., the people who created it and those who maintain it) logic, a better not better question might be why American students are getting their [æsɪz] kicked internationally. So, please stop asking or talking about the

DOI: 10.4324/9781003204756-9

Black-White Achievement Gap. Better still, stop talking about achievement gaps. **It's not the shoes**! It's because we ain't white and we are in the "Unequal Opportunity Race" (see https://vimeo.com/25362993).

All these people doing this "Why can't . . .?" work act like Black children weren't educated before *Brown v. Board of Education of Topeka*. I think some people believe *Brown I* and *II* were about getting Black children in schools with white children so their whiteness could rub off. It wasn't. Black people weren't asking to have their children sit next to white children—they were asking to have the same resources that white schools received. They wanted equality and equity because they hadn't received it in the hundreds of years of our existence in this country. They wanted their **40 acres and a mule**. Instead, they got mass firings of Black teachers; Black children sitting next to white kids in classrooms they had to get to under the protection of law enforcement and/or busing to white schools instead of the reverse; white teachers who hated them and didn't want to teach them; tracking as the new segregation within schools; white flight; privatization of schooling (which is why there has been a movement for the government to fund private education through vouchers along with the rise of charter schools to the detriment of public education funding, which is already scarce due to years of underfunding and massive cuts); and the dissolution of multi-class Black neighborhoods that housed the Black literati and working-class alike. They pulled the **okey-doke** because that's what equality has looked like in the U.S.

> I wanted to make a statement that the whole problem of Black children going to school and not learning standard English is a relatively recent phenomenon. It is not the case that Black people used to go to school came out the way they went in, okay? I went to school during the 1940s and 50s. We didn't go to school as speakers of Black English. We went to school understanding that the purpose of school was to clean up whatever you took in. . . . Since desegregation you've had to deal with the weight of color. When we went to school, we just went to school. You didn't go to school as a Black child, you just went to school as a child. . . . The weight of race is something Black people have

to carry today. When I went to school, I did not carry the weight of race.... During the period of segregation there was not such a thing in your mind as you were going to a Black school.... You were simply going to school and the assumption was that you were going to school to learn because you had something to do there you couldn't do away from school, and that's learn something.

> (Professor Richard Wright, Howard University, as quoted from his appearance on the Gordon Elliot television show in January 1997, as quoted in Baugh 2000, 109–110)

This is a recurring message in Baugh (2000): This nation will not heal and cannot move forward until it redresses not only the linguistic consequences of slavery in America (i.e., linguistic justice) but all consequences for a racial reckoning (Lanehart 2007, as well as the many calls for reparations).

How and When We Enter White Educational Spaces . . . and Some Definitions

It matters how and when people enter these educational spaces. According to the late anthropologist John Ogbu in his seminal work *Minority Education and Caste* (1978), how minoritized immigrants get to a country—voluntarily or involuntarily—matters. *Voluntary minoritized immigrants* don't have the invisible shackles of enslavement or colonization of the place they choose to enter. They chose to go where they went on their own accord. *Involuntary minoritized immigrants*, or caste-like minoritized immigrants, were enslaved and colonized and brought to spaces they did not choose or want to go. This situation exists around the world, but Obgu's focus was the U.S. and the impact it had on American slave descendants, especially the educational and linguistic impacts. Ogbu's collaboration with anthropologist Signithia Fordham, who also studies how race influences Black children's educational experiences in classrooms, led to his interest in her work on *acting white* (Fordham and Ogbu 1986). Her concept of "acting white" (Fordham 1996) as well as *racelessness* (1988) and *gender passing* (1993) are extensions of DuBois's *double consciousness* (1903) and Smitherman's *push-pull* (1977).

Acting white is the concept that Black students who achieve school or academic success and/or have an interest in learning are acting white. ☺ A retort, of course, is, "What is acting Black?" It completely overlooks or dismisses the long history of Blacks and education, as well as a history of Africans and civilization that did not begin with chattel slavery in the Americas. It also is the short-sighted view that Black education only began when white folks made it legal for Blacks to learn to read and write. You do know Black folks existed before slavery, right? I think "acting Black" is upholding the dreams, fortitude, perseverance, and persistence of our ancestors and our heritage of excellence and greatness. "Acting Black" is knowing who you are and whose you are. It's knowing that your story began not on the Middle Passage but in Mother Africa. "Acting Black" is knowing that we are a remarkable people and that our children are **young, gifted, and Black**. Telling me I'm "acting white," then, is you **calling me outta my name**. Remember, **we don't play that**.

Racelessness is the concept that high-achieving Black students are pulled between white norms of success and Black culture and community solidarity. I talk about my own experiences with this in *Sista, Speak!* (Lanehart 2002) and reference others who have done the same, such as David Mura, a third-generation Japanese American poet and memoirist whose parents were interned in the U.S. during World War II:

> What I am now trying to do in my writing and my life is to replace self-hatred and self-negation with anger and grief over my lost selves, over the ways my cultural heritage has been denied to me, over the ways that people in America would assume either that I am not American or, conversely, that I am just like them; over the ways my education and the values of European culture have denied that other cultures exist. I know more about Europe at the time when my grandfather came to America than I know about Meiji Japan. I know Shakespeare and Donne, Sophocles and Homer better than I know Zeami,

Basho or Lady Murasaki. This is not to so say I regret what I know, but I do regret what I don't know.

(1988, 163)

Booyah! Mic drop. This gives me **all the feels** because I have lived this. I have walked this walk, and I know the journey of this realization. Some don't make it (I won't name some of the well-known ones but I'll let you fill in the blank here). I'm glad I made it.

Gender passing is Black girls resisting the concept of femaleness as white middle-class womanhood and articulating their Blackness in all the ways that try to make them see themselves as less than. It's anti-*respectability politics* and the *cult of true womanhood*. It means, yes, we can be angry because we have a right to be. Yes, we can be loud if we want to (do you even hear us?). Yes, we can let our curves show in our **thick**ness. Yes, we can **wear our hair natural and nappy**. We can be **unapologetically Black** with our **Black Girl Magic. Say that!**

"Acting white," "racelessness," and "gender passing" are all about race and identity, language and identity, gender and identity, etc.—they're about our stories and being ripped apart from/by our identities with another force trying to impose an alien identity onto us (this is the stuff of science fiction/fantasy–like hive mind or body snatching, but we have an answer for that: Afrofuturism). These all exemplify racism as a parasite or virus latched onto our bodies and minds as hosts that play havoc with our culture, language, mind, body, and just living our lives as highly melanated humans. Can you see how we've got all of these concepts for trying to explain the space that Black children are allowed to take in schools and education because these spaces were not meant for us and they will never love us? If Black children are to thrive in educational contexts that were not meant for them and that will never love them, then what does that say about **when and where we enter**?

While we're at it, let's go ahead and define styleshifting, codeswitching, bidialectalism, and contrastive analysis a bit more than I have already. *Styleshifting* is the notion that within a language, people shift from one dialect to another or one style to another. For example, one might switch from Southern English to whatever people think of as "good" English. In the literature, this term is mostly used for Black folks switching from AAL/USEB to WAmE, or what people consider "good" English or academic English or classroom English or, you get the point, I hope. However, for Black people, styleshifting is more than just shifting from AAL/USEB to whatever the other variety is. Making that shift often means engaging in racelessness. There is a wonderful book by two **sistas**, Charisse Jones and Kumea Shorter-Gooden, titled *Shifting: The Double Lives of Black Women in America*, that explains this battle for Black women and how it entails both racism and sexism. It was the book about **misogynoir** and how Black women tryna **get ovah** before Moya Bailey coined the much-needed term in 2010 while a graduate student at Emory University (2013, 2021).

After a while, though, some Black scholars began to question the use of the term "styleshifting" since "codeswitching" seemed better. *Codeswitching* had been used exclusively to describe how bi- and multilingual people switched between different languages they knew. So, a Spanish-English bilingual person may use both Spanish and English while speaking with someone who is likely proficient to some degree in both Spanish and English. I would do this often when I used both Latin and English in my notes and journals. In some instances, I just found myself recalling or using Latin words and phrases faster or that seemed more suited than English. I must say, I did something similar with mathematics symbols based on my time as a math major in college. Using the symbols just seemed easier and faster in some non-math-related writing instances. The idea of codeswitching and the actual articulation are more complicated than this because there are nuances to how it manifests and what is seen as codeswitching. Those complexities led these Black scholars to use "codeswitching" instead of "styleshifting" when referring to AAL/USEB and WAmE use because AAL/USEB speakers were not simply shifting the style of their speech but shifting between linguistic/language and cultural codes that represented different languages of identity. Jamila Lyiscott's TED Talk, "Three Ways to Speak English" (2014), where she does spoken word in response to a white lady calling her (a Black woman) "articulate" (https://youtu.be/k9fmJ5xQ_mc) aligns with this argument.

Given the idea of styleshifting or codeswitching, that takes us to "contrastive analysis" and "bidialectalism" as ways to "fix or repair daily" Black children in schools. (If you get the joke, high fives.)

Contrastive analysis as a study is the systematic comparison between two different languages in order to identify their similarities and differences in establishing their language genealogies. As a pedagogy with Black children, it is used to show them what one might say in AAL/USEB and then compare that to how one might say the "right," I mean same, thing in WAmE or SAmE, sort of like Google Translate. Seeing the differences is supposed to help Black children see that using WAmE or SAmE was as easy as, well, Google Translate: Type in the sentence in your language and then see the SAmE (get it?) version come out. The idea was manifested in *Bridge*, a cross-cultural reading program and series of books created by Simpkins and colleagues (1977), who were all Black. They created these books to help Black children learn to read because it was believed that AAL/USEB was interfering with literacy. However, negative reactions of Black educators and school boards who believed the curriculum was being dumbed down for Black children and the defensive attitude of the publishers in reaction doomed the *Bridge* readers until recently. The idea is that contrastive analysis is benign in its presentation. The ideology behind contrastive analysis is bidialectalism.

Bidialectalism coincided with researching AAL/USEB and "fixing" Black children in the 1960s as a way to make Black children use WAmE or SAmE in the classroom since they recognized that they were bringing AAL/USEB to schools with them. Imagine that! ☺ The pedagogical strategy said to tell children there was a time and a place for their home language, but that "home" language wasn't white, I mean, right or school language. "School" language was WAmE, though of course they called it SAmE. While the idea seemed like a compromise to telling Black children outright that their language was bad/wrong/**ignant**, they instead just said there was no place for it in school—not even on the playground. They had no idea about how language learning or child development worked—or they just didn't care when it came to Black children. I guess SOTL (scholarship on teaching and learning) only applied to white children. They just knew you couldn't bring AAL/USEB—and certainly not AAVL/VUSEB—into schools. They comforted themselves by believing that they were trying to do right by these poor, unfortunate children (you know, "kill the Indian" mentality). But they **had another thing coming**.

While SAmE has been a prominent goal for educating AAL/USEB-speaking children, another one has been tackling the issue of reading and literacy proficiency. Reading is foundational in education. Reading proficiency is an indicator of whether a child will drop out of school. There are many factors that contribute to why children leave or are pushed out of school (see Morris 2015), but reading and literacy are what we can address in this book because that falls into what sociolinguists and educational linguists can contribute. As I indicated earlier in this chapter, reading/literacy is how a lot of scholars entered the conversation on AAL/USEB, in particular in the 1960s and 1970s. White liberal educators were trying to get Black children to learn WAmE/SAmE and trying to teach them to read and write. AAL/USEB was seen as a barrier to making that happen. While there had been varying results about whether or how AAL/USEB interfered with reading and writing proficiency, Labov (2001) concluded that AAVL/VUSEB did, in fact, interfere with reading and writing proficiency (e.g., the silent -*e* rule just didn't work for AAVL/VUSEB-speaking children). There are many other linguistic factors involved in the learning of WAmE for children whose native variety is AAL/USEB. But, as Foster (1997), Ladson-Billings (1994/2009), and many other researchers have shown, good (Black) teachers **work it out, honey**.

We Ain't Havin It!: Let's *Get on the Good Foot*

Approaches to studying AAL/USEB in educational contexts have primarily involved trying to remake Black children into white children in how they talk, what they read and write, how they act, how they live, how they be. A Southern white professor at the University of Texas at Austin (my alma mater!), James Sledd,[1] spoke to trying to turn Black children into white children:

> Because people who rarely talk together will talk differently, differences in speech tell what groups a man [sic] belongs to.

---

1 I never had the opportunity to meet Dr. James Sledd, personally. He had already retired by the time I was an undergraduate student at the University of Texas at Austin. I was introduced to his writings by his colleagues at the university. However, I knew that if Docta G gave him props in her article "English Teacher, Why You Be Doing the Thangs You Don't Do?" then I knew I could—and can—too.

> He [sic] uses them to claim and proclaim his [sic] identity, and society uses them to keep him [sic] under control. The person who talks right, as we do, is one of us. The person who talks wrong is an outsider, strange and suspicious, and we must make him [sic] feel inferior if we can. That is one purpose of education. In a school system run like ours by white businessmen, instruction in the mother tongue includes formal initiation into the linguistic prejudices of the middle class.
>
> (Sledd 1969, 1307)

> Bidialectalism is the attempt to require [B]lack children in the schools to learn middle-class white English for use on all occasions which the middle-class white world considers worth its while to regulate, so that by mollifying their white masters young [B]lacks may achieve the upward mobility in the mainstream culture which otherwise the whites will permanently deny them. The bidialectalist does not argue that one language or dialect may in itself be better than another. Instead, he [sic] imagines a nightmare world in which white prejudice must remain as an eternal obstacle to [B]lack advancement unless [B]lack children consent to remake themselves in a white image.
>
> (Sledd 1973, 770)

That's the way of the world (Earth, Wind, and Fire [1975], y'all).

You would think that with Sledd's work and Labov's (1972) seminal work, "The Logic of Nonstandard English," and other white liberal (male) scholars that would have been the end of deficit theory, bidialectalism, and linguisticism. But you know **we understood the assignment**: Pre K–12 Schools and the Academy are not meant for us, and they are not meant to love us or our scholarship. Baker-Bell (2020, 5) spells it out for you:

"You on the Wrong Side of History, Bro." *Linguistic Justice* Is for Teachers Like You!

Teacher: In order to dismantle white supremacy, we have to teach students to code-switch!

Baker-Bell: If y'all actually believe that using "standard English" will dismantle white supremacy, then you not

> paying attention! If we, as teachers, truly believe that code-switching will dismantle white supremacy, we have a problem. If we honestly believe that code-switching will save Black people's lives, then we really ain't paying attention to what's happening in the world. Eric Garner was choked to death by a police officer while saying "I cannot breathe." Wouldn't you consider "I cannot breathe" "standard English" syntax?

Yeah, I, I mean she, said it. Y'all all heard it. **She said what she said**!

In addition to Baker-Bell's linguistic justice is another story to be told to show how this chapter is going to play out: *Fugitivity*—Blackness that "exploits and subverts the very invisibility that white patriarchal imperialism imposes on them" (Moody 2018)[2]—and *abolitionism*, as described by Ruth Wilson Gilmore on the Rustbelt Abolition Radio episode "What Do We Mean by Abolition?" (https://rustbeltradio.org/2017/01/01/ep01/):

> I am an abolitionist. Abolition. Abolition is a plot against racial capitalism, which is all capitalism, not just some of it. It is a plot in a narrative sense. It is a plot in which the arc of change is always going resolutely toward freedom. It is a plot in a geographic sense. It is a plot in which we aim to make all space, not just some space, free in two senses. Free in the sense that

---

2 This is a very short article that says a lot. Besides supporting #CiteASista and #CiteBlackWomen, which means I purposefully did not cite a (white) man, this sista is **fire**. Her specialty is Black women's auto/biography and life writing. The full quote I'd like to share is: "If you assume [B]lack women's life writings locate a free subjectivity within white patriarchal imperialist spaces, rather than in a self-conscious and choreographed fugitivity, then you will not read the texts they write. For even before Phillis Wheatley engaged in eighteenth-century transatlantic migrations, [B]lack women's life narratives have inscribed, and continue to document, our fugitive disidentifications. To disregard [B]lack women's fugitivity is to risk misreading [B]lack women's lives and life writings. Anti-[B]lackness everywhere has always required [B]lack women to construct a fugitive selfhood that exploits and subverts the very invisibility that white patriarchal imperialism imposes on them" (Moody 2018, 636).

it cannot be alienated—which is to say, sold by anybody to anybody—and free in the sense of non-exclusive. There is no boundary or border that we keep somebody in or keep somebody out. That is abolition. That's the plot. That's my plot. It is an internationalist impulse that is part of what many of us call the Black Radical Tradition, which is open for all [it's not just for Black people].

It doesn't get much Blacker than that. Oh, wait, yes it does:

> While the Underground Railroad and runaway slaves like Harriet Tubman are iconic, the purpose of their escapes and absolute refusal of enslavement *is a away that you live your life and understand yourself.* This means that I cannot locate myself in the radical traditions of people like Harriet Tubman and then turn around and say that there is something about white institutions that I must simply accept. I am choosing Black [R]adical [T]raditions and [F]ugitivity and [A]bolition instead.
>
> (Kynard 2021)

Now that you know how it is and how it's gon be, **let's get it started in here** (Black Eyed Peas 2004).

We Come From a Remarkable People

Black people care about education. **Periodt!** They care about schooling. And in the midst of all those things that stood in their way for an education, they persisted. Enslaved Blacks maintained their orality and encoded it into ways of being in spite of everything telling them not to. They carry this on to this day. We see it in the continued existence of AAL/USEB despite everything every day that has tried to kill it, to kill them, and has failed. That is one of the reasons why Lucille Clifton's poem "won't you celebrate with me" (1993)[3] has been my email signature for so many years:

---

3 To hear Lucille Clifton read her powerful poem, see https://youtu.be/XM7q_DUk5wU.

It's Not the Shoes, Bruh! You Black! 205

won't you celebrate with me
what i have shaped into
a kind of life? i had no model.
born in Babylon
both nonwhite and woman
what did i see to be except myself?
i made it up
here on this bridge between
starshine and clay,
my one hand holding tight
my other hand; come celebrate
with me that everyday
something has tried to kill me
and has failed.[4]

Our history of perseverance, of persisting in spite of it all, is reflected in our language, our culture, our identities, our lives, **yet and still**. I cannot write this chapter or do this work without believing and knowing that **a change is gonna come** as we each play our part.

White settler-colonial schooling and education perspectives show a profound failure of imagination and will to teach Black American children. You cannot teach Black children if you don't love Black children (just see Uncle Jimmy 1979 again). And you certainly can't teach them if your goal is to teach them to hate themselves. And just to be clear: Teaching Black children to codeswitch or be bidialectal for the sake of making white people comfortable is **educational malpractice** (Baugh 1999). It is akin to "kill the Indian to save the child" mentality and **we are not here for it**! We have seen the evidence of how that turned out in Canada and the U.S. for Native Americans/Indigenous Peoples but we wanna ack like that didn't happen to Black children? (I feel the introductory narration of *The Six Million Dollar Man* coming on: "We can rebuild him. We have the technology. We can make him better than he was. Better,

---

4 Lucille Clifton, "won't you celebrate with me" from *The Book of Light*. Copyright © 1993 by Lucille Clifton. Reprinted with the permission of The Permissions Company, LLC on behalf of Copper Canyon Press, coppercanyonpress.org.

stronger, faster.") That's how we get nonsense saying Black children "acting white" when they want to learn, when they want an education. Just make sure it's not an **edumacation**.[5]

Don't **get it twisted**. I am all for everyone learning multiple languages. Research has shown the benefits of being at least bilingual. Why you think all them white parents enrolling they kids in bilingual schools so much so that there's no room for regular POC to get their kids in those schools? Why you think there's a whole podcast on how "nice" white parents took over a public school in New York City serving mostly Black and Latinx students and wanted the preferred "foreign" language to be French?[6] Why you think Black folks speaking a non-English language is seen as a novelty act by white folks or that the assumption is that Black folks don't or cain't speak a non-American English language? C'mon, man. They🍎 don't🍎 wanna🍎 teach🍎 our🍎 kids🍎! **Yet and still**. Richard and Oracene Williams—in the midst of coming out of Compton in the 1980s (that's right, the Rodney King, Crips and Bloods, crack epidemic 1980s)—raised a family of Black professional women, most notably Venus and Serena Williams. They educated—not **edumacated**—their girls to become Black women who know who they are and where they come from. Carla O'Connor's 1997 article, one of my favorites, takes down the whole theory of "acting white" and talks about the impact on Black children who were raised by Black parents that instilled Black language and culture in them so they could **know the assignment** and not be fooled (see Uncle Jimmy again). Their parents were imbued with Blackness. They all had a Richard and Oracene Williams in their lives. They would not be moved from their Blackness, their language, their culture, and they thrived in schools because they are **young, gifted, and Black**.

---

[5] There is a great example of what edumacation will do for you in Gloria Naylor's *Mama Day*.

[6] *Nice White Parents* is a *New York Times* podcast that examines the relationship between white "liberal" parents and the public school down the block over the course of 60 years.

The Research: Language and Linguistic Justice for Black Children

Rickford et al. (2013) provide over 1,600 references on AAVL/VUSEB, English-based creoles, Latinx English, Native American English, and other English vernaculars in the U.S., as well as Aboriginal English in Australia in educational contexts in their comprehensive, annotated, topic-coded bibliography. It is the place you should start if you're at all interested in investigating and contributing to the conversation on AAL/USEB and/in education. I only wish there was an updated, second edition on the way to include the latest research (hint hint if the authors are reading this).

Hollie (2018), LeMoine (1999), and Richardson (2003) address teachers and their beliefs of AAL/USEB in classrooms and how they might use culturally and linguistically relevant pedagogy. These are expansions on and in conversation with work by Gloria Ladson-Billings and her concept of *culturally relevant pedagogy/teaching* (1992, 1994, 1995/2009, 2014), then Geneva Gay's *culturally responsive teaching/pedagogy* (2000/2010/2018), and then Django Paris's *culturally sustaining pedagogy* (2012). The idea is that the culture, language, and literacy practices of Black students matter. Children don't enter schools as empty vessels to be filled. Their sociocultural and historical contexts matter and everything they bring with them to the classroom. Attempts to separate their culture and language, or "kill the Indian" mentality, don't work for educating Black children—or any (BIPOC) children.

Craig and Washington (2006) address issues around AAL/USEB in schools from the perspective of speech-language pathology and the problems of the instruments and measures that struggle to distinguish speech-language pathologies from speech-language differences, or variation (i.e., AAL/USEB). Researchers at the University of Massachusetts Amherst changed the instruments instead of changing the child because they didn't believe the child was broken (Seymour et al. 2003a, 2003b, 2005). The system was broken, and the instruments used to diminish the child were broken. So, like

Star Trek's Captain James Tiberius Kirk, they changed the conditions of the test so Black children could win.[7]

Baugh's *Out of the Mouths of Slaves* (1999) provides a scathing analysis of how AAL/USEB is (mis)perceived, (mis)addressed, and (mis)characterized by schools, public policies, and educators who are, therefore, guilty of language and educational malpractice of African American, AAL/USEB-speaking children and youth. Though this book was published a couple of years after the Oakland Ebonics Controversy (see Chapter 3), it contains research essays that were previously published. Still, I think that makes the case even more of how persistent this issue has been and how arguments have consistently been made, proven, and made and proven again that language and educational malpractice are part of a history of systemic racism that is embedded in schools, pedagogies, and curricula.

April Baker-Bell's *Linguistic Justice* (2020) provides a new approach to addressing AAL/USEB in educational contexts: Tackle systemic, institutional racism and white supremacy and an education system that was not meant for Black children. It is the book **we have been waiting for**. And not just the book. **TOP**[8] **got next/ now**. In addition to *Linguistic Justice* and NCTE's (National Council of Teachers of English) *Students' Right to Their Own Language* (https://ncte.org/statement/students-right-to-their-own-language/),

---

7 I'm Team Star Trek. *Star Trek: The Original Series* (Roddenberry 1966–1969). It only lasted for three seasons, but it is a huge science fiction entity. There have been several movies based on TOS (the original series), including the memorable *Star Trek II: The Wrath of Kahn* (Meyer 1982). In *Star Trek II*, we learn that the Kobayashi Maru was a no-win test that Starfleet cadets took to assess their command capabilities—but Kirk beat the test. His son tells him that he cheated, but Kirk replies that he simply changed the conditions of the test. Classic Kirk. Interestingly, the latest *Star Trek* series, *Star Trek: Discovery* (Fuller and Kurtzman 2017–2022), which has a Black woman as the main character, has an episode titled "Kobayashi Maru" for the season 4 premiere on Paramount+. The episode frequently references *Star Trek II: The Wrath of Kahn*. In a nod to my other favorite science-fiction series, *Doctor Who* (Newman, Webber, and Wilson 1963–1989), and *New Who* (2005–present) in particular, "spoilers."

8 This is an inside reference. If I told you, I'd have to **murck** you.

Baker-Bell and her TOP[9] on the 2020 CCCC (Conference on College Composition and Communication, a part of NCTE) Special Committee on Composing a CCCC Statement on Anti-Black Racism and Black Linguistic Justice, or, Why We Cain't Breathe—Bonnie J. Williams-Farrier, Davena Jackson, Lamar Johnson, Carmen Kynard, and Teaira McMurtry—pushed for better linguistic justice advocacy from NCTE and classroom teachers. The culmination of their work was *This Ain't Another Statement! This Is a DEMAND for Black Linguistic Justice!* (https://cccc.ncte.org/cccc/demand-for-black-linguistic-justice) as a new policy demand for NCTE and CCCC to live by and advocate. That list demands that:

1 Teachers stop using academic language and standard English as the accepted communicative norm, which reflects White Mainstream English!
2 Teachers stop teaching Black students to codeswitch! Instead, we must teach Black students about anti-Black linguistic racism and white linguistic supremacy!
3 Political discussions and praxis center Black Language as teacher-researcher activism for classrooms and communities!
4 Teachers develop and teach Black Linguistic Consciousness that works to decolonize the mind (and/or) language, unlearn white supremacy, and unravel anti-Black linguistic racism!
5 Black dispositions are centered in the research and teaching of Black Language!

They ain't playin, y'all (Morgan 2021). Forget the trope of the **Angry Black Woman**. We have a right to be angry. I am the mother of a Black son and I can't not be angry. As Dr. David Banner, aka The Hulk, says in Marvel's *The Avengers* (2012) when the enemy was **cuttin up**, "That's my secret, Captain [America], I'm always

---

9 April Baker-Bell was my first NCTE Cultivating New Voices among Scholars of Color Program (CNV) mentee. CNV began in 2000 and has been fulfilling its mission of cultivating SOC in leadership and scholarship in language, literacy, teacher education, English, and cultural studies. All of Baker-Bell's co-conspirators on the committee have been involved in CNV in some capacity. **Keep on keepin on**, CNVers.

angry." It's my superpower. And **shonuff**, it's TOP's superpower too. Like I said: They🍵 ain't🍵 playin🍵.

You saw the previous quote from Baker-Bell (2020) about codeswitching. That was an exchange between her and a male teacher, who was a Black man 🍵. I don't want to get too deep in the weeds on that one, but suffice it to say, colonized, edumacated minds are for real. I'll refer you to my review of the book (Lanehart 2021) for more on that if you're interested. But before I go, I want you to let the chapter titles from Baker-Bell (2020) marinate:

Chapter 1, Black Language Is Good on Any MLK Boulevard
Chapter 2, What's Anti-Blackness Got to Do Wit It?
Chapter 3, Killing Them Softly
Chapter 4, Scoff No More
Chapter 5, Black Linguistic Consciousness
Chapter 6, THUG [The Hate You Give][10] Life: Bonus Chapter: Five Years after Leadership Academy

Finally, I want you to know what linguistic justice is from the lady herself:

Linguistic Justice, the book and the framework, is about Black Language and Black Liberation. It is an antiracist approach to language and literacy education. It is about dismantling Anti-Black Linguistic Racism and white linguistic hegemony and supremacy in classrooms and in the world. As a pedagogy, Linguistic Justice places Black Language at the center of Black students' language education and experiences. Linguistic Justice does not see White Mainstream English as the be-all and end-all for Black speakers. Linguistic Justice does not side-step fairness and freedom. Instead, it affords Black students the same kinds of linguistic liberties that are afforded to white students.

---

10 This title is in reference to the popular young adult novel by Angie Thomas that was made into a movie, *The Hate You Give*, and often abbreviated as THUG. It's also in reference to Tupac's theory, THUG LIFE, an acronym for "**The Hate U Give** Little Infants Fucks Everyone" (Baker-Bell 2020, 124)

Within a Linguistic Justice framework, excuses such as "that's just the way it is" cannot be used as justification for Anti-Black Linguistic Racism, white linguistic supremacy, and linguistic injustice. Telling children that White Mainstream English is needed for survival can no longer be the answer, especially as we are witnessing Black people being mishandled, discriminated against, and murdered while using White Mainstream English, and in some cases, before they even open their mouths.
(Baker-Bell 2020, 7)

That is abolitionist talk right there. And it's **right on time**.

Language of Black America on Trial: The Ann Arbor "Black English" Trial and the Oakland Ebonics Controversy

Language and linguistic scholars as well as educators and other social scientists began serious scholarship on AAL/USEB in the 1960s and 1970s because of concerns that working-class African American students were academically less successful after school desegregation was mandated by the U.S. Supreme Court with the *Brown I* and *II* decisions in 1954 and 1955 because of their language and culture. Mind you, as schools began to take the decisions seriously (i.e., obey the law), Black teachers were fired because they weren't white enough (cough), I mean, good enough to teach in white schools 👀; Black children were bussed to white schools because white children couldn't possibly be bussed to Black schools 👀; and the Black schools that remained segregated due to neighborhood school policies were supposed to get better funding to make them equal to white schools. (Can we talk about how that worked out for HBCUs?) These are the lies people told themselves so they could sleep better at night, I guess. **Chile, please**!

I was one of those Black kids who was bussed across town in elementary from my MLK, working-class, Black neighborhood to an all-white neighborhood and school. I rode the bus with my Black neighborhood kids and made friends with white kids. I liked my school. But I'd liked all of my schools because I was that kid: The "lame," the teacher's pet, the **Blerd**. And I remained that kid, even after that fateful day in fourth grade at Henry Wadsworth Longfellow Elementary School when my white male teacher I regularly ate lunch with in the cafeteria yelled at my friend Troy to "get your BLACK hands off of that!" His face was all red and he was visibly angry. No one verbally said anything to the teacher, but I know my heart broke a little bit and I was **shook** for a moment. Today, that teacher would be suspended. Back then, that was **just another Tuesday**. But the problem was the Black children and their language and culture, huh? (😒 and snark) I still think there are people who believe our skin color will rub off on them or whatever we touch. I guess that's why all those water fountains, restrooms, lunch counters needed to be separate 😒. That doesn't explain the literacy tests for voting, but they did the mental gymnastics to make that work then—and we are headed back in that direction if we're not careful given the assaults on the Voting Rights Act of 1965; the Supreme Court appointee trickery in 2016, 2017, 2018, and 2020; and governors and state legislatures dismantling voting rights. C'mon, man! Don't be **bamboozled**.[11]

Within 15 years of *Brown* and 10 years of language and linguistics scholars probing, all hell broke loose: *Martin Luther King Jr., Elementary School Children v. Ann Arbor School District*, aka, the *Ann Arbor* "Black English" Trial, in 1979. The Ann Arbor case was filed on behalf of several working-class, AAVL/VUSEB-speaking African American students at Martin Luther King Jr. Elementary School who were being labeled as "educationally retarded" and "learning disabled" for failing to make satisfactory academic progress (Smitherman 1981). Chambers (1983) details how the negative attitudes of teachers toward the students' AAVL/VUSEB had created a psychological barrier to their academic achievement. No kidding 😒. Yes, teachers were an impediment to the academic achievement of Black children! And **water is wet**.

Unfortunately, despite winning the battle, we lost the war. The Ann Arbor School District Board decided not to appeal the decision and, as a result, the ruling only applied to their federal district court's jurisdiction. Had they appealed and lost again, the ruling

---

[11] Watch Spike Lee's 2000 film *Bamboozled*.

would have applied nationally. However, in the case of California, since interested parties were following the trial, it decided to be proactive and respond to the issues involved in the case. The Los Angeles Unified School District, for example, created the Academic English Mastery Program directed by Noma LeMoine for 20 years (LeMoine 1999). I need to give a shout out to her colleague Sharroky Hollie, who also wrote a book to help teachers in classrooms implement the program (Hollie 2018) since this is one of the recurring themes of what teachers ask: "I believe and support what you're saying, but how do I translate what you're saying into daily action, pedagogy, and curricula in my classrooms and schools?" Because of the *Ann Arbor* decision, teachers in the district were required to take 40 hours of training to learn about AAL/USEB. They did the training and learned about AAL/USEB, but it didn't prepare them to be better teachers with the new knowledge. They needed to translate that knowledge into pedagogy and curricula. That's why books like Baker-Bell (2020), Hollie (2018), and LeMoine (1999) are so important. And that's why sociolinguists and educational linguists need to continue to be agents of change in reading and literacy of AAL/USEB-speaking Black children. That's why Lisa Green's and others' work on African American child language acquisition and development is so important.

Twenty years later, we have the Oakland Unified School District (OUSD) Board making national news and causing a firestorm—as Rickford and Rickford (2000) put it—over its plan to deal with educating African American students whose language, as they believed, was the reason they were performing poorly in schools (not racism, not white supremacy, not segregation by tracking, not redlining, not poverty, not . . . you get the point). The Oakland Ebonics Resolution recognized Ebonics as the primary language of African American students in their schools and recommended maintenance of Ebonics in addition to the acquisition and mastery of SAmE (sound familiar). What was different about the Oakland Ebonics Resolution is that it required teachers to not just learn about Ebonics and AAL/USEB research like the *Ann Arbor* case, but to learn AAL/USEB. The resolution, therefore, was saying that OUSD should be part of bilingual education funding because Ebonics as a language is, therefore, the same as asking teachers to know, for example, Spanish when they are working with children whose native language is Spanish. And even though they backtracked on this and did a "**my bad**, you must have misheard me," this was a **boss**, **bodacious** move. As such, folks **weren't having it**. Black folks didn't like it because they were still saying AAL/USEB was just "bad" English just like they did with the *Bridge* readers. Brown folks and bilingual educators **weren't having it** because they didn't want to have to include Ebonics as a language that impinged on their bilingual education funding. White folks and others **weren't having it** because they said Ebonics, AAL/USEB, and anything to do with "legitimizing" Black folks' language and communication was just malarkey and a scam for money (you know, because Black folks are always tryna steal money from the government and white folks—😒, suck teeth, and the Annalise Keating[12] meme with her purse, see https://tenor.com/search/annalise-keating-gifs—you'll know it when you see it). If the excerpt from Baugh's (2000) *Beyond Ebonics* provides you with any indication of how his book brilliantly tackles the Ebonics Controversy, then you know it's a must read. Perry and Delpit (1998), Ramirez et al. (2005), and Wolfram (1998) explore the linguistic, ideological, educational, sociocultural, and political origins and implications of these controversies, but Smitherman (2015) provides historical overviews of these AAL/USEB education controversies.

As My Dad Would Say, "Stop *Pussyfootin Roun* the Issue:" Because Racism

In "Understanding the Why of Whiteness: Negrophobia, Segregation, and the Legacy of White Resistance to Black Education in Mississippi," Jamel Donnor (2019) eloquently explains why 60 years after *Brown I* and *Brown II* we still haven't resolved Negrophobia (i.e., fear of Black people) and racism both *in* education and

---

12 Annalise Keating, played by the fabulous Academy Award-winning actress Viola Davis, is the fictional Black woman superstar lawyer and main character on the Shonda Rhimes legal drama *How to Get Away with Murder* (Rhimes 2014–2020). Her memes expressing African American Women's Language are not to be missed—or messed with.

It's Not the Shoes, Bruh! You Black! 215

as education. What's striking is that Mississippi has gotten away with **pussyfootin roun** the issue for all this time and with impunity because Negrophobia is built into the legal system and social fabric of the U.S.—not US. It's why white people can shoot Black people and legally claim they were justified due to fear—even when they did the attacking and then claimed self-defense because the Black person had the gall to fight back (Wise 2021), like Sandra Bland and Trayvon Martin. Black people fighting back is a legal claim for murder by a white person because Negrophobia is consciously or subconsciously recognized by white jurors and the judicial system as justified (Donnor 2019). This is white, systemic racism.

The impact of racism on Black language and lives, on Black education and success, cannot be overstated. There are people who dismiss the existence of racism and the impact of racism on not just Black people but all people by saying that since slavery and involuntary servitude were abolished with the Thirteenth Amendment to the U.S. Constitution in 1865, then racism ended. **That's not how this works; that's not how any of works** 🙎‍♀️. You don't wake up the next day when a law passes like that and say, "Okay, I no longer believe in white supremacy and institutional racism; I now believe Black people are equal humans and should be made whole for what we, white people, have done to them." Again, **that's not how any of this works** 🙎‍♀️. We know that's not true because Black people were never remunerated and reparations is a moot topic of discussion for most white people and the U.S. government and its policies. It's why we went from slavery to property and business thefts, segregation, slave patrols, mass incarceration, Jim Crow, literacy tests for voting, redlining, and more. It's why Black children are told to be like white children as if somehow turning metaphorically and psychologically white will somehow make them white. Whiteness is more than skin color; it's a state of mind. Remember the **HNIC** Professor Golightly from Derrick Bell's (1992) *Space Traders*? Remember James Sledd's "compassionate, liberal educators . . . will change the color of a student's vowels because they cannot change the color of their students' skins" (Sledd 1969, 1312)? The **okey-doke** is real, y'all, and it's racist **AF**. White people, especially white men, actually believe they are now the people who are most discriminated against. White men believe they receive the most discrimination in the U.S. and it's why they "struggle" for jobs. I am not making this up, but it does feel like *The Twilight Zone*.

Fortunately, we have some wonderful Black scholars who are changing the game. They are making demands and taking names. They are shining a light on linguisticism and educational malpractice through critical race scholarship, Black Feminisms, Afrofuturism, Abolitionism, Fugitivity, and just plain **speaking truth to power**. We will not sacrifice our children to try to cash that U.S. **[gʌmənt] check** that we know has insufficient funds.[13] We gon **make a way outta no way** because **that's how we do** and that's how we be. **Keep on keepin on**. **Fight the power!**

Questions, Discussion, and Further Inquiry

1 What's problematic about how scholars/linguists ask and approach these questions: Why are Black children struggling readers? Why are Black children struggling writers? Why don't Black children speak like white children?
2 What was the impact of *Brown I* and *II* on the education and language of Black children?
3 What does "I want my 40 acres and mule" mean?
4 What is *double-consciousness*, and how does it impact Black language and Black people?
5 What is bidialectalism?
6 After bidialectalism, then what?
7 What is acting white? Racelessness? Gender passing?
8 "English Teacher, Why You Be Doing the Thangs You Don't Do?" What does Smitherman (1972) mean here?
9 What is the distinction and impact between voluntary and involuntary immigrants and how they are minoritized and integrated into society?
10 When did Blackness come into being or existence?
11 Has there always been racism? If not, what was before it?
12 What is the difference between *styleshifting* and *codeswitching*?

---

13 This is in reference to Dr. Martin Luther King Jr.'s "I Have a Dream" speech in 1963 at the Lincoln Memorial in Washington, DC.

13 If Black children are to thrive in educational contexts that were not meant for them and that will never love them, then what does that say about when and where we enter and how we claim a history of a people who will not be denied educational equity and success?
14 What is *linguistic justice*?
15 Do you believe that using "SAmE" will dismantle white supremacy? How or why not?
16 Do you believe that codeswitching will save Black people's lives? How or why not?
17 What is *fugitivity*? How does fugitivity fit into conversations around AAL/USEB, linguistics, education, and society?
18 What is *abolitionism*? How does abolitionism fit into conversations around AAL/USEB, linguistics, education, and society?
19 Why you think all them white parents enrolling they kids in bilingual schools so much so that there's no room for regular POC to get their kids in those schools? Why you think there's a whole podcast on how "nice" white parents took over a public school in New York City serving mostly Black and Latinx students and wanted the preferred "foreign" language to be French?
20 Why you think Black folks speaking a non-English language is seen as a novelty act by white folks or that the assumption is that Black folks don't speak a non-American English language?
21 How do you enact linguistic justice praxis in every classroom?
22 How do you understand **the assignment** is when comes to educating Black students?

References

Bailey, Moya. 2013. New Terms of Resistance: A Response to Zenzele Isoke. *Souls: A Critical Journal of Black Politics, Culture, and Society* 15.14: 341–343. DOI: 10.1080/10999949.2014.884451

Bailey, Moya. 2021. *Misogynoir Transformed: Black Women's Digital Resistance*. New York: New York University Press.

Baker-Bell, April. 2020. *Linguistic Justice: Black Language, Literacy, Identity, and Pedagogy*. London: Routledge and NCTE.

Baugh, John. 1999. *Out of the Mouths of Slaves: African American Language and Educational Malpractice*. Austin, TX: University of Texas Press.

Baugh, John. 2000. *Beyond Ebonics: Linguistic Pride and Racial Prejudice*. New York: Oxford University Press.

Bell, Derrick. 1992. Space Traders. In *Faces at the Bottom of the Well: The Permanence of Racism*, edited by Derrick Bell, 197–242. New York: Basic Books.

Brown v. Board of Education of Topeka, 347 U.S. 483 (1954).

Brown v. Board of Education of Topeka, 349 U.S. 294 (1955).

Chambers, John, Jr., ed. 1983. *Black English: Educational Equity and the Law*. Ann Arbor, MI: Karoma.

Clifton, Lucille. 1993. Won't You Celebrate with Me. In *The Book of Light* (25). Port Townsend, WA: Copper Canyon Press.

Craig, Holly, and Julie Washington. 2006. *Malik Goes to School: Examining the Language Skills of African American Students from Preschool—5th Grade*. Mahwah, NJ: Lawrence Erlbaum.

Delpit, Lisa. 2006. *Other People's Children: Cultural Conflict in the Classroom*. New York: The New Press.

Donnor, Jamel K. 2019. Understanding the Why of Whiteness: Negrophobia, Segregation, and the Legacy of White Resistance to Black Education in Mississippi. In *Understanding Critical Race Research Methods and Methodologies: Lessons from the Field*, edited by Jessica T. DeCuir-Gunby, Thandeka K. Chapman, and Paul A. Schutz, 13–23. London: Routledge.

Fordham, Signithia. 1988. Racelessness as a Factor in Black Students' School Success: Pragmatic Strategy or Pyrrhic Victory? *Harvard Educational Review* 58.1: 54–85.

Fordham, Signithia. 1993. "Those Loud Black Girls": (Black) Women, Silence, and Gender "Passing" in the Academy. *Anthropology & Education Quarterly* 24.1: 3–32.

Fordham, Signithia. 1996. *Blacked Out: Dilemmas of Race, Identity, and Success at Capital High*. Chicago: University of Chicago Press.

Fordham, Signithia, and John U. Ogbu. 1986. Black Students' School Success: Coping with the "Burden of 'Acting White'." *The Urban Review* 18.3: 176–206

Foster, Michèle. 1997. *Black Teachers on Teaching*. New York: The New Press.

Gay, Geneva. 2000/2010/2018. *Culturally Responsive Teaching: Theory, Research, and Practice*. New York: Teachers College Press.

Hollie, Sharroky. 2018. *Culturally and Linguistically Responsive Teaching and Learning: Classroom Practices for Student Success*, 2nd ed. Huntington Beach, CA: Shell Education.

Jones, Charisse, and Kumea Shorter-Gooden. 2009. *Shifting: The Double Lives of Black Women in America*. New York: Harper Collins.

King, Martin Luther, Jr. 1963. *I Have a Dream*. Washington, DC: Lincoln Memorial Mall. www.npr.org/2010/01/18/122701268/i-have-a-dream-speech-in-its-entirety

Kynard, Carmen. 2021. Reflections from Black Feminist Compositionistas on Research, Teaching, and Writing. Presentation at the annual convention of the National Council of Teachers of English. Online.

Labov, William. 1972. The Logic of Nonstandard English. In *Language and the Inner City: Studies in the Black English Vernacular*, 201–240. Philadelphia: University of Pennsylvania Press.

Labov, William. 2001. Applying Our Knowledge of African American English to the Problem of Raising Reading Levels in Inner-city Schools. In *Sociocultural and Historical Contexts of African American English*, edited by Sonja L. Lanehart, 299–318. Amsterdam: John Benjamins.

Ladson-Billings, Gloria. 1992. Reading between the Lines and Beyond the Pages: A Culturally Relevant Approach to Literacy Teaching. *Theory into Practice* 31.4: 312–320.

Ladson-Billings, Gloria. 1994/2009. *The Dreamkeepers: Successful Teachers of African American Children*. San Francisco: Jossey-Bass.

Ladson-Billings, Gloria. 1995. Toward a Theory of Culturally Relevant Pedagogy. *American Educational Research Journal* 32.3: 465–491.

Ladson-Billings, Gloria. 2014. Culturally Relevant Pedagogy 2.0: AKA the Remix. *Harvard Educational Review* 84.1: 74–84.

Lanehart, Sonja L. 2002. *Sista, Speak! Black Women Kinfolk Talk about Language and Literacy*. Austin, TX: University of Texas Press.

Lanehart, Sonja L. 2007. If Our Children Are Our Future, Why Are We Stuck in the Past?: Beyond the Anglicists and the Creolists, and Toward Social Change. In *Talkin' Black Talk: Language, Education, and Social Change*, edited by H. Samy Alim and John Baugh, 132–141. New York: Teachers College Press.

Lanehart, Sonja. 2021. The Struggle is Real Every🖤 Single🖤 Day🖤: Doing Black Linguistic Consciousness. *American Speech* 96.2: 286–292. DOI: 10.1215/00031283-9142460

LeMoine, Noma. 1999. *English for Your Success: A Language Development Program for African American Children Grades Pre-K—8*. Maywood, NJ: The Peoples Publishing Group, Inc.

Martin Luther King Jr., Elementary School Children. v. Ann Arbor School District, 473 F. Supp. 1371 (E.D. Michigan 1979).

Moody, Joycelyn K. 2018. Fugitivity in African American Women's Migration Narratives. *Canadian Review of Comparative Literature* 45.4: 636–638.

Morgan, Marcyliena. 2021. Counterlanguage Powermoves in African American Women's Language Practice. *Gender & Language* 15.2: 289–299. DOI: 10.1558/genl.20317

Morris, Monique W. 2015. *Pushout: The Criminalization of Black Girls in Schools*. New York: The New Press.

Mura, David. 1988. Strangers in the Village. In *The Graywolf Annual Five: Multi-Cultural Literacy*, edited by Rick Simonson and Scott Walker, 135–153. St. Paul, MN: Graywolf Press.

Naylor, Gloria. 1988. *Mama Day*. New York: Ticknor & Fields.

O'Connor, Carla. 1997. Dispositions Toward (Collective) Struggle and Educational Resilience in the Inner City: A Case Analysis of Six African-American High School Students. *American Educational Research Journal* 34.4: 593–629.

Ogbu, John U. 1978. *Minority Education and Caste: The American System in Cross-Cultural Perspective*. New York: Academic Press.

Paris, Django. 2012. Culturally Sustaining Pedagogy: A Needed Change in Stance, Terminology, and Practice. *Educational Researcher* 41.3: 93–97.

Perry, Theresa, and Lisa Delpit, eds. 1998. *The Real Ebonics Debate: Power, Language, and the Education of African American Children*. Boston: Beacon.

Ramirez, J. David, Terrence G. Wiley, Gerda de Klerk, Enid Lee, and Wayne E. Wright, eds. 2005. *Ebonics: The Urban Education Debate*, 2nd ed. Clevedon, UK: Multilingual Matters.

Richardson, Elaine. 2003. *African American Literacies*. London: Routledge.

Rickford, John R., and Russel J. Rickford. 2000. The Ebonics Firestorm. In *Spoken Soul: The Story of Black English*, 161–218. New York: John Wiley & Sons.

Rickford, John R., Julie Sweetland, Angela E. Rickford, and Thomas Grano. 2013. *African American, Creole, and Other Vernacular Englishes in Education: A Bibliographic Resource*. London: Routledge.

Seymour, Harry N, Thomas W. Roeper, and Jill de Villiers. 2003a. *Diagnostic Evaluation of Language Variation: Criterion Referenced*. San Antonio, TX: The Psychological Corporation.

Seymour, Harry N, Thomas W. Roeper, and Jill de Villiers. 2003b. *Diagnostic Evaluation of Language Variation: Screening Test*. San Antonio, TX: The Psychological Corporation.

Seymour, Harry N, Thomas W. Roeper, and Jill de Villiers. 2005. *Diagnostic Evaluation of Language Variation: Norm-Referenced*. San Antonio, TX: The Psychological Corporation.

Simpkins, Gary, Charlesetta Simpkins, and Grace Holt. 1977. *Bridge: A Cross-Cultural Reading Program*. Boston: Houghton Mifflin.

Sledd, James. 1969: Bi-Dialectalism: The Linguistics of White Supremacy. *English Journal* 58.9: 1301–1315, 1329.

Sledd, James. 1973. After Bidialectalism, What? *English Journal* 62.5: 770–773.

Smitherman, Geneva. 1972. English Teacher, Why You Be Doing the Thangs You Don't Do? *English Journal* 61.1: 59–65.

Smitherman, Geneva. 1977. *Talkin and Testifyin: The Language of Black America*. Boston: Houghton Mifflin.

Smitherman, Geneva, ed. 1981. *Black English and the Education of Black Children and Youth: Proceedings of the National Symposium on the King Decision*. Detroit: Center for Black Studies, Wayne State University.

Smitherman, Geneva. 2015. African American Language and Education: History and Controversy in the Twentieth Century: A Commentary on Ebonics. In T*he Oxford Handbook of African American Language*, edited by Sonja Lanehart, 547–565. Oxford: Oxford University Press.

Wolfram, Walt. 1998. Language Ideology and Dialect: Understanding the Oakland Ebonics Controversy. *Journal of English Linguistics* 26.2: 108–121.

Filmography

Bennett, Harve, executive producer. 1973–1978. *Six Million Dollar Man*. ABC. 99 episodes + 6 tv movies.

Fuller, Bryan, and Alex Kurtzman, creators. 2017–2021. *Star Trek: Discovery*. CBS All Access/Paramount+. 44 episodes.

Lee, Spike, director. 2000. *Bamboozled*. 40 Acres and a Mule Filmworks and New Line Cinema. 135 minutes.

Meyer, Nicholas, writer and director. 1982. *Star Trek II: The Wrath of Kahn*. Paramount Pictures.

Newman, Sydney, C. E. Webber, Donald Wilson, creators. 1963–present. *Doctor Who*. BBC Studios.

Rhimes, Shondra, producer. 2014–2020. *How to Get Away with Murder*. ABC Studios and Shondaland. 90 episodes.

Roddenberry, Gene, creator. 1966–1969. *Star Trek: The Original Series*. Paramount. 79 episodes.

Whedon, Joss, director. 2012. *The Avengers*. Walt Disney Studios. 143 minutes.

Discography

Black Eyed Peas. 2004. Let's Get It Started. Bonus Track 14 on *Elephunk* re-issue. A&M Records.

Earth, Wind, and Fire. 1975. That's the Way of the World. Track 2 on *That's the Way of the World*. Columbia.

Digital Media

Baker-Bell, April, Bonnie J. Williams-Farrier, Davena Jackson, Lamar Johnson, Carmen Kynard, and Teaira McMurtry. 2020. **This Ain't Another Statement! This is a DEMAND for Black Linguistic Justice!* https://cccc.ncte.org/cccc/demand-for-black-linguistic-justice

Conference on College Composition & Communication. 1974. *Students' Right to Their Own Language*. https://ncte.org/statement/students-right-to-their-own-language/

Crenshaw, Kimberlé. 2010. *Unequal Opportunity Race*. African American Policy Forum. https://vimeo.com/25362993

Gilmore, Ruth Wilson. 2017. "What Do We Mean by Abolition? Rustbelt Abolition Radio. January 1. https://rustbeltradio.org/2017/01/01/ep01/

Joffe-Walt, Chana, host. 2020. *Nice White Parents*. Serial Productions Podcasts and *The New York Times*. 6 episodes.

Lucille Clifton reads "won't you celebrate with me." 2021. Uploaded by Mellon Foundation. April 5. https://youtu.be/XM7q_DUk5wU.

Lyiscott, Jamila. 2014. Three Ways to Speak English. TED Talk. Uploaded by TED, June 19. https://youtu.be/k9fmJ5xQ_mc.

Wise, Tim. 2021. Ahmaud Arbery's Killers Gambled and Lost, But the Game Remains Rigged. *Medium*. https://aninjusticemag.com/ahmaud-arberys-killers-gambled-and-lost-but-the-game-remains-rigged-f754d8002b4d

Chapter 10

"*If You Don't Know Me by Now* . . ."[1]

Introduction: *"You Cain't Do Wrong and Get By"*

My maternal grandmother, my original *Sista, Speak!*, who's on the cover of the book, would say, when need be, "**You cain't do wrong and get by**." For too many years, what some considered scholarship and research in language use in African American communities was us being **done wrong**. AAL/USEB was believed to be "baby talk" or worse, shoddy research was accepted, we were told we were abusing our children by what some called our lack of culture via deficit theories, we were tormented by **respectability politics**, women were ignored and excluded from research, and deficit perspectives of AAL/USEB were used to harm our children in their education, schooling, and success. And, to top it off, we were made to feel as if we were the problem. We are at the end of this book, but you still have work to do. **You ready**?

As I said, I couldn't do all the things in this book, but I did what I said I would do. That's enough to get you started. From **the get go**, you knew my subjectivities, positionalities, and just plain where I was coming from. I named, called out, and called to in each chapter. I pushed you to confront your subjectivities, attitudes and beliefs, ideologies, and more so we could have real talk about this **thang**. I showed you the good, the bad, and some of the ugly and situated

---

1 I'm going to give you this one: Harold Melvin & the Blue Notes with Teddy Pendergrass singing the lead in this 1972 number one R&B single. **Ooh, chile**!

DOI: 10.4324/9781003204756-10

it all from a critical discourse, critical sociolinguistics, Black Feminisms, and, in some ways, an Afrofuturism perspective. I provided background information for context from my inter-, multi-, trans-disciplinary interests and studies to get us to a place where we have to **name a thing a thing** for ourselves and others. I helped confront the systemic, institutional racism and white supremacy from within and without "scholarship" on Black folks that uses research on language use in African American communities as a proxy (i.e., it's not the language; it's because we Black). If more people would **call a thing a thing** and know what it feels like to be deemed a problem to a solution that can't be attained until we say the name, then maybe we could all do better and be better humans.

From there we confronted the history and development of AAL/USEB through the different theories that are grounded in subjectivities and positionalities whether they admit such or not. And from that whole discussion, the take-away for me is that they don't have the goods. They can't know and we (i.e., Black folks) don't know, but we do know we come from a remarkable people. We **did that thang**, and we will not go quietly into a racist night that would tell us we and our language are less than. We see that in all aspects of our lexicon and grammar. There are currently several dictionary projects going on that are addressing AAL/USEB in lexicography. We have AAL/USEB everywhere whether you choose to see it or not. We are across the country in every region and geographic space **making it do what it do**. We are complicated, complex, and multifaceted in our language beyond region or whether there are lakes, rivers, and mountains. It didn't just take land, water, and land masses to separate us in the U.S. Being woman, being deaf, being two degrees beyond WHAM was enough. And in the midst of all that, we still had AAWL, SAAL/SUSEB, Black ASL, HHNL, and so much more, as discussed in Chapter 7. Why would anyone ever think we are a homogeneous people? We got Spoken Soul; we are part of an Ebonics nation.

To show all of that off is how we use our Spoken Soul to speak ourselves into something beyond what men say we are.[2] We are

---

2 Just in case you don't get this, it's a reference to the Bible, Matthew 16.

Blackfamous and **Blacktainment**. We are soul and more soul. We are Black Twitter and Black excellence so you cannot make me **eat the [dæm] cake**. **You better recognize**! Afrofuturism lets us interrogate race and language from a variety of angles across time and space because time is not linear in Afrofuturism. Our time doesn't start with plantations filled with enslaved peoples. We must never forget enslavement—just like Jews don't forget the Holocaust or Japanese Americans don't forget U.S. internment camps or Native Americans/Indigenous Peoples don't forget attempted genocide and how their land was stolen. We are more than that; our language is more than that. We can see that in TikTok and Instagram, television and films, music, and digital media. We can use all that to stop lettin folks **pussyfoot roun** and let them do the work that needs to be done because **they cain't keep doin wrong and expect to keep gettin by**. That's not how this works. **That's not how any of this works**. Did you get all of that?

Things I Didn't Discuss That You Might Consider

There's so much more to AAL/USEB that I just didn't do because of constraints. However, that doesn't mean you can't do more. For example, we have people setting the record straight about how African American children acquire and develop their AAL/USEB. They acquire language just like anybody else. They are capable of bi- and multilingualism just like anybody else. One thing we (re-)learned and should have already known is that African American children don't wake up at two or three or five years old already using the full grammar of AAL/USEB. They acquire language in stages of development just like other children. So, no, they don't have or use all the "features" of AAL/USEB when they leave the womb or start Pre-K. We gotta do better if this is a lesson we had to (re-)learn.

Another big area regards terms of reclamation. There are many terms used to denigrate Black people because that's how anti-Black racism and discrimination work. The same for (Black) women, LGBTQ+, and other social demographic groups that are meant to be lower than (wealthy) WHAM. *Reclamation* is a process where offensive terms are "reclaimed" from their pejorative intentions and then ameliorated by the offended party. Such has been the case with one of the most controversial racial epithets: the *N-word*. When I say "controversial," I mean controversial in Black communities. It is not controversial in its original intent to slander and demean Black people. Black folks still know and understand that. However, the reclamation of the N-word is only seen as such by some people in Black communities. The reclamation process for those in Black communities involves conforming the word to Black linguistic norms. So, the N-word is reclaimed according to AAL/USEB norms as seen in Example 17 in Chapter 5; hence [nɪgə] and not [nɪgɚ]. Also not OK but certainly reflective of my undergraduate history professor's Southern linguistic identity expression: [nɪgɹə]. I cringed each and every time he said it, and I still remember it these more than 30 years later. Other examples of reclamation are [bɪtʃ] and *queer*, both used and applicable in our heterogeneous, intersectional, Black communities.

Another area that could use more breadth and depth is sexuality and gendered identities. Though AAWL is understudied, it is still better studied than sexuality and gendered identities overall. There is so much to learn and investigate around Black sexuality and gendered identities in particular that I don't think we have even gotten to appropriate ways of talking about and investigating the work that needs to be done. These are complex and complicated research endeavors that require new tools in addition to some of the old ones. AAL/USEB research has been hyper-focused on some things and lacking in imagination and inclusion on others. That conversation needs to change, and I hope some of **you are the change we need to see**.

There are certainly more areas in need of further discussion and research, but this is an introductory book. It does not and cannot attempt to cover everything there is. That's just not possible or realistic. Even the *Oxford Handbook of African American Language* (Lanehart 2015) could not and does not cover everything despite trying to be as comprehensive as possible. There's so much more I could have included and discussed here and in Lanehart (2015) that I didn't or only broached instead of going into more detail because of constraints. But what I hope I did was at least whet your appetite, open your mind for exploration and deep dives, and provide a perspective that was engaging and thoughtful.

"Whatcha Know Good?": **What I Hope You Did, Learned, and Hope to Do**

As you saw throughout this book, I highlighted words and phrases that represent aspects of Black language, life, and culture. However, on all but a few instances, I leave that exploration for what I mean and what they mean in their context in the text up to you to investigate. What does, for example, "Eat the cake!" mean, and why did I use it where and how I did? What does, "Say my name!" or "When and where we enter" mean and come from? Some instances aren't as deep as those and are simpler to decipher or discover, like "What we not gon do," "Put some respeck on my name!?," "We bout to ride up on . . .," or "We gon be alright." All those highlighted words and phrases matter, and I hope you enjoyed (re-)discovering and (re-)engaging them.

I hope you read every word, of course, and that you learned something regardless of your level of familiarity and engagement with Black language, life, and culture as well as your subjectivities and positionalities. I hope you want to engage and learn more about sociolinguistics; Black language, life, and culture; and all the things that make AAL/USEB so important and so exciting to explore in the 21st century. I hope you had engaging and informative conversations with friends and family, classmates and colleagues, and even strangers on a plane/train/bus. I hope you were all in. And even if you weren't or didn't do all the things, I hope you did at least enough to leave this space better informed than when you arrived. Remember, **stay ready. You got next, you got now**.

Questions, Discussion, and Further Inquiry

1 What are other reclaimed words you are familiar with and their histories?
2 What is your perspective on reclamation and how it critiques social constructs from the perspective of the demeaned social group? What does reclamation say about social and linguistic norms?
3 What does, "Eat the cake!" mean, and why did I use it where and how I did?
4 What does, "You cain't do wrong and get by" mean, and why did I use it where and how I did?

5 What does "What does it feel like to be a problem?," "Say my name!," or "When and where we enter" mean, and why did I use them where and how I did?
6 What do you know now that you didn't know before reading this book?
7 What will you do differently now than you did before reading this book?
8 What's left for you to explore? What do you want to know more about?

Reference

Lanehart, Sonja, ed. 2015. *The Oxford Handbook of African American Language*. Oxford: Oxford University Press.

Discography

Harold Melvin & the Blue Notes. If You Don't Know Me by Now. Track 1 on *I Miss You*. Philadelphia International Records.

AAL and Black culture words and phrases

A$AP 161
acting a fool 23
AF (as f∧k) 8, 158, 185, 215
ain't she the woman 158
alhamdulillah 161n11, 162
Allahu akbar 162
all the feels 185, 198
all the things 47, 186
all those things and a bag of chips 29
all up in here 183
assignment, understanding the 25, 26, 202, 206

back in the day 31
bad (in the good way) 26, 79
bædæs 179, 185
bamboozled 212
bank, making 181, 182
be all up in here 9
because racism 52
bednot 187
be ready 13
Big Freedia 180
Bismillah 162
Blackademic 27
Black and it's beautiful 179
Blackfishing 184, 188
Black Girl Magic 198
Blackity Black Black 11, 181
Blerds (Black nerds) 32, 211–212

bodacious 214
bofum 187
booyah 198
boss 214
bright/light and (damn near) white 149
brothas and sistas 46, 179
Bruh 48, 61, 194

cain't get enough 181
call a spade a spade 33, 46
calling a thing a thing 9, 224
call me outta my name 47, 197; don't call me outta my name 53
cappin 163
a change is gonna come 205
check yo self before you wreck yo self 13
cheese [g∧mənt] 182
"child, don't play with me today" 48
Chile, please! 211
cipha/cipher 161, 161n12
clapped back 101, 154
is complicated like that 25
the cookout 26, 183
crazy 163
CREAM 161, 163
credit to his race 22
crunkness 125n1
cutting up 209

deen 161
dhikr 162
did not come to play 180
did that thang 180, 224
dissing 22, 23
done wrong 223
don't call me outta my name 53
don't get it twisted 101
dope 155
dozens, doin the 163
drop knowledge 161

Eat the cake, Anna Mae 189
eat the [dæm] cake 225
educational malpractice 205
edumacated/edumacation 22, 206, 210
er'ybody 186

fam 185
fear of a Black planet 179
feeling some kind of way 36
feel some kind of way about 144
fight the power! 216
fire 203n2
for all the world to see 187
for real for real 18
40 acres and a mule 195
fronting 145

G 161
the get go 223
get it twisted 2, 13, 101, 206
get on the good foot 200
get ovah 199
get ready 13, 14
girrrrl 180
[gʌmənt] check 216
[gʌmənt] cheese 182
GOAT 49, 79
goes IN 163
good and ready 180
got it goin on 27
got next 126, 208
got this on lockdown 179
grown 165

had another thing coming 200
haram 162
hard headed 124
hipped 144
HNIC 215
hoes 180
House Negro 21
how and when we enter 196
how does it feel to be a problem 24
how we do 8, 159, 216
how we gon play this? 41
h/t 154, 177

I can do bad all by myself 70
If you [dõ] know, you [bɛrə] [æks] somebody 183
if you don't know me by now 223
ignant 19, 200
I'm going to school you 30
Inshallah 162
in the house 124
ioneem 187
is complicated like that 25
"I see you" 154
it's a Black thang 178
it's about to be lit up in here 139
it's not the shoes (!) 22, 195
it's not the shoes, Bruh! 194

Jig-a-Bobo 180
jive talk 184
June Bug, Ray Ray, and Pookie 124
just another Tuesday 20, 212

keep on keepin on 141, 209n9, 216
kept it moving 180
King James Version of the real deal in language 29
KRS-One 161

let it all hang out 12
let's do this thang 14
"Let's get it on" 9
let's get it started in here 204
let's just be real for a moment 144
let's turn this mutha out 14

AAL and Black culture words and phrases 231

"little" usage 157
Lord, [hæmɝsi] 184

make a way outta no way 216
make it do what it do 224
make you wanna holler, throw up both your hands 188
making bank 181, 182
mannish boy who is smellin himself 122
"Massa, we sick" 20, 128
mic-drop moments 49, 198
murck 208n8
my bad 214
my jam 155

nah 48, 61
name a thing a thing 9, 224
nitty gritty 155
not all skin folk yo kinfolk 128
nuff said 180, 184
NWA 161

okey-doke 195, 215
okurrr 154
Ooh, chile! 49, 184, 223n1
owned 184

peace 161
Periodt! 70, 155, 204
play, did not come to 180
problem: how does it feel to be 24; what's it feel like to be 46, 51
props 9, 45
pussyfootin roun 214, 215
pussyfoot roun 225
put some respeck on it 53, 184
put some respeck on my name 41

ratchet 19, 97, 182
real 183
respeck 178n4; put some on it 53, 184; put some on my name 41
right on time 211
rooting for everybody Black 8, 25
RZA 161

say it loud, I'm Black and I'm proud 154
Say My Name! 52
Say that! 198
shawtys 139, 166
shaytan 160n9, 161, 162
shonuff 210
shook 212
showed out 180
showed up 180
shut yo mouf! 29
shut yo mouth! 143
sipping tea 129
Sirat al-mustaqeem 161
sistas 198
slay 180, 181, 185
some folk don't believe fat meat is greasy 78
speaking truth to power 216
stay ready 227
stop messin 187
studn bout 49
sundown towns 180
swagger 129

takes it home 156
talmbout 145–146, 187
thang 223
that's how we do 216
that's not how any of this works 225
that's not how it works; that's not how it works at all 215
that's the way of the world 194, 202
that's what you're not going to do here 27
they ain't playin 209
they ain't slick 179
they cain't keep doin wrong and expect to be gettin by 225
thick 198
a thing a thing, (naming or calling) 9, 224
things that make you wanna go hmmmm 188

This is why we can't have nice things 177
THUG LIFE 210n10
took care of business (TCB) 180
Top Five 155
Topsy and Bopsy 180
turned this mutha out 180
24/7 28, 79

unapologetically Black 198
understand/understood the assignment 25, 26, 202, 206
uppity 129

water is wet 212
we are not here for it 205
wear our hair natural and nappy 198
we bout to ride up 75
we come from a remarkable people 204
we didn't know we needed 179
we do language 1
we don't play 154
we don't play that 197
we have been waiting for 208
well . . . 45
went to be with the Lord 153
weren't having it 214
we straight 41
Whatcha know good? 177, 227
what's good? 75
what's it feel like to be a problem 46, 51
what's the move 6
what we not gon do 78
when and where we enter 198
"when you know better, do better" 31
where my big white Bible African Americans at 29
where we at 116
where we enter 116
Where your people at? 122
whew, chile! 31
white is right 128
white meat 165, 166, 187
a whole thing 154
who we were when 51
Word! 158
Word from the mother 103
word is bond 161
work it out, honey 200
wypipo 146, 186
wypipologist 186

y'all ain't ready 14
Yassss, queens! 154
yet and still 147, 205, 206
YOLO (à la Drake 2012) 28
"You are so articulate" 25
you are the change we need to see 226
you better recognize! 225
you cain't do wrong and get by 223
you got next 227
young, gifted, and Black 184, 197, 207
youngbloods 182
you ready 223
yt 146

Index

AAL/USEB (African American Language/U.S. Ebonics): children who speak AAL 116, 200–201; consensus hypotheses 67–69; contrasted with AAVL/VUSEB 102; Deficit Hypothesis 59–61; directions for future research 225–226; Divergence/Convergence hypothesis 69–70; lexical and slang terms 79; (Neo-)Anglicist Origins Hypotheses 61–67; (Neo-)Creolist Origins Hypotheses 61–67; origins of 58–70; patterns, systems, and structure 103–104; as performative Blacktainment 181–184; regional and geographic variation 122–133; sexuality and gendered identity 164–166; unique qualities 78–79; *see also* grammar, descriptive, of AAL/USEB

AAL/USEB (African American Language/U.S. Ebonics), linguistic systems and features: baited indirectness 94–95; and church language 114–115; complementizer constructions 91; directness 93; discourse features 91–95; existential constructions 91; indirectness 93–94; inflections 111; locative constructions 91; loud-talking 96–97; marking 96; morphological features 83–87; negation 90; nonverbal communication 114; nouns and pronouns 89–90; phonological features 79–83, 111–113; pointed indirectness 94; questions 90–91, 109–111; quotative constructions 91; reading 95–96; semantic license 95; semiotic resources 95–97; signifying 91–92; speech events 113–114; verbal markers 104–109; verbal tense marking 87–88; women's language 97–101; word classes and word formation 104; *see also* grammar, descriptive, of AAL/USEB

AAVE (African American Vernacular English) 23, 44, 123

AAVL (African American Vernacular Language) 42, 44, 129, 151, 187; contrasted with AAL/USEB 102, 122; in educational system 200–201, 212

abolitionism 203–204, 216

Academic English Mastery Program 213

Index

accent 32
"acting Black" 197
"acting white" 196–197, 206
adolescent male influence on language 128–129, 151
African American church services and language 114–115, 139, 148, 179
African American English (AAE) 42, 52, 68, 132–133, 145–146, 151
African American English: A Linguistic Introduction (Green) 103
African American Language (AAL) 41–42; early scholarship concerning 43; others' perceptions of 18–19, 36; varying terms for 43–44
African American Policy Forum 188
African Americans, definitions of term 117–11
African American Women's Language (AAWL) 97–101, 152–158, 164, 165
African American Women's Language (Lanehart) 153–154
African diaspora 45–46, 149
Africanisms in the Gullah Dialect (Turner) 43
Afrofuturism 53, 75, 178–181, 185, 198, 224–225
Afropessimism 53
Alexander, Dr. Benjamin H. 19–20, 21
Alim, H. Samy 158, 159, 163
American Sign Language (ASL) 140; *see also* Black ASL (American Sign Language); signed language
Anderson, Bridget 131
Angelou, Maya (poet) 19, 23, 31
Angles, Saxons, and Jutes 61, 65
Anglicist (Neo) Origins Hypotheses 61–67

"Angry Black Woman" stereotype 157, 209–210
Anita Hill-Clarence Thomas Senate Judiciary Hearing 99–100
Ann Arbor "Black English" trial 20, 21–22, 212–213
Annalise Keating (*How to Get Away with Murder*) 214
anti-Black racism 153
anti-respectability politics 198
Arbery, Ahmaud (hate crime victim) 178
Articulate While Black (Alim & Smitherman) 158
aspectual markers in AAL/USEB *see* verbal markers in AAL/USEB
Atlanta Black Star (digital publication) 188
author's personal background 29–106, 75–76, 153, 211–212

"baby talk," AAL/USEB considered to be 59, 129, 223
Badu, Erykah (singer/songwriter) 159
Bailey, Beryl 117
Bailey, Guy 69, 102, 129, 130
Bailey, Moya 199
Bailey, Richard W. 95, 51
baited indirectness 104–105
Baker-Bell, April 52, 160, 202, 208–209, 210, 213
Baldwin, James (writer) 21–22, 25, 38, 125–126, 205, 206
BAME (Black, Asian, and Minority Ethnic), use of term 47
Baptista, Marlyse 67
Barrett, Rusty 166
Baugh, John 60, 109, 196, 208, 214
Bayley, Robert 140, 141
Bébé's Kids (animated film) 117
Bell, Derrick 21, 215
Bereiter, Carl 59
Beverly, Frankie (singer/songwriter) 183

Beyoncé (singer/songwriter) 185–186
Beyond Ebonics (Baugh) 214
bidialectalism 52, 198–200
BIPOC (Black and Indigenous People of Color), use of term 63n2
"Black," definitions of term 117–11
Black ASL (American Sign Language) 140–141
Black ASL Project, The (Gallaudet University project) 140
Black Feminism 29, 159, 164–165, 180, 185, 224; *see also* women
Black Guy Who Tips, The (podcast) 188
Black Kirby (Jennings & Robinson) 181
Black Language Podcast, The 188
Black Language Syllabus (website) 160
Black Me Up (podcast) 188
Black Muslims 160–161
Black Panther (film) 181
Black Reconstruction 150
Black Standard English (BSE) 141–148
Black Twitter 186–187
Black women's hair 154
Blackademics 27
blackface 183
Blackfamous 182–183
Blackfishing 188
#BlackLivesMatter 69
Blackness in the Americas, self-reference and identity 45–51
Blacktainment 181–184
Blacula (film) 182
Blake, Renée 159
Bland, Sandra (hate crime victim) 215
Blavity (website) 188
Blaxploitation films 182
Blerds (Black nerds) 32, 211–212
Blige, Mary J. (singer/songwriter) 159, 186

Blind men and the elephant story 77
Blow, Charles (journalist) 186
BME (Black and Minority Ethnic), use of term 47
Bono (singer/songwriter) 61
Book of Rhymes: The Poetics of Hip Hop (Bradley) 163
Boondocks, The (television show) 21
Bradley, Adam 163
Brandy (singer/songwriter) 159
Bridge (reading program) 200
Bridges, Beau (actor) 22
British Black Music/Black Music Congress 46
British English 62, 66–67
Britt, Erica 139
Brown, Bobby (singer/songwriter/dancer) 185
Brown, H. Rap (civil rights activist) 113
Brown, James (singer/songwriter) 10, 185
brown paper bag test 149
Brown v. Board of Education of Topeka 35, 190, 195, 211, 214
Bucholtz, Mary 122–124, 166
Burling, Robbins 43
Butler, Octavia (writer) 181

call and response 114–115; *see also* African American church services and language
camouflaged forms in AAL/USEB 145
Campbell-Kibler, Kathryn 166
"capping" 92, 100, 163
Cardi B (rap artist) 159, 166
Caribbean creoles 62–63
Caribbean English 68
Carpenter, Adam 163
Caxton's printing press 33–34
CCCC (Conference on College Composition and Communication) 209

Index

Chambers, John, Jr. 212
Champion, Tempii B. 139
Chappelle, Dave (comedian) 20, 186
church language *see* African American church services and language
#CiteBlackWomen/#CiteASista 203n2
Clark, Heather D. 140
Cleopatra Jones (film) 182
Clifton, Lucille (poet) 204–205
Clinton, George (musician/singer/songwriter) 181
CNN Headline News (television show) 28
CODA (film) 141
codeswitching 52, 198–199, 210
collaborative speech 157
colonialism: colonial-white settler practices 63–64; and enslavement 196; settler-colonial economy 127; slavery and language development 126–127; white settler-colonial practices 63–64
Color Purple, The (Walker) 95, 20
colorism 148–150
complementizer constructions in AAL/USEB 91
contrastive analysis 52, 198–200
Coogler, Ryan (film director) 181
Cooper, Brittney 186
cooperative or collaborative speech 98
copula 62, 67
CORAAL (Corpus of Regional African American Language) 131–133
Cornelius, Brianna 166
Cosby, Bill (actor/comedian) 23, 186
Cottom, Tressie McMillan 186, 189
covert prestige 26
Cox, Renee 181
Craig, Holly 207

Crenshaw, Kimberlé (lawyer/civil rights advocate) 10–11, 164–165
Creole Exceptionalism 65
creole languages: as contested concept 32–33; definitions 64–66; lack of evidence for AAL/USEB as a widespread creole 68; Gullah Geechee as 126–127
Creolist (Neo) Origins Hypotheses 61–67
Critical Discourse Analysis 29
Critical Race Theory 29
crunk feminism 125
Crunk Feminist Collective 125
Crystal, David 76
Cukor-Avila, Patricia 129, 130
Cullinan, Danica (filmmaker) 140
cult of true womanhood 198
cultural appropriation 177–178, 182
culturally relevant pedagogy 207
culturally sustaining pedagogy 207
culturally-toned diminutives 157
Cunningham, Irma Aloyce Ewing 126

Da Brat (rap artist) 159
Dark Girls (documentary) 50
Dash, Julie (filmmaker) 127
Daughters of the Dust (film) 127
Davis, Ossie (actor) 25–26
Davis, Viola 184, 214n12
DBGFs (distinctively Black grammatical features) 145–146
DeBose, Charles 108, 139
deficit theories 223; Deficit Hypothesis 59–61
definitions and naming 117–11; "Black" contrasted with "African American" 46–51
DeGraff, Michel 67
Delpit, Lisa 214
descriptive grammar of AAL/USEB *see* grammar, descriptive, of AAL/USEB

Index

desegregation 43, 70, 148, 194, 195, 211
dialects, contrasted with languages 28–29
digital blackface 188
digital media 187–189
Dillard, Joey L. 43
directness contrasted with indirectness 93–95, 155
discourse features: in AAL/USEB 91–95; in African American Women's Language (AAWL) 97–101
discourse genres 153
Divergence/Convergence hypothesis 69–70
Django Unchained (film) 20, 128
Doctor Who (television show) 29n5
Doja Cat (rap artist) 159
Dolemite (film) 182
Dolezal, Rachel 19, 128
Donnor, Jamel K. 35, 214–215
Du Bois, W.E.B. (William Edward Burghardt) 36, 128, 150, 197
Due, Tananarive (writer) 181, 186

Ebonics 11, 19–20, 23, 44–46; and Afrofuturism 178–181; Ebonics jokes 183–184; U.S. Ebonics (USEB) 51–53
Ebonics Controversy, Oakland 20, 45–46, 51, 183, 208, 213–214
Ebonics: The True Language of Black Folks (Williams) 45
ecological hypotheses and theory 59, 67–69
education in U.S. and use of AAL/USEB: Ann Arbor "Black English" trial 212–213; Black history of perseverance 204–206; and fear of Black people 214–216; and linguistic justice 201–204; Oakland Ebonics controversy 213–214; overview 194–196; research concerning linguistic justice 207–211; schools as white educational spaces 196–201
education levels and personal ideologies 153
Elliott, Missy (rap artist) 159, 186
embodied sociolinguistics (Bucholtz) 180–181
Engelmann, Siegfried 59
English language, history of (HEL) 30, 33
Essence (magazine) 188
essentialism 122–124
Etter-Lewis, Gwendolyn 117, 97–98, 155, 157
Eve (rap artist/actress) 159
existential and other constructions in AAL/USEB 91, 110

Faculty of Color (FOC) 11
Faraclas, Nicholas 108
Farrington, Charlie 131, 132
Fasold, Ralph 43, 132
Fat Albert and the Cosby Kids (television show) 23
feminism *see* African American Women's Language (AAWL); Black Feminism; women
Fiasco, Lupe (rap artist) 162
Fielder, Tim (illustrator/animator) 181
Five Percent Nation 160–161, 162
Floyd, George (hate crime victim) 178
folk/perceptual linguistics research 18
Ford Foundation Fellowships 73, 95
Fordham, Signithia 196–197
Foster, Michèle 117, 154–155, 157, 201
Foxy Brown (film) 182
Franklin, Aretha (singer/songwriter) 184–185
Freedom Summer (2020) 178, 188

Freire, Paulo 22
fugitivity 203–204, 216

Gallaudet University 140
Gates, Daryl (LAPD Chief of Police) 94
Gay, Geneva 207
Gay, Roxane (writer/social commentator) 189
Gaye, Marvin (singer/songwriter) 188
Gender and Language (G & L) (journal) 165
gendered identities and language 164–166, 226
gender passing 197, 198
Gibbs, Norman Alexander (actor) 184
Gilmore, Ruth Wilson (prison abolitionist) 203–204
GirlTrek (podcast) 188
Glow Up, The (podcast) 188
Gooden, Shelome 113
Good Times (television show) 158
grammar: definitions of 76–77; descriptive contrasted with prescriptive 13n9, 27, 31, 77; grammar study, limitations of 75–76; knowing grammar contrasted with knowing about grammar 76
grammar, descriptive, of AAL/USEB 75–116; camouflaged forms 145; directness contrasted with indirectness 93–95; discourse features 91–101; existential, locative, and other constructions 91, 110; inflections 111; lexical level 104; morphosyntactic level 111; negation 90, 109; nouns and pronouns 89–90; overview 75–78; patterns, systems, and structure 103–104; phonological features 79–83; phonological level 111–113; preverbal markers 84–87, 108–109; questions 90–91, 110; semiotic resources for conversation signifying 95–97; speech events and paralinguistic levels 113–115; syntactic level 104–111; verbal tense marking 87–88
grammaticalization 145–146
Great Migration 51, 69, 102, 150
Green, Al (singer/songwriter) 184
Green, CeeLo (singer/songwriter) 61
Green, Lisa 13, 103–104, 113, 115–116, 139, 213
Green, Misha (screenwriter/director/producer) 180
Grio, The (website) 188
Gullah Geechee 42, 63, 68, 126–127
Gunter, Kaylynn 131
Gutenberg Bible 34

Haddish, Tiffany (comedian/actress) 181, 182
hair, significance of in Black community 50, 154
Hannah, Dawn 67
Hannah-Jones, Nikole (journalist) 186
Hansberry, Lorraine (writer) 147
Harriot, Michael 35, 182–183, 186–187
Harris, Wendell A. 70
Hart, Kevin (comedian/actor) 181, 182, 186
Harvey, Steve (comedian) 181, 182
Hate You Give, The (film)
HBCUs (Historically Black Colleges and Universities) 128, 129, 211
Here to Slay (podcast) 188–189
Hill, Anita (lawyer) 99–100
Hill, Jemele (journalist) 186
Hill, Joseph 140–141

Hill, Lauryn (singer/songwriter) 159
"Hip Hop Lives" (KRS-One) 159
Hip Hop Nation Language (HHNL) 53, 158–163
Hip Hop Word Count database 160
Hispanic communities 149
history of the English language (HEL/HOTEL) 30, 33
Hodge, Aldis (actor) 22
Holliday, Nicole R. 113
Hollie, Sharroky 207, 213
Hoover, Mary Rhodes 129, 142–143, 144, 146
Hopkinson, Nalo (writer) 181
"House Negroes" 21
Houston, Whitney (singer) 185
Hudson, Barbara Hill 154
Hull, Gloria T. 153
Hurston, Zora Neale (writer) 106–117, 159
Hutcheson, Neal (filmmaker) 140

Ice Cube (rap artist/actor/filmmaker) 13
Ice-T (rap artist/actor) 94–95
identity, complexity of 53
Ideology of Emancipation (Lanehart) 153
Ideology of Opportunity (Lanehart) 153
Ideology of Progress (Lanehart) 153
Ifill, Sherrilyn (lawyer/civil rights advocate) 186
immigration, voluntary contrasted with involuntary (Ogbu) 196
impostor syndrome (imposter phenomenon) 2n2
Indigenous Peoples 205
indirectness in AAL/USEB 93–95, 113
inflections in AAL/USEB 111
Instagram and cultural appropriation 177–178, 182
International Gender and Language Association (IGALA) 165

International Phonetic Alphabet (IPA) xii–xiii, 13
Intersectionality Matters (podcast) 188
Intersectionality Theory (Crenshaw) 29, 164
involuntary minoritized immigrants 196
Islam and Hip Hop culture 160–161

Jackson, Davena 209
Jackson, Mahalia (singer) 185
Jackson, Michael (singer/songwriter) 26
Jackson, Millie (singer/songwriter) 183
Jackson, Reverend Jesse 19, 23
Jackson, Samuel L. (actor) 20, 128
Jacobs-Huey, Lanita 154
jargon, 32; *see also* slang
Jay-Z (rap artist) 163
Jemisin, N.K. (writer) 181
Jennings, John (illustrator) 181
Jim Crow laws 150
jive talk 184
Johnson, Lamar 209
Jones, Charisse 199
Jones, Grace (actress) 181
Jones, Taylor 132–133

Keating, Annalise (*How to Get Away with Murder*) 214
Kendall, Tyler 131, 132
Kid Fury (rap artist) 188
Kikongo language 67
King, Carole (singer/songwriter) 184
King, Martin Luther, Jr. 22, 128, 129, 160–161
King, Sharese 132
knowing grammar contrasted with knowing about grammar 76
KRS-One (rap artist) 159
Kwa language 67
Kynard, Carmen 160, 209

Labov, William 43, 59, 60, 69–70, 78, 102, 201, 202
Ladson-Billings, Gloria 201, 207
Lamar, Kendrick (rap artist) 20, 163, 186
Lane, Nikki 166
Lanehart, Sonja, personal background 29–106, 75–76, 153, 211–212
Language and Life Project (NCSU) 130, 140
Larsen, Nella (writer) 150
latching (turn-taking mechanism) 99–100
Latifah, Queen (rap artist/actress) 159
Latinx communities 149
laughter 155–156
Lee, Margaret 117
LeMoine, Norma 207, 213
Lemonade (Beyoncé album) 185
Let's Do It Again (film) 23, 182
Levert, Gerald (singer/songwriter) 183
lexical and slang terms, AAL/USEB 79
Lil' Kim (rap artist) 159
Lil Nas X (rap artist) 166
lingua franca 64n3
linguistic denial 23–25
linguistic justice 201–204, 210–211
Linguistic Justice (Baker-Bell) 208
linguistic prejudice 19–23
linguistic pride and acceptance 25–26
linguistic racism (linguisticism) 183–184
linguistic shame 23–25
linguistics, definitions of 154
Linguistic Society of America 154
linguisticism (linguistic racism) 183
literacy and education 35–36
"little" usage in AAWL 157
Lizzo (rap artist) 159, 186
locative constructions in AAL/USEB 91

"Logic of Nonstandard English, The" (Labov) 59–60, 78, 202
Lopez, Qiuana 166
Los Angeles Unified School District 213
loud-talking 96–97
Lovecraft Country (television show) 178, 180
Lucas, Ceil 140, 141
Lumbee English 130
Lyiscott, Jamila 199
Lyte, MC (rap artist) 159

Malcolm X (civil rights activist) 129, 160–161
Malcolm X (film) 183
Malik, Ayesha 160–163
Mama Day (Naylor) 73
Mande language 67
Mandingo (film) 182
mansplaining 2n3
Mappers Delight XR (tool) 160
"marking" (form of conversation signifying) 96, 101, 114
Marshall, Kerry James (artist) 181
Martin, Trayvon (hate crime victim; #BlackLivesMatter) 61, 215
Maximum Distance Minimum Displacement (exhibit) 160
MCAAL/MCUSEB (Middle-Class AAL/USEB) 148–152
McCabe, Allyssa 139
McCaskill, Carolyn 140, 141
McLarty, Jason 131
McMurtry, Teaira 209
Megan Thee Stallion (rap artist) 159, 166, 186
Mellon Foundation Fellowships 73
Mfume, Kweisi (NAACP; politician) 19
Middle-Class African American Language (Weldon) 148
middle-class language use 148–152
miles-hercules, deandre 166

Minaj, Nicki (rap artist) 159, 186
Minority Education and Caste (Ogbu) 196
misogynoir (M. Bailey) 125, 199
Mitchell-Kernan, Claudia 117, 43, 96–97, 143, 152
mock Ebonics 183
Monáe, Janelle (singer/songwriter/actress) 146, 181, 186
"MONTERO" (Lil Nas X) 166
Moody, Simanique 126
Morgan, Joan 159
Morgan, Marcyliena 117, 95, 151, 152, 154, 155–156, 159, 209
Morgan, Tracey (actor/comedian) 182
morphological features of AAL/USEB 83–87
Morrison, Toni 25, (writer) 47–49, 52–53, 64, 116; GIF from Charlie Rose interview 64
Mufwene, Salikoko 23, 42, 67, 68, 69, 126
Mules and Men (Hurston) 159
Mura, David 197–198
Murphy, Eddie (actor/comedian) 182
Mutu, Wangechi (visual artist) 181
My Soul Is My Own (Etter-Lewis) 155

naming and definitions 117–11
naming and self-reference 63–64
Nation of Gods and Earths (NGE) 160, 162
Nation of Islam (NOI) 160–161, 162
Native Americans 205
Naturalization Act (1790) 50
Naylor, Gloria (writer) 73
NCTE (National Council of Teachers of English) 208–209
negation in AAL/USEB 90
"Negrophobia" 214–215
Nelson, Alondra 181
Neo-Anglicist Origins Hypotheses 61–67

Neo-Creolist Origins Hypotheses 61–67
New Who (television series) 208n7
Nice White Parents (podcast)
Niger-Congo languages 45, 67
Noname (rap artist) 159, 186
nonverbal communication 114
nouns and pronouns in AAL/USEB 89–90
N-word, use of 14, 22n4, 226

Oakland School Board Ebonics Controversy (1996-1997) 19–20, 45, 213–214
Obama, President Barack 50, 184
obscenity 14
Occupy Wall Street movement 60–61
O'Connor, Carla 206
Ocracoke English 130
Ogbu, John 196–197
Okorafor, Nnedi (writer) 181
one-drop rule 50
One Night in Miami (film) 22
-onics jokes 183
ORAAL (Online Resources for African American Language) 132
Orr, Eleanor Wilson 60
OSHUN (Hip Hop duo) 160
Out of the Mouths of Slaves (Baugh) 208
Owens, Candace (influencer) 186
Oxford Handbook of African American Language, The (Lanehart) 106, 41, 133, 226
Ozawa v. United States (1922) 50

Paris, Django 207
Parliament Funkadelic (music collective) 181
Passing (Larsen) 150
patterns perspective 103–104
Peculiar to Your Mind (Lanehart) 95
People of Color (POC), use of term 11, 63n2

Perry, Theresa 214
Perry, Tyler (actor/filmmaker/
    playwright) 182
Peter Principle (Peter) 2n2
phonological features of AAL/
    USEB 79–83, 111–113
pidgin languages 64–65
Piece of the Action, A (film) 23
playing the dozens 113, 163
podcasts, Black 188–189
pointed indirectness in AAL/
    USEB 94
Poplack, Shana 62, 67
Pough, Gwendolyn 13, 159
prescriptive grammar 24
preverbal markers of tense, mood,
    and aspect in AAL/USEB 84–87
Prince (singer/songwriter) 185
printing press and language
    development 33–34

Quartey, Minnie 132
question formation in AAL/USEB
    90–91, 109–111
quotative constructions in AAL/
    USEB 91

racelessness 197, 198–199
racism: anti-Black racism 153;
    definitions 34–35; linguistic
    racism 183–184; systemic racism
    208, 215–216; white racism 35
Rahman, Jacquelyn 139
Raisin in the Sun, A (Hansberry) 147
Rambsy, Howard, II 92
Ramirez, J. David 214
Rap Almanac (database) 160
Rap Genius (digital media
    company) 160
Rap Research Lab 160
rapping 114, 115, 159–160
Read, The (podcast) 188
"reading" (form of conversation
    signifying) 95–96, 113, 155
received pronunciation (RP) 32

reclamation, terms of 225–226
Red Table Talk (podcast) 188
Reed, Ishmael (poet) 92
Reid, Joy (journalist) 186
reported speech 97–98, 157
respectability politics 22, 128, 154,
    198, 223; (anti-)respectability
    politics 198
restructuralist hypotheses and
    theory 59, 67–69
Richardson, Elaine "Docta E" 117,
    159, 207
Rickford, John Russell 95, 53, 139,
    183, 184, 207, 213
Rickford, Russell John 53, 183,
    184, 213
Robinson, Stacey (visual artist) 181
Rock, Chris (comedian/actor) 154,
    182
Rodgers, Carolyn 92
Root, The (online magazine) 35, 188
Rose, Charlie (journalist) 48–49, 64
Ross, Loretta (singer/songwriter) 11
Rowe, Ryan 132
rural/urban variations in AAL/
    USEB 127–131

Salt-N-Pepa (Hip Hop duo) 159
Samaná (Dominican variety of
    English) 67
SAmE (Standard American
    English): contrasted with SAAL/
    SUSEB 142, 143; definitions and
    overview 29–31; use of term 144
schools *see* education in U.S. and
    use of AAL/USEB
Scott, Stuart (sports commentator)
    28, 181
segregation 70, 150
semantic license 95
semiotic resources 95–97
separation, physical, and language
    variation 69
settler-colonial economy 127;
    see also colonialism

sexuality and language 164–166, 226
Shaft (film) 182
Shifting: The Double Lives of Black Women in America (Jones & Shorter-Gooden) 199
Shorter-Gooden, Kumea 199
Shousterman, Cara 159
signed language 122, 140–141
signifying 91–92, 113, 155, 157–158; semiotic resources for conversation signifying 95–97
Signing Black in America (film) 140
Silk Sonic (music duo) 186
Simone, Nina (singer/songwriter) 186
Simpkins, Gary 200
Sista, Speak! (Lanehart) 95, 148, 153, 197, 223
Sister Souljah (writer/activist) 159
slang 27–28, 32; and lexical terms AAL/USEB, 79
Sledd, James 50, 201–202, 215
"smart talk" 91–92, 100, 156, 157–158
Smiley, Rickey (comedian) 183
Smith, Jada Pinkett (actress) 154
Smith, Will (actor/rap artist) 154
Smitherman, Geneva "Docta G" 117, 11, 25, 43, 51, 52, 78, 91, 95, 103, 114, 127, 128, 158, 159, 197, 214
social media 177–178, 182
sociolinguistics 164–165, 180–181, 224
soul music 184–186
Souls of Black Folks, The (DuBois) 36
Southern/Northern variations in AAL/USEB 127, 129, 130–131
Space Traders (Bell) 215
Sparkle (film) 182
Spears, Arthur K. 14, 109, 128, 139, 143, 144–145, 146–148

Specter, Arlen (U.S. senator) 99–100
speech events in AAL/USEB 113–114
Spoken Soul 53, 184, 224
Spoken Soul (Rickford & Rickford) 44, 53
Stanback, Marsha Houston 157
Standard African American Language (SAAL/SUSEB) 141–148; middle-class language use 148–152
Standard American English (SAmE) *see* SAmE (Standard American English)
Standard English 21
Stanford University 95
Star Trek 208n7
Star Trek: The Next Generation 128
Stewart, William 43
Stoop, The (podcast) 188
Students of Color (SOC) 11
Students' Right to Their Own Language (NCTE) 208
styleshifting 198–199
substrate languages 64n4
substratist hypotheses 67–69
Sunni Islam 160, 162
Sun Ra (composer) 181
Super Fly (film) 182
superstrate languages 64n5
Sweet Sweetback's Baadasssss Song (film) 182
"sweet talk" 157
syntax 76
systemic racism 208, 215–216

Tagliamonte, Sali 62
Talented Tenth (W.E.B. Du Bois) 21
Talkin and Testifyin: The Language of Black America (Smitherman) 11, 103, 158
Talkin that Talk (Smitherman) 158
Talking Black in America (film) 140
"talking that talk" 100–101

Tatum, Beverly Daniel 75
Taylor, Breonna (hate crime victim) 178
Taylor, Orlando 43, 124, 141–143, 143–144, 146
Teena Marie (singer/songwriter) 183
terms of reclamation 225–226
Therapy for Black Girls (podcast) 188
This Week in Blackness (podcast) 188
Thomas, Clarence (U.S. Supreme Court justice) 99–100
Thomas, Erik 69
"Three Ways to Speak English" (Ted Talk, Lyiscott) 199
TikTok and cultural appropriation 177–178, 182
toasts 114
Traditional Black Church 179
Training Day (film) 183
Trina (rap artist) 159
Troutman, Denise 101, 156–157, 158
Tulsa Race Massacre (1921) 179, 180
Turner, Lorenzo Dow 43, 126
Twice as Less (Orr) 60

"Understanding the Why of Whiteness" (Donnor) 214–215
Under the Blacklight (podcast) 188
"Unequal Opportunity Race" (video) 195
University of Arizona, Tucson 106, 41
University of Georgia 95, 76
University of Michigan 73, 47
University of Texas at Austin 201n1
University of Texas at San Antonio (UTSA) 95–106
Unrelated Kin (Etter-Lewis & Foster) 155

"Unspeakable Things Unspoken" (Morrison) 47–49
Uptown Saturday Night (film) 23, 182
Urban Dictionary (crowdsourced online) 160
urban/rural variations in AAL/USEB 127–131
U.S. Ebonics (USEB) *see* Ebonics

Variation in African American English (Jones) 132–133
variations: physical separation and language variation 69; regional 53; regional and geographic, in AAL/USEB 122–133
variety (term for linguistic systems) 31–32
verbal genres 155
verbal markers in AAL/USEB 104–109
verbal tense marking in AAL/USEB 87–88
Vernacular Black English (VBE) 143
vernacular languages 32; in educational contexts 207; *see also* AAVE (African American Vernacular English); AAVL (African American Vernacular Language);
Very Smart Brothas (podcast) 188
Villarreal, Daniel 113
voluntary minoritized immigrants 196

Walker, Alice (writer) 95, 20
Walking Eagle (Native American term) 131
WAmE (White American English) 67, 70, 78–79, 144, 153, 200–201
"WAP" (Cardi B) 166
Washington, Denzel (actor/producer) 183
Washington, Julie 207
Watchmen (film) 178, 179–180

Weissler, Rachel 157
Weldon, Tracey 126, 139, 148, 150–151
West, Crissle (writer) 188
West, Kanye (rap artist/singer/songwriter/producer) 21
West African languages 67
WHAM (White, Heterosexual, and Male) 164
Where's My 38 Acres? (podcast) 188
White, Al (actor) 184
"white", definitions of term 117–11
White American English (WAmE) 67, 70, 78–79, 144, 153, 200–201
white gaze 51, 52, 78, 116
white racism 35
white settler-colonial practices 63–64; *see also* colonialism
white supremacy 208; *see also* racism
Whiteside, Briana 92
Williams, Frederick 142
Williams, Katt (comedian/actor) 183
Williams, Oracene (tennis coach) 206
Williams, Richard (tennis coach) 206
Williams, Robert L. 25, 45, 51, 53
Williams, Serena (tennis player) 206
Williams, Venus (tennis player) 206
Williams-Farrier, Bonnie J. 209
Winfrey, Oprah (talk show host/producer/actress/philanthropist) 31
Wolfram, Walt 43, 69, 101, 102, 129–130, 132, 140, 214
women: African American Women's Language (AAWL) 97–101; 152–158, 164, 165; Black women's hair 154; Black women's laughter 155–156; Black women teachers 154–155; cult of true womanhood 198; lack of inclusion in research 122; stereotypes of Black women 157–158; *see also* Black Feminism
Women of Color (WOC) 11
"won't you celebrate with me" (Clifton) 204–205
"woofing" 114
word classes and word formation in AAL/USEB 104
Word from the Mother (Smitherman) 158
Wright, Kelly 13
Wright, Richard (writer) 195–196
Wu Tang Clan (Hip Hop group) 162

Zeigler, Mary 117
zero copula 62, 67, 84